T0305145

A Research Agenda for Creative Tourism

Elgar Research Agendas outline the future of research in a given area. Leading scholars are given the space to explore their subject in provocative ways, and map out the potential directions of travel. They are relevant but also visionary.

Forward-looking and innovative, Elgar Research Agendas are an essential resource for PhD students, scholars and anybody who wants to be at the forefront of research.

Titles in the series include:

A Research Agenda for Creative Tourism

Edited by

NANCY DUXBURY

Researcher and Co-coordinator, Cities, Cultures, and Architecture Research Group, Centre for Social Studies, University of Coimbra, Portugal

GREG RICHARDS

Professor of Placemaking and Events, Breda University of Applied Sciences and Professor in Leisure Studies, Tilburg University, the Netherlands

Elgar Research Agendas

Cheltenham, UK • Northampton, MA, USA

Published by
Edward Elgar Publishing Limited
The Lypiatts
15 Lansdown Road
Cheltenham
Glos GL50 2JA
UK

Edward Elgar Publishing, Inc.
William Pratt House
9 Dewey Court
Northampton
Massachusetts 01060
USA

A catalogue record for this book
is available from the British Library

Library of Congress Control Number: 2018960564

This book is available electronically in the **Elgar**online
Social and Political Science subject collection
DOI 10.4337/9781788110723

ISBN 978 1 78811 071 6 (cased)
ISBN 978 1 78811 072 3 (eBook)

Typeset by Servis Filmsetting Ltd, Stockport, Cheshire
Printed on FSC approved paper
Printed and bound in Great Britain by Marston Book Services Ltd, Oxfordshire

Contents

Figures

Tables

Contributors

Manuela Blapp holds a Master of Arts in Tourism Destination Management from Breda University of Applied Sciences, in the Netherlands. She is a tourism professional with diverse work experience in sales, marketing, and operations in the travel trade, hospitality, and airline industry. Her research interests include sustainable tourism development, destination management, creative tourism, and authenticity in tourism. Manuela published 'Creative tourism in Balinese rural communities' in *Current Issues in Tourism* (2017, with Ondrej Mitas).

Patrick Brouder, PhD, is British Columbia Regional Innovation Chair at Vancouver Island University, Canada, and a Senior Research Fellow in the School of Tourism and Hospitality, University of Johannesburg, South Africa. He serves as Chair of the Economic Geography Group of the Canadian Association of Geographers and is on the Steering Committee of the International Polar Tourism Research Network (IPTRN). Patrick is a resource editor for *Tourism Geographies* and an editorial board member for *Polar Geography*. He is co-editor (together with S. Anton Clavé, A. Gill, and D. Ioannides) of *Tourism Destination Evolution* (2017), an edited volume bridging economic geography and tourism studies.

Marie-Andrée Delisle started her own firm in 1988 as a tourism development consultant for public and private organizations. Her travels through over 65 countries as a globetrotter, consultant, trainer, and travel trade journalist have given her opportunities to meet with numerous cultures while conducting various assignments. She earned her Master's degree in Tourism Planning and Management at the Université du Québec à Montréal (UQAM) in 2004 and co-authored a book on alternative tourism, *Un autre tourisme est-il possible?* (2007). A senior consultant and university lecturer, Marie-Andrée is completing her doctoral studies at UQAM and is currently working on her thesis on creative tourism as a PhD candidate.

Nancy Duxbury, PhD, is a Researcher at the Centre for Social Studies, University of Coimbra, Portugal, and a member of the European Expert Network on Culture. She is Principal Investigator of the project 'CREATOUR: Creative Tourism Destination Development in Small Cities and Rural Areas'. Nancy's research has examined culture in local sustainable development, culture-based development in smaller communities, cultural mapping, and creative tourism. Recent books are: *Cultural Mapping as Cultural Inquiry* (2015), *Culture and Sustainability in European Cities: Imagining Europolis* (2015), *Cultural Policies for Sustainable Development* (2018), and *Artistic Approaches to Cultural Mapping: Activating Imaginaries and Means of Knowing* (2019).

Magnus Luiz Emmendoerfer, PhD, is Associate Professor at the Universidade Federal de Viçosa (UFV), Viçosa, Minas Gerais, Brazil. He is Chair of the Doctoral Program in Public Administration at UFV, and Researcher and Coordinator of the Research Group on Management and Development of Creative Territories. Magnus's research has examined creative tourist regions, tourism policy, innovation, and entrepreneurship in the public sector.

Jaana Erkkilä-Hill is Professor in Fine Art at University of Lapland, Finland. She graduated with an MA in Fine Art from the Finnish Academy of Fine Arts and completed her doctoral degree, Doctor of Art, from Aalto-University, Helsinki. Jaana worked as a Director of the Nordic Art School in Kokkola (2006–09) and as a Director of Research and Development for Art and Culture in Novia University for Applied Sciences (2009–13), before her current appointment as Professor. She has published academic texts on arts-based and artistic research. Her art practice covers painting, printmaking, installations, and creative writing.

Isabel Freitas is Associate Professor with Aggregation at Portucalense University, Portugal. She holds a PhD in History, is correspondent of the Portuguese Academy of History, and Director of the Department of Tourism, Heritage and Culture. She is a collaborator in the Landscape, Heritage and Territory Laboratory (Lab2PT) research centre at the University of Minho and is integrated in the Portucalense University Research Centre, REMIT. Isabel is coordinator of several projects at Portucalense University in the areas of heritage, culture, and tourism, and a collaborator in several other projects concerned with valorization of the territory. In the scope of these projects, she is the author of several publications on themes related to territory, water, and borders within the framework of peninsular relations.

Ricardo Gôja is a PhD student in Geography and a Researcher in the CREATOUR-Lab2PT (Landscape, Heritage and Territory Laboratory) team at the University of Minho, Portugal. In 2012, he graduated in Geography and Planning and in 2015, obtained a Master's degree in Planning and Territory Management from the University of Minho. Ricardo's areas of interest are Geographic Information Systems, creative tourism, enogastronomic tourism, and territory planning.

Olga Gracheva worked as a business consultant in marketing, start-up creation, sales, and communications for five years following 15 years working as a manager and owner of fashion wear manufacturing company ULITA in Saint-Petersburg, Russia. After moving to Leningradskaya oblast, together with her husband Viktor Grachev (sculptor), in 2010, the not-for-profit non-governmental organization 'Kaykino Creative Projects' was established as a centre for innovative solutions in social and economic development through cultural and creative communicative instruments. Olga graduated from the Stockholm School of Economics Russia, and has a State University Diploma as a teacher. Since 1998, she has organized more than 25 art exhibitions, as well as cultural projects.

Brent Hanifl is the Director of Marketing at Explore La Crosse, La Crosse, Wisconsin, USA. He gained experience in planning and implementing tourism initiatives in Wisconsin, Oregon, and New Mexico. He managed the Santa Fe Creative Tourism Initiative from its initial stages through to successful maturity. Working for the Arts and Business Alliance of Eugene, Brent co-founded 'Create! Eugene', a month-long art workshop festival and *plein air* competition. He has an undergraduate degree in Tourism and a Master of Science in Arts Management with research focused on the economic value of creative tourism in Santa Fe, New Mexico, from the University of Oregon.

Mirja Hiltunen (Doctor of Art, MEd) is Professor of Art Education in the Faculty of Art and Design, University of Lapland, Finland, and Docent in the University of Oulu. She devised a performative art strategy as part of her work in art teacher education and has been leading community-based art education projects in Lapland for over 20 years. Mirja's particular interests are site-specificity, performativity, and socially engaged art and art education. She has presented numerous international research papers and published her work in art education journals and books and in art exhibitions.

Daniela Angelina Jelinčić is a Senior Research Adviser at the Institute for Development and International Relations in Zagreb, Croatia. She holds a PhD in Ethnology. Her specific interests are in cultural tourism, creative industries, cultural policy, creativity, experience economy, and social innovations. Daniela teaches these subjects at several universities and business schools, and at the UNESCO Chair for Cultural Heritage Management and Sustainable Development in Köszeg, Hungary. She is the author of: *Innovations in Culture and Development: The Culturinno Effect in Public Policy* (2017); *ABC of Cultural Tourism* (2008, 2009); *Culture in a Shop Window* (2010); and *Culture, Tourism, Interculturalism* (2010). She served as the Council of Europe expert for cultural tourism.

Timo Jokela is Professor of Art Education at the Faculty of Art and Design, University of Lapland, Finland. His expertise is in environmental art and especially snow and ice. His theoretical academic studies focus on the phenomenological relationship between art and nature, environmental art, community art, and art education. Jokela works actively as an environmental artist taking local cultural heritage as a starting point.

Salla-Mari Koistinen works as a Project Manager in the Master's Degree Programme of Applied Visual Arts and Nature Photography, University of Lapland, Finland. She is also a doctoral candidate at the Faculty of Art and Design, with a research focus on participatory methods of art and design.

Hélder da Silva Lopes is a PhD student at the University of Minho, Portugal (Geography and Regional Planning) and the University of Barcelona, Spain (Geography, Territorial Planning and Environment Management – Natural Systems and Global Changes). He is a Researcher at the Landscape, Heritage and Territory Laboratory (Lab2PT), in the Space and Representations (SpaceR), Water Research Institute (IdRA), and Climatology groups. Hélder is Vice-President of the Students' Association of Geography and Planning (GeoPlanUM). His main research interests are tourism and climate, urban geography, urban tourism, rural tourism, bioclimatology, environmental management, urban morphology, urban climate, climate changes, natural risks, health and tourism, and Geographic Information Systems.

Marina Matetskaya is Associate Professor in the Management Department of the National Research University – Higher School of Economics in Saint-Petersburg, Russia. She holds a PhD in Economics from the Faculty of Economics at Saint-Petersburg State University. Marina's research interests include cultural policy, economics, and management in arts and creative industries, place management, and tourism development.

Olga Matos holds a PhD in Archaeology and is Adjunct Professor at the Polytechnic Institute of Viana do Castelo (IPVC) and an Integrated Researcher at the Landscape, Heritage and Territory Laboratory (Lab2PT), University of Minho, Portugal. She works in the areas of cultural heritage, museology, interpretation, and cultural tourism. Olga has participated as a researcher in national and international projects, in jury competitions, in several national and international congresses as a speaker, and also has an important number of publications in her areas of interest.

Satu Miettinen (Doctor of Arts) is Professor of Service Design as well as Dean of the Faculty of Art and Design at the University of Lapland, Finland. Her research interests are in the areas of service design, including social and public service development, citizen engagement, and digital service development, and she has a strong design research interest for complex, extreme, and marginal contexts. Satu is a Visiting Lecturer in Service Design for PUC in Chile and Hokkaido University in Japan, and has been a Visiting Professor at Stanford University, USA; Tongji University, China; and the University of Trento, Italy. Among her research projects, she is coordinating the Arctic design lab that is part of the DESIS network, looking at design solutions for circumpolar areas and conditions. She is an active artist and designer in the area of socially engaged art.

Ondrej Mitas researches quality of life with a focus on tourists' emotions, including emotion biometrics during leisure and tourism experiences and the role of tourism experiences in happiness and well-being. Ondrej brings an eclectic background to his research, with qualifications in arts studies with a minor in Computer Programming (BA), tourism with a minor in Landscape Architecture (MS), and a PhD from Penn State, USA (2008) on tourists' emotions with a minor in Psychology. Besides working as a Lecturer in Research Methods and an Applied Academic Researcher at Breda University of Applied Sciences, the Netherlands, since 2008, Ondrej is an active artist of flying kinetic sculptures and mixed graphic media.

Miguel Pereira holds a Master's degree in Tourism and Regional Development from the Catholic University of Portugal (Portugal) and the University of Santiago de Compostela (Spain), graduating with the thesis 'The Geographic Information System in planning and municipal tourism management: Barcelos as a case study' (2007). He completed his PhD from the University of Santiago de Compostela, University of Vigo, and University of A Coruña in 2014. Miguel has a postdoctoral

Degree in Augmented Reality Applied to Tourism from the Laboratory of Landscape, Heritage and Territory (Lab2PT) (2015–17). He is Commissioner for Administrative Modernization (Cartography and Geographic Information Systems) in the Atlantic Axis of the Northwest Peninsular (since 2007).

Paula Remoaldo is Associate Professor with Habilitation in Human Geography in the Department of Geography of the Institute of Social Sciences, University of Minho, Portugal. She received her PhD in Human Geography in 1999 from the University of Minho with the collaboration of Louvain-la-Neuve University, Belgium. Paula is Head of the Department of Geography and Director of the Laboratory of Landscape, Heritage and Territory (Lab2PT) at the University of Minho. Her main research fields are cultural tourism, mega events, creative tourism, urban tourism, and regional and local development.

Vítor Ribeiro is Professor of Geography in the Department of Geography of the Institute of Social Sciences, University of Minho, Portugal, and at the Department of Teacher Training at Paula Frassinetti's School of Education. He holds a PhD in Geography and Regional Planning from the University of Minho/Universidad Complutense de Madrid (Spain). He also has a postdoctorate from the University of Minho in the field of Educational Technology. He is an Integrated Member of the Laboratory of Landscape, Heritage and Territory (Lab2PT) of the University of Minho. Vítor's main subjects of research are in the areas of transport geography, Geographic Information Systems, tourism and regional and local development, crime geography, and geographical education, having several research publications in journals and books in these fields.

Greg Richards is Professor of Placemaking and Events at Breda University of Applied Sciences and Professor of Leisure Studies at the University of Tilburg in the Netherlands. His recent publications include the *SAGE Handbook of New Urban Studies* (with John Hannigan, 2017) and *Small Cities with Big Dreams: Creative Placemaking and Branding Strategies* (with Lian Duif, 2018).

Matea Senkić holds a Master's degree in Sociology from the Faculty of Humanities and Social Sciences, University of Zagreb, Croatia. She works in the Department for Culture and Communication at the Institute for Development and International Relations in Zagreb. Matea has been involved in projects focusing on cultural tourism, cultural heritage revitalization, and cultural policies as well as those dealing with development of strategic planning for local heritage development. She is particularly interested in the study of cities, their ethnic and cultural diversities, popular culture, alternative cultural practices and tourism, artivism, grassroots initiatives, experience economy, and contemporary tourism practices.

U-Seok Seo is a Professor in the Department of Urban Sociology at the University of Seoul, Korea, and also served as Chair of the Department of Culture, Arts and Tourism at the Graduate School of Urban Sciences from 2008 to 2016. His research areas include cultural sociology, urban sociology, cultural policy, and research methodology. He recently edited academic monographs focused on Seoul, including *Humanities Research on Seoul* (2016) and *Seoul Sociology* (2017). He currently serves as editor-in-chief of *Review of Culture and Economy* published by the Korean Association of Cultural Economics and is on the Committee for Culture City Seoul of the metropolitan government.

Alexandra Svyatunenko is a student in the Master's programme 'Experience Economy: Hospitality and Tourism Management' at the National Research University – Higher School of Economics in Saint-Petersburg, Russia. Alexandra is a member of a project on tourism development in rural areas (Leningrad oblast, Volosovo) with the non-governmental organization 'Kaykino Creative Projects', supported by the Timchenko Charity Foundation.

Siow-Hooi Tan is Associate Professor in Economics at the Faculty of Management, Multimedia University, Malaysia. She earned her PhD from the Faculty of Economics and Management, Universiti Putra Malaysia. Her research interests primarily focus on behavioural economics, tourism economics, and corporate social responsibilities.

Siow-Kian Tan is a Senior Lecturer of the Faculty of Management, Multimedia University, Malaysia. She holds a PhD degree from the Institute of Creative Industries Design, National Cheng Kung University, Taiwan. The focus of her research is service design, tourism management, creative tourism, and creative industries.

Thanakarn (Bella) Vongvisitsin is a Senior Researcher at Perfect Link Consulting Group, Thailand. Her interest in tourism inclusiveness and diversity has given her many opportunities to be one of the most respected persons representing international gender diversities in Asia. She has been awarded a PhD scholarship and is completing her Doctor of Philosophy at the School of Hotel and Tourism Management, Hong Kong Polytechnic University.

Jutamas (Jan) Wisansing holds a PhD in Tourism Marketing and Management from Lincoln University, New Zealand. She is a Founder and Managing Director leading an innovative team at Perfect Link Consulting Group, 'a consortium of experts' in Thailand. Working closely with diverse ranges of public and private sectors in Asia, her research and initiatives specialize in capacity-building programmes, tourism marketing, destination branding, creative tourism, sustainable culinary supply chain management, greener business, hotel and tourism occupational standards, organization development and sustainable tourism development, and community participation in sustainable development.

Acknowledgements

The editors gratefully acknowledge the contributions of the contributing authors – your diverse research approaches, contextualized insights, and unique perspectives reflect the richness and variety found within the field of creative tourism today. The depth of commitment and care evident in the research and practice settings you have presented in this volume is inspiring. We believe the opportunity to bring together such an international collection of creative tourism situations and perspectives is an important milestone in the field of creative tourism and a foundation for continued conversations and exchanges going forward.

Greg would like to acknowledge the important contributions made to the field by the many individuals and organizations involved in creative tourism research, development, and networking over the years. Although these are too numerous to mention here, some of the key figures include Caroline Couret and the Creative Tourism Network, Elena Paschinger, Crispin Raymond, Carlos Fernandes, Jan Wisansing, Esther Binkhorst, and Rebecca Wurzburger. Without their creative inspiration the field would not have developed in the many fruitful directions it has taken around the world.

Nancy would like to express gratitude for the insightful exchanges among her research colleagues and 'creative tourism pilot' practitioners within the project CREATOUR: Creative Tourism Destination Development in Small Cities and Rural Areas, which is illustrating the potential creative tourism can hold for meaningful, culture-informed development in small cities and rural areas. This work has also highlighted the on-the-ground challenges involved in designing and implementing creative tourism initiatives, the importance of research–practice connectedness, and the critical need to advance research on creative tourism and to improve knowledge sharing about leading practices, experiences, lessons learned, issues encountered and addressed, emerging trends, critical and questioning perspectives, and the wide variety of developments internationally. She hopes this book is a contribution towards this objective. She would also like to acknowledge the support provided for time to work on this book from the CREATOUR project (no. 16437), which is funded by the Portuguese Foundation for Science and Technology (FCT/MEC) through national funds and co-funded by FEDER through the Joint Activities Programme of COMPETE 2020 and the Regional Operational Programmes of Lisbon and Algarve.

Finally, we wish to express our gratitude for the support of our editor at Edward Elgar Publishing, Katy Crossan, who patiently accompanied us on this journey.

1 Towards a research agenda for creative tourism: developments, diversity, and dynamics

Nancy Duxbury and Greg Richards

Creative tourism is a niche tourism area that has emerged both as a development of cultural tourism and in opposition to the emergence of 'mass cultural tourism'. While creative tourism is fed by the general growth in cultural tourism, at the same time it caters to people who want more out of their cultural experiences. Creative tourism demand is driven by travellers seeking more active and participative cultural experiences in which they can use and develop their own creativity. Responding to these demands, and in the context of providing alternative approaches to tourism development in many locations, interest in creative tourism is rising internationally.

Although no data are available on the volume of creative tourism, there are some indications of the growth in demand. For example, the percentage of young travellers worldwide indicating that they had used their holidays to develop their creative potential rose from 18 per cent in 2012 to over 30 per cent in 2017 (WYSE Travel Confederation, 2017). Within the cultural tourism market, accounting for just under 40 per cent of all international travel and widely expected to continue growing (UNWTO, 2018),[1] experience-seeking travel has seen significant growth with an increasing demand for engaging and creative experiences. In Europe, a well-established cultural tourism market, travellers are 'increasingly interested in discovering new destinations' especially if 'these offer authentic activities that teach them about local culture' (CBI, 2018, n.p.). Altogether, the drive for more engaging culture-based experiences means that the demand for creative tourism is likely to increase in the future.

This volume brings together 30 authors working within and researching creative tourism from different disciplinary perspectives and different origins. Many of these chapters also make strong links between theory and practice. Each chapter provides a window on current investigations in creative tourism, illustrating the variety of research interests, approaches, and geographic contexts informing and influencing the development of the field. Taken together, these cases encapsulate the growing diversity and scope of creative tourism and the expanding body of literature on this topic. From these varied perspectives, we asked each author to suggest future research streams to extend the conceptual questions and pragmatic issues with which they are engaged.

In this opening chapter, we present an overview of the evolving and diversifying world of creative tourism, discuss the changing contexts for research in this field, and introduce the chapters in this volume. In the closing chapter, we synthesize contributors' suggestions and advice to outline the main research gaps and to elaborate key thematic areas for investigation to advance creative tourism research.

What is creative tourism? An evolving field

While travel has long been associated with artistic pursuits and creative experiences, in many ways the creative tourism field was launched in 2000[2] when Greg Richards and Crispin Raymond defined creative tourism as:

> Tourism which offers visitors the opportunity to develop their creative potential through active participation in courses and learning experiences which are characteristic of the holiday destination where they are undertaken. (p. 18)

This definition corresponds to what can be viewed as *creative tourism 1.0* featuring the development of small-scale creative experiences and learning activities, provided mainly by creative entrepreneurs as a supplement to other creative production (Richards, 2015). This type of creative tourism focuses on offering informal, hands-on workshops and creative experiences and is, in general, production-focused. As Crispin Raymond (2007) describes it, based on his experiences in developing creative tourism in New Zealand, these 'workshops take place in small groups at tutor's homes and places of work; they allow visitors to explore their creativity while getting closer to local people', providing 'an authentic feel for a local culture' and forming the basis of 'a more sustainable form of tourism' (p. 145).

Soon, policies began to be developed related to creative experiences in specific destinations and Internet portals were launched to market and distribute creative tourism (Binkhorst and den Dekker, 2009; Richards and Wilson, 2006), which can be labelled the *creative tourism 2.0* phase. This phase reflects a macro consumption-related perspective, with creative activities used to attract tourists to a destination. In this context, in 2006 the United Nations Educational, Scientific and Cultural Organization (UNESCO) Creative Cities Network took up and defined the creative tourism concept as:

> Creative tourism is travel directed toward an engaged and authentic experience, with participative learning in the arts, heritage, or special character of a place, and it provides a connection with those who reside in this place and create this living culture. (p. 3)

A variation to this approach linked creative tourism with community-based tourism and community development thinking. For example, in *Turismo creativo: el fin de la competitividad* (*Creative Tourism: The End of Competition*), Sergio Molina Espinoza (2011) presented a creative tourism that incorporates development processes focusing on community participation, interests, and expectations, and highlights an appreciation of the local culture, environment, and people. In this vision, creative tourism beomes a platform for collaboration among a variety of stakeholders, a process enabled by strategic partners such as public sector institutions, non-governmental organizations (NGOs), and private entrepreneurs. The overall objective is to use tourism as a stimulus to serve the economic and social development of the community, with attention to who is involved in tourism development and to whom the benefits of tourism flow. These ideas continue to resonate internationally, as can be seen in many of the chapters in this volume.

Contextualizing these developments, a shift of focus from tangible resources (e.g., built heritage, museums, monuments, beaches, mountains) to intangible resources (e.g., image, identity, lifestyles, atmosphere, narratives, creativity, media) could be observed in cultural tourism more generally. With a need to develop new types of distinctive cultural tourism, destinations began realizing the growing importance of their symbolic and intangible cultural dimensions (their 'soft cultural infrastructure') in defining their experiential sense of place, promoting their cultural vitality and energy, and as key differentiators in a global tourism marketplace. This focus on intangible cultural resources places people at the heart of cultural tourism, bringing forward important issues of intergenerational cultural sustainability, representation, and intellectual property. It also directs attention to the attractiveness of 'new' creation processes, creative places, and the spirit of creative milieu to tourists.

Consequently, over the past decade, the scope of activities incorporated within the concept of creative tourism has expanded. With the growing presence of the 'creative economy', connections between tourism, creative economy enterprises and activities, and the places they inhabit grew more evident, leading to *creative tourism 3.0*. This broadening integration of tourism and the creative economy led to the development of a wider range of creative experiences as well as more passive forms of creative consumption by tourists (Long and Morpeth, 2016; OECD, 2014). A growing array of studies of the relationship between tourism and the creative economy examined the development of creative economy policies, specific creative sectors and activities, the role of knowledge and networks in tourism, and the growth of specific creative tourism experiences (e.g., Fahmi et al., 2017; Fernandes, 2011; Gretzel and Jamal, 2009; Richards, 2011; Stolarick et al., 2011; Wattanacharoensil and Schuckert, 2016). Reflecting these development patterns, in a 2014 report for the Organisation for Economic Co-operation and Development (OECD), *Tourism and the Creative Economy*, Greg Richards re-defined the creative tourism concept to take these trends into account:

> Knowledge-based creative activities that link producers, consumers and places by utilising technology, talent or skill to generate meaningful intangible cultural products, creative content and experiences. (p. 7)

Destinations promoting creative experiences are faced with the challenge of fixing relatively mobile creative skills, knowledge, and ideas within their locale. Duxbury et al. (forthcoming, 2019) point to the importance of deeply embedding place-specificity in creative tourism activities and experiences, especially in non-urban areas. Growing mobility has also highlighted the importance of networks as 'conduits of knowledge flows and a means to generate creative experiences' (Richards, 2018, p. 16). This highly networked environment has engendered *creative tourism 4.0*, characterized by a shift towards 'relational tourism' based on the co-creation of experiences facilitated through peer-to-peer networks (Richards, 2014). This can be viewed as a micro consumption-related perspective blending into prosumption, with tourists designing or co-creating their creative activities and experiences in a particular destination.

It is important to note that while these four types of creative tourism activities developed in a roughly sequential basis, they should be viewed as *overlays*, with all four dimensions strongly evident today. This also means that what is referred to as 'creative tourism' may be linked to very different types of creative activities and creative contexts, and there is no consistent application of the definitions or terminology relating to creative tourism. A range of definitions have emerged, reflecting different contexts and accenting various dimensions depending on the intentions of the person defining it.

For example, in the CREATOUR research-and-application project (creatour.pt), which focuses on the development of creative tourism in small cities and rural areas in Portugal, the vision of creative tourism is centred on active creative activity encouraging personal self-expression and interaction between visitors and local residents, inspired by local endogenous resources (place and people), and designed and implemented by local residents for community benefit. In reviewing the various definitions of creative tourism that have been published, the CREATOUR team selected four aspects that resonate most strongly with the type of creative tourism activities the project aims to catalyze: active participation, creative self-expression, learning, and a link to the local community. The types of activities developed to date incorporate both workshops (creative tourism 1.0) and more free-form platforms for creative co-creation (creative tourism 4.0).

Researching creative tourism: an emerging field

As the contexts for creative tourism have diversified and the nature of tourism–creativity connections have evolved and expanded, research has accompanied these developments, providing insights and reflections from a wide variety of local and national contexts. While there is not sufficient space here to review the evolution of this research in detail, in a general way the trajectories of research on creative tourism have moved from identifying the emergence of creativity-based tourism activities, to examining creative tourist motivations and behaviours, the nature of the creative tourism experience, the general forms of organizations supplying creative tourism products, the relationships between tourists and their destination, and the impacts of this activity in the communities in which they occur. Many researchers have also worked to bridge their findings and analyses with frameworks for developing new creative tourism initiatives and policies.

The chapters in this volume demonstrate that the field of creative tourism research is much broader than a focus on the creative tourism activity and the experience it offers. Much research remains to be conducted about creative tourists, with a need to better understand both intentional and incidental creative tourists/travellers, and there still is a large gap in our knowledge about the producers of creative tourism offers and experiences. We also observe growing attention to the settings and locales in which these activities take place and how creative tourism initiatives can be strategically designed and levered for both visitor and local benefit. Research on programmes/strategies/policies to frame, inform, nurture, and support creative tourism is rising: ranging from artisan mapping/directories and development programmes, to training and promotional organizations, to strategies for linking creative tourism to local development and planning. A challenge in all this work is to acknowledge and embrace the complementarity of bottom-up innovations and idiosyncratic, unpredictable developments while making room for policy, planning, and collaborative governance frameworks.

At this juncture, we feel it is a timely moment to offer three overarching challenges to researchers. The first challenge is a conceptual one: to build from the prevailing series of definitions of creative tourism and develop a more integrated model. We suggest that defining the field of creative tourism now requires a new framework for organizing the disparate elements that comprise this evolving set of practices, and it may require an integrally dynamic approach, approximating a kaleidoscope perhaps, which would enable the inclusion of an array of types of creative tourism activities and accommodate a wide range of socio-cultural and geographic contexts. Towards this objective, we offer an initial organizing framework that attempts to summarize some of the main aspects of creative tourism development and research (Figure 1.1).

The framework centres on the 'creative core' of creative tourism, which is basically the learning process that is the focus of interactive workshops and creative experiences. These types of activities were the original inspirations for the creative tourism concept, and the idea of involving visitors in the creativity of the destination through learning about local culture, skills, and ideas is still one of the most powerful inspirations for creative tourism development. But the rapid expansion of creative tourism from this original creative tourism 1.0 form has seen a series of new layers added to the field over time. One important dimension of the expansion of creative tourism has been the engagement of visitors as co-creators of their own experiences. This moves away from the formal setting of the workshop, in which the learning environment is usually provided by the producer, to a broader context of creative interaction between local and mobile creatives. In many destinations there is also a trend towards adding creative spectacles as a means of developing more engaging content (Richards and Wilson, 2006). In these settings, which include events, art displays, and architecture, the visitor is basically a passive consumer of

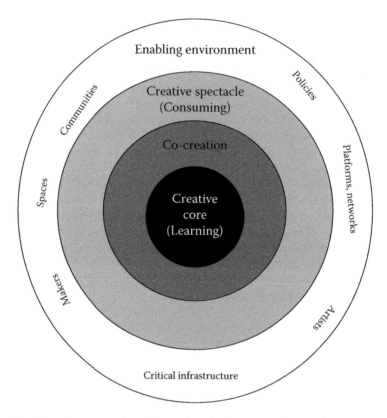

Figure 1.1   The main aspects of creative tourism development and research: an organizing framework

the creativity of others. Finally, creative experiences would not be available without a broad range of creative resources in the local enabling environment. These include creative individuals, communities, and organizations; the spaces and places in which locals and visitors can interact creatively; and the supporting policies for development and marketing. Taken together, the different layers of Figure 1.1 reflect the many different approaches to creative tourism that have emerged over the years, and which are reflected in this volume.

The second challenge is to more explicitly acknowledge and critique the temporal, conceptual, and geographic contexts in which the research and conceptualization in the field has progressed. As creative tourism practices continue to change, the context in which creative tourism is interpreted and understood also evolves. Critically revisiting earlier works in light of situations and challenges today is an important task for the field as it moves forward. For example, when creative tourism was discussed in the early years of the twenty-first century, 'creative cities', 'creative class', and the 'creative economy' were still-emerging ideas that were only beginning to gain notice in policy and planning contexts. Jumping forward to today, we have over a decade and a half of experiences, trajectories, and critiques of these topics, and their diffusion in a wide variety of international contexts. How can this work assist us in re-conceiving and critically examining creative tourism trajectories and their impacts? While various notions of creativity remain a strong presence, continuing to influence policy and planning interest in creative tourism as well as some areas of creative tourism research, they share the stage with other societal trends and developments shaping the world today – and travel and tourism within this.

This brings us to the third challenge, to link creative tourism research to the major challenges facing our societies and the planet. As research on creative tourism moves forward, the field should proceed with a heightened cognizance of the significant roles travel and tourism play in constructing and shaping our interconnected world, and the ways in which we imagine and understand it, others, and ourselves. Mitigating the more negative aspects of tourism, for example, in terms of environmental sustainability and in relation to the socio-cultural well-being of *in situ* communities, could form an important dimension of this. In this context, research could take on a more 'future forming' orientation, to 'bring into focus new and far-reaching potentials of inquiry' (Gergen, 2014, p. 288) and to play an active role in envisioning, informing, and empowering alternatives. Today, we recognize the great need for connections on a human level globally and to our planet, and the essential importance of intercultural learning and sharing experiences. The forces of imagination and creative expression provide us with important tools with which to revitalize and extend cultural traditions and practices, to immerse ourselves in different worldviews and perspectives, and to build renewed visions and pathways for the future, inspiring and informing the world we are collectively constructing. Creative tourism can play an important role in this trajectory going forward.

About this volume

This volume brings together 30 authors working within and researching creative tourism. Their chapters investigate and reflect on the field of creative tourism and its meaningful articulation in diverse settings:

- World Heritage Sites in Malaysia
- The Indonesian island of Bali
- 13 small communities in Thailand
- Small town 'creative outposts' in British Columbia, Canada
- Community-engaged projects in rural Russia
- The snowy cultural and natural landscape of Lapland, Finland
- Gangneung, Korea's 'coffee city'
- The pioneering creative tourism city of Santa Fe, New Mexico, United States
- A participatory museum in Zagreb, Croatia
- The creative neighbourhoods of Montréal, Canada
- The culture-rich city of Ouro Preto, in the state of Minas Gerais, Brazil
- The virtual landscape of creative tourism networks and platforms.

The volume is divided into four main parts in which the gaze of the research progressively broadens outward, beginning with research that focuses on the creative tourist and his or her individual experiences; progressing to give greater consideration of the symbiotic relationships between different forms of creative tourism activity and the local contexts in which it occurs: moving on to the challenges of development processes, articulating local impacts, and informing local strategies and policies; and, finally, presenting an international review of the offers of creative tourism platforms and networks that organize and promote creative tourism activities on a collective basis. Following from this array of research perspectives, the volume ends with a concluding chapter that synthesizes and elaborates on the contributors' suggested future research trajectories in creative tourism.

Part I: The Creative Tourist and Creative Tourism Experiences presents three chapters focused on understanding the creative tourist and examining core elements of the creative tourism experience: taking creative action, authenticity, and emotions.

Siow-Kian Tan and Siow-Hooi Tan's chapter, 'Nurturing the creative tourist in Malaysia', is based on in-depth interviews and observations at George Town and Melaka, Malaysia's World Heritage Sites. It aims to identify possible routes that could be used to encourage creative tourists, particularly at such heritage sites. Informed by literature on the formative influences of awareness/consciousness, social justice concerns, and sense of place, they search for the keys that motivate people to move beyond awareness to take the actions that are vital for a creative experience. The study aims to examine how awareness, creativity, and action-oriented knowledge – all vital for nurturing creative tourists – can be applied to learning processes related to intrapersonal and development aspects of creativity, a gap in the research to date. They then turn to analyze the different stakeholders involved in heritage sites, examine how they could play a role in nurturing creative tourists, and identify some challenges and barriers to encouraging creative tourism in this context.

Authenticity is often presented as a key element of creative tourism but is often incorporated in an uncritical manner. In 'The role of authenticity in rural creative tourism', Manuela Blapp and Ondrej Mitas critically examine the role of authenticity in creative tourism in rural areas of the Indonesian island of Bali. They argue that to develop creative tourism in rural areas and prevent commodification, the theoretical assumptions and definitions behind ideas of authenticity must be carefully considered. Extending the discussion in the literature on this topic, their chapter analyzes how different theories of authenticity are applied in creative and community-based tourism literature and suggests a synthetic theory of authenticity applicable to creative tourism development in rural areas. This theory is explored in the context of five Balinese villages using a microethnographic approach with participant observation and expert as well as tourist interviews.

Daniela Angelina Jelinčić and Matea Senkić's chapter, 'The value of experience in culture and tourism: the power of emotions', seeks strategies to design meaningful experiences into cultural and creative tourism attractions and activities. Looking to research on the experience economy, the authors find that meaningful experiences are based on creating different innovative, spectacular, and sensory stimuli that engage tourists to identify with them and/or to participate and co-create. In other words, to achieve a 'real' response in a tourism experience, it is necessary to stimulate emotions with which tourists are able to identify. As Jelinčić and Senkić elaborate, tourists increasingly seek experiences that reflect their own personal stories, and successful experience creation must include this personal identification with the attraction. The chapter provides a transdisciplinary theoretical background on experience creation drawing from the fields of psychology, culture, and tourism to introduce the concept of tourist emotional engagement. The authors examine this concept in the context of an experience co-(re)creation exhibit within the Museum of Broken Relationships, in Zagreb, Croatia. The authors contend that since emotions instigate response behaviours, a participatory creative activity such as writing personal experiences (as integrated into this exhibit) can provide an experience for self-healing and transformation.

In *Part II: Forms of Creative Tourism Destinations*, four types of creative tourism initiatives are presented in very different settings, with research that investigates and reflects on the interaction between creative tourism activities, the places that inform, inspire, and nurture these experiences, and local dynamics that may be catalyzed in these creative tourism experiences.

Patrick Brouder's chapter, 'Creative tourism in creative outposts', focuses on the subtle, yet palpable, role of creative processes that contribute to rural peripheral tourism innovation and regional development. Creative outposts are defined as rural peripheral communities that face challenging socio-economic environments but meet these challenges by deploying endogenous creative capital resulting in a palpable shift towards a more sustainable socio-economic environment. As Brouder observes, the 'island-like' status of these outpost communities opens up both the possibility for and the challenge of increased local interaction and cooperation. He argues that tourism has proven to be tenacious in rural peripheral areas and that creative tourism has a clear role in the long-term resilience of rural communities. In order to illustrate the challenge of, and the necessity for, understanding the potential of creative tourism in creative outposts, three cases from rural British Columbia, Canada (Ashcroft, Fernie, and Salt Spring Island) are presented.

In 'Stories of design, snow, and silence: creative tourism landscape in Lapland', Satu Miettinen, Jaana Erkkilä-Hill, Salla-Mari Koistinen, Timo Jokela, and Mirja Hiltunen discuss how the creative tourism landscape in Lapland has been constructed and transformed into a topography of artistic collaboration, walking, and gazing. They introduce Arctic design and artistic production as creative contexts that allow people to both participate and develop a cluster of events aimed at increasing art, creativity, and innovation in the Arctic. Three case studies are presented. The first case study, 'Lapland Snow Art and Design', represents snow and ice forming the landscape and location for artistic production and tourist activity.

The second case study, 'Travelling Laboratories for Artistic Thinking', studies the artist's way of producing a tourism experience through performance and mediation in silence and walking. The third case study, 'Master's degree programme of Applied Visual Arts and Nature Photography', introduces a contemporary discussion on creating the tourist gaze in the Arctic through photography. The case studies are analyzed using art education as an embodied practice and in terms of collaborative design processes in creative tourism. The chapter discusses active engagement and ways of introducing creative and cultural activities as tools for collaboration between tourists and local communities, and the positioning of community members as visitors in their own topography.

U-Seok Seo's chapter, 'Coffee tourism as creative tourism: implications from Gangneung's experiences', discusses the diverse relationships between creativity and coffee tourism in Gangneung, South Korea. The chapter outlines how the rise of coffee tourism has been possible in a small city such as Gangneung and how the city's use of creativity contributed to this achievement. Coffee tourism in Gangneung provides creative tourism opportunities like learning various knowledges about coffee and participating in a variety of coffee-related DIY experiences. The author suggests a more differentiated understanding of creative tourism is needed to understand a variety of these creative tourism developments (such as a 'snack culture' type). Creative spaces have been made in cafés, which function as cultural spaces, with some linked to popular media and visiting celebrities. The creative convergence evident in Gangneung's experiences means coffee tourism now plays a pivotal role in fostering favourable circumstances for culture-based urban regeneration through attracting taste-oriented visitors and enhancing place image.

Closing this part, Marie-Andrée Delisle's chapter, 'Montréal: a creative tourism destination?', challenges the assumption that creative tourism initiatives are a 'natural' aspect of the life of a well-known 'creative city'. Her research finds that although widely considered a 'creative' destination, Montréal somehow has not invested in creative tourism. She points to the intense programming of the 375th anniversary of the city in 2017 as an opportunity for its population to participate directly in imagining the city in a creative way and to actively engage in the celebration of their city at a community level – an event-based decentralized platform that also helped facilitate the immersion of visitors in the local culture and way of life. She asks: From this base, how can creative tourism be fostered in the city? The research conducted for this chapter found that artists and artisans may not be aware of the opportunity available for them to offer creative workshops to visitors. There are numerous workshops already offered to the local population, so adapting those for visitors may represent an easy transfer, but one would need to motivate the artists and artisans into extending their activities as workshop productions for visitors, and the process would have to be facilitated. Various examples and some interviews with key stakeholders illustrate these topics. In closing, the chapter suggests seeds for the implementation of creative tourism workshops in Montréal's neighbourhoods.

Part III: Creative Tourism in Local Development turns to examination of development models and processes and addresses the issue of how to measure and monitor the multidimensional impacts of creative tourism on local communities.

Brent Hanifl begins this part with the chapter 'Creative tourism in Santa Fe, New Mexico', which provides an overview of the development of a major, pioneering creative tourism initiative in the United States. Hanifl then discusses research undertaken to identify the economic value of 'creative tourism' activity in Santa Fe, including efforts to assess the scope, nature, and extent of creative tourism activities and to identify and assess the economic value of creative tourism in the city. Hanifl describes efforts to evaluate the characteristics of a thriving arts and culture sector to support creative tourism activities, and raises the important issue of directing investments in creative tourism towards developing activities of interest to creative tourists versus investments to brand a place as a creative tourism destination.

In 'Local impacts of creative tourism initiatives', Jutamas (Jan) Wisansing and Thanakarn (Bella) Vongvisitsin present an integrated monitoring system called 'Linkages and Leakages' which has been developed combining the lessons learned from a pilot project in six designated areas in Thailand with a synthesis of extensive information on impact evaluations and indicators applicable to measuring various aspects of social, economic, and environmental sustainability at a community level. The resulting Community Benefitting through Creative Tourism (CBCT) model maps out impacts and benefits from end to end across the entire creative tourism value chain. This comprehensive and local-friendly tool was leveraged by a multi-stakeholders' co-creation and facilitated by the Designated Areas for Sustainable Tourism Administration (DASTA). It has been designed as a locally owned and led process for monitoring, managing, and enhancing the sustainability of creative tourism initiatives. Three intertwined sustainable dimensions – articulating an ecologically, socio-culturally, and economically sustainable and equitable environment – enable community leaders to delineate the need for empowerment and capacity-building programmes, local sourcing strategies, and starting up community enterprises and their social capital-building structures (social networks and trust).

Marina Matetskaya, Alexandra Svyatunenko, and Olga Gracheva's chapter, 'The development of creative tourism in rural areas of Russia: issues of entrepreneurial ability, cooperation, and social inclusion', examines the experience of several projects initiated by NGOs that aim to support the initiatives of local residents in the field of rural creative tourism. The chapter highlights the particular characteristics and features of rural areas that make rural tourism initiatives differ from those of city tourism. Along with governmental support measures and private investments, the authors contend that rural projects have a number of advantages in terms of collaborating with local communities, including craftspeople/artisans, who present a specific category of business unit. Combining a literature review with case study research, Matetskaya, Svyatunenko, and Gracheva discuss management tools employed by tourism projects in rural areas, approaches to community engagement in tourism-related projects, and creative tourism models and challenges in rural areas.

Closing this part, and linking creative tourism to local policy development in an urban context, Magnus Luiz Emmendoerfer's chapter, 'Creative tourist regions as a basis for public policy', presents the concept of 'creative tourist regions' to support the elaboration and implementation of public policies in support of creative tourism at the municipal level, drawing from case study research in Ouro Preto, Brazil. Informed by comparisons between the concepts of creative tourism and community-based tourism, as well as ideas from creative economy and public policy, the idea of the creative tourist region is elaborated as the basis for public policy that respects and congregates the diversity of existing cultural and market expressions in an area and represents it with an intent to induce tourism. Emmendoerfer also proposes elements that can help plan and monitor local public policies in regards to both tourism activities and creative ventures. Attention to collective actions among stakeholders and collaborative governance underpin this work.

Part IV: Creative Tourism Networks and Platforms presents the initial findings of an international examination of creative tourism networks and platforms. As mentioned earlier, many of these networks were established to profile and promote creative tourism to attract tourists to a specific destination (local, regionally, or nationally defined) but these organizations have not been systematically examined. In 'Good and not-so-good practices in creative tourism networks and platforms: an international review', Paula Remoaldo, Olga Matos, Isabel Freitas, Hélder da Silva Lopes, Vítor Ribeiro, Ricardo Gôja, and Miguel Pereira report on the first systematic international review of these organizations and structures, conducted within the framework of the CREATOUR project. This chapter reports the primary findings of an investigation of the websites of these networks and platforms, carried out in 2017, to identify and analyze existing practices and initiatives undertaken by each institution. The study reinforces our observations that a consensus has not yet been reached worldwide regarding the concept of creative tourism. The main results show that not all initiatives referred to as 'creative experiences' have identifiable creative content or focus. The fact that most of the identified initiatives stem from southern Europe also suggests that many are driven by a desire to diversify tourism, rather than to develop creativity per se.

In the closing chapter of this volume, 'Towards a research agenda in creative tourism: a synthesis of suggested future research trajectories', Nancy Duxbury and Greg Richards provide an overview of the main themes for future research that have been suggested in this volume and point out potentially fruitful future research avenues within the tourism field and related to it. The chapter is organized into nine thematic areas: the creative tourist, creative tourism experiences, creative supply, marketing creative tourism, the development of creative tourism experiences and destinations, assessing creative tourism development, the role of local communities in creative tourism, placemaking through creative tourism, and creative tourism networks and platforms.

NOTES

1 According to an August 2017 report from London-based market research forecasters Technavio, the global cultural tourism market is expected to grow at a compound annual growth rate of almost 36 per cent between 2017 and 2021, and will be valued at US$10.02 trillion by 2021.

2 Richards (2010) outlines the genesis of the creative tourism concept. He notes that the idea arose in the mid-1990s within the EUROTEX project when a group of researchers and practitioners were looking at ways to enhance the sales of craft products to tourists: 'Through discussions with craft producers and interviews with tourists, we quickly realised that many visitors were interested in seeing how craft products were made, and many wanted to learn craft skills for themselves. As a result, we decided to develop craft experiences which allowed the visitors to get involved with the production process, either by seeing craft producers at work or by learning particular textile production techniques' (p. 79). These ideas became the inspiration for what would be called creative tourism.

References

Binkhorst, E. and T. den Dekker (2009), 'Agenda for co-creation tourism experience research', *Journal of Hospitality Marketing and Management,* **18** (2–3), 311–27.

CBI, UK Ministry of Foreign Affairs (2018), *What are the Opportunities for Cultural Tourism from Europe?*, accessed 13 October 2018 at https://www.cbi.eu/marketinformation/tourism/culturaltourism/culturaltourismeurope/.

Duxbury, N., S. Silva and T.V. de Castro (forthcoming, 2019), 'Creative tourism development in small cities and rural areas in Portugal: insights from start-up activities', in D.A. Jelinčić and Y. Mansfeld (eds), *Creating and Managing Experiences in Cultural Tourism*, Singapore: World Scientific Publishing.

Fahmi, F.Z., P. McCann and S. Koster (2017), 'Creative economy policy in developing countries: the case of Indonesia', *Urban Studies,* **54** (6), 1367–84.

Fernandes, C. (2011), 'Cultural planning and creative tourism in an emerging tourist destination', *International Journal of Management Cases,* **13** (3), 629–36.

Gergen, K.J. (2014), 'From mirroring to world-making: research as future forming', *Journal for the Theory of Social Behaviour,* **45** (3), 287–310. doi:10.1111/jtsb.12075.

Gretzel, U. and T. Jamal (2009), 'Conceptualizing the creative tourist class: technology, mobility, and tourism experiences', *Tourism Analysis,* **14** (4), 471–81.

Long, P. and N.D. Morpeth (2016), *Tourism and the Creative Industries: Theories, Policies and Practice,* London: Routledge.

Molina Espinoza, S. (2011), *Turismo creativo: el fin de la competitividad* (*Creative Tourism: The End of Competition*), Santiago, Chile: Escritores.

OECD (2014), *Tourism and the Creative Economy*, Paris: OECD.

Raymond, C. (2007), 'Creative Tourism New Zealand: the practical challenges of developing creative tourism', in G. Richards and J. Wilson (eds), *Tourism, Creativity and Development*, London: Routledge, pp. 145–57.

Richards, G. (2010), 'Creative tourism and local development', in R. Wurzburger, T. Aageson, A. Pattakos and S. Pratt (eds), *Creative Tourism: A Global Conversation*, Santa Fe, NM: The City of Santa Fe, pp. 78–90.

Richards, G. (2011), 'Creativity and tourism: the state of the art', *Annals of Tourism Research,* **38** (4), 1225–53.

Richards, G. (2014), 'Creativity and tourism in the city', *Current Issues in Tourism,* **17** (2), 119–44.

Richards, G. (ed.) (2015), *Creative Tourism Trend Report Volume 1*, Arnhem: ATLAS.

Richards, G. (2018), 'Cultural tourism: a review of recent research and trends', *Journal of Hospitality and Tourism Management,* **36**, 12–21.

Richards, G. and C. Raymond (2000), 'Creative tourism', *ATLAS News*, no. 23, 16–20.

Richards, G. and J. Wilson (2006), 'Developing creativity in tourist experiences: a solution to the serial reproduction of culture?', *Tourism Management*, **27**, 1209–23.

Stolarick, K.M., M. Denstedt, B. Donald and G.M. Spencer (2011), 'Creativity, tourism and economic development in a rural context: the case of Prince Edward County', *Journal of Rural and Community Development*, **5** (1–2), 238–54.

Technavio (2017), *Global Cultural Tourism Market 2017–2021*, Toronto: Technavio.

UNESCO Creative Cities Network (2006), *Towards Sustainable Strategies for Creative Tourism. Discussion Report of the Planning Meeting for 2008 International Conference on Creative Tourism, Santa Fe, New Mexico, U.S.A., October 25–27, 2006*, accessed 16 October 2018 at http://unesdoc.unesco.org/images/0015/001598/159811e.pdf.

UNWTO (2018), *Report on Tourism and Culture Synergies*, Madrid: UNWTO.

Wattanacharoensil, W. and M. Schuckert (2016), 'Reviewing Thailand's master plans and policies: implications for creative tourism?', *Current Issues in Tourism*, **19** (10), 1045–70.

WYSE Travel Confederation (2017), *New Horizons, Preliminary Results*, Paris: UNWTO and UNESCO.

PART I

The creative tourist and creative tourism experiences

2 Nurturing the creative tourist in Malaysia

Siow-Kian Tan and Siow-Hooi Tan

The creative tourist is an important stakeholder in creative tourism as they are the 'prosumers' of the creative tourism products/experiences. The growth in 'prosumption', a process in which the consumer becomes a producer of the products and experiences they consume, coincides with the emergence of a new breed of tourists labelled 'skilled consumers' or 'creative consumers' (Richards, 2011; Richards and Wilson, 2006) or 'creative tourists' (Raymond, 2003). No matter what term is applied, they all refer to tourists who actively create their experience at the destinations they choose. The creative tourist is a participant, someone who learns by doing and finds enjoyment and fulfilment in developing his or her new abilities; in other words, the interactive traveller is a creative tourist (Raymond, 2003). Creative tourists are no longer satisfied with pure observation of cultural spectacles; rather, they look for active participation.

Creative tourism can be seen as an alternative path towards a more sustainable tourism and it depends far more on the active involvement of tourists. Nevertheless, there is a great diversity of creative tourists, from families who take part in a craft-making class at their holiday destination, to artists who stay in an art-residency – all can be called 'creative tourists'. While every (ordinary) tourist has the potential to be a creative tourist, only those tourists who encounter a creative experience may be called a creative tourist (Tan et al., 2014). Tan et al. (2013) propose that 'inner reflections' and 'outer interactions' together construct a tourist's creative experience, and awareness or consciousness of these inner and outer interactions is crucial for a tourist to become a creative tourist. Nevertheless, and although the importance of creative tourists to a more sustainable ecosystem has been acknowledged, we still know little about how to ensure more tourists have creative experiences.

This chapter aims to identify the possible routes that could be used to encourage creative tourists, particularly at heritage sites. First, we review the literature on the formative influences of awareness/consciousness. Then we examine the literature on social justice concerns and sense of place in order to know what motivates people to take action, as awareness itself does not guarantee taking the actions that are vital for a creative experience. The concepts of creativity and action-oriented knowledge are subsequently reviewed as potential tools for action-taking. We then analyze the different stakeholders at heritage sites and examine how they could play a role in nurturing creative tourists. Finally, some challenges and barriers to encouraging creative tourism are identified.

Awareness/consciousness and life experiences

Awareness/consciousness is influenced and constituted cognitively by individual experiences, and it comes from our daily life experiences. Howell and Allen (2016) categorize these repeated/ongoing and/or 'ordinary' experiences under 12 groups: people (with whom we have direct personal contact), media, formal and informal education, outdoor/nature experiences, work (paid or voluntary), negative experiences/events, impacts of climate change, organizations/campaigns/groups, grandchildren/children, travel/living abroad, religion/spirituality, and waste/frugality. They propose that the continuity of our daily life experiences is vital in influencing our awareness of environmental issues such as climate change. They also suggest that in order to motivate people to take action, social justice concerns, such as fairness and climate justice, and biospheric-oriented concerns, such as impacts on wildlife and landscapes, are vital.

Awareness, social justice concerns, and sense of place

When people are concerned about an issue, such as the conditions of a place that is deteriorating, or have a sense of loss due to something that is missing, or have a sense of injustice about something that is unfair, they will be motivated to take action (Chapin III and Knapp, 2015; Howell and Allen, 2016; Tan et al., 2018). This is because affective ties to places may motivate people to be better informed and, hence, make decisions beneficial to their communities (Adams et al., 2010).

According to Tan et al. (2018), sense of place consists of sense of loss, sense of justice, and sense of mission. Yet not everyone who has a sense of loss or a sense of justice will have a sense of mission. Sense of mission needs to be evoked in order to motivate someone to take an action. Awareness is one of the sources of sense of loss, sense of justice, and sense of mission; however, in order to foster people to do something, creativity is needed. This raises two questions: What is creativity? and How can people 'use or apply' creativity? This also requires an understanding of creativity itself.

Creativity, knowledge, and actions

Creativity can be seen from different perspectives. In their 4-c model of creativity, Kaufman and Beghetto (2009) identify four types of creativity: big-c, which focuses on eminent creativity; little-c, which looks more at everyday creativity; mini-c, which highlights the intrapersonal and development aspects of creativity; and pro-c, which focuses on professional expertise. Based on this model, mini-c and little-c can be found in anyone; and from mini-c, everyone has a potential to develop their little-c, pro-c, and even big-c.

Tan et al. (2018) study the dimensions of creativity from different perspectives and acknowledge that the components of creativity include curiosity, life experiences linked together, and the demands of society. Nevertheless, how these components have been integrated remains understudied. According to Jensen (2002), knowledge that encourages people to take action consists of four dimensions: first, knowledge about effects (what kind of problem is it?); second, knowledge about the root causes (why do we have the problems we have?); third, knowledge about strategies for change (how do we change things?); and, the last, knowledge about alternatives and visions (where do we want to go?). Of these, knowledge about strategies for change is a vital trigger that may motivate people to take actions. However, *how* these four dimensions of knowledge have been integrated to better motivate people to take action requires further discussion. In short, although awareness, creativity, and action-oriented knowledge are vital for nurturing creative tourists, how these different components have been applied in this mini-c learning process has been overlooked. The current study aims to bridge these gaps.

Methods

This study uses qualitative content analysis of in-depth interviews and observations conducted in George Town and Melaka (Malaysia's World Heritage Sites) between March 2015 and May 2017. Representatives of non-governmental organizations, tourists, and traditional craftspeople were interviewed. A total of 20 documents, including interview transcripts, field-notes, and textual documents (such as books, brochures, and maps) were analyzed and used to discuss how different stakeholders or local communities could play roles in nurturing creative tourists. Associations or 'Kongsi' (the company of a family clan), grandparents/parents/neighbourhoods, and traditional traders or craftspeople were selected as they represent the linkage of the present and the past and could provide rich information and stories for the public. As creative tourists are expected to contribute to a more sustainable ecosystem, by nurturing more creative tourists, these stakeholders may find some solutions to the problems they currently face, such as the loss of a sense of cohesiveness in associations, sense of belongingness to a neighbourhood, and issues of inheritors for traditional crafts and arts.

This study uses Tan et al.'s (2018) sense of place model (shown in Table 2.1, row 1), which consists of awareness/consciousness, creativity, sense of loss, sense of justice, sense of mission, and sustainability goals; and Jensen's (2002) four dimensions of action-oriented knowledge (shown in Table 2.1, row 2): knowledge about effects, knowledge about root causes, knowledge about strategies for change, and knowledge about alternatives and visions, to discuss 'what has been done', and 'what can be done' to nurture creative tourists.

Table 2.1 Using a sense of place model and four dimensions of action-oriented knowledge to nurture creative tourists

Sense of place model		Aware/conscious about . . .			Sustainability goals
Four dimensions of action-oriented knowledge		Sense of loss	Sense of justice	Sense of mission (Creativity tools)	
		What is the problem? (Effects)	Why do we have the problems we have? (Causes)	How do we change things? (Change strategies)	Where do we want to go? (Vision)
Stakeholders	Background				
Associations/ Kongsi	• The history and the background of these associations • The association's functions	• Lost their function to unite the people from the same villages • Loosened their connections with their ancestors' hometowns or villages	• Not able to attract young generations to join • Youth do not understand the meaning of these associations	Old plus new, linking different life experiences together: • The heritage building may serve as a museum to exhibit the history and development of the associations • Apps should be designed in order to connect these associations	• To create a sense of belongingness among the youth • Creative tourists who are aware of self and culture
Grandparents/ Parents/ Neighbourhood	• Grandparents' generation was born in an era of scarcity • Had more opportunities to learn in outdoor environment	• Young generations not appreciating what they have • They seldom reuse the existing materials as everything new	• Parents give the best to their children, including the expensive e-gadgets	Curiosity as a means: • Traditional childhood games that can be played everywhere can be displayed to attract the attention of the young	• To 'awaken' the young to appreciate the resources they have • Creative tourists who are aware

Traditional traders/craftsmen	• The history and development of these traditional trades and crafts	• More appreciative of the materials they had owned	• Lost their functions and identity	is available at cheaper cost	• No demand as people are not aware of their existence	Demands of the society: • Knowing what is needed by the society • Adding aesthetic factors into the product/experience	of the younger generations and environment	• To revive and transform the traditional crafts and to nurture more 'prosumers' who appreciate their own culture • Creative tourists who are aware of their own culture

Source: Tan et al. (2018) and Jensen (2002).

In the following section, a brief background about these stakeholders is presented, followed by a synthesis of the problems faced by them (to know about the effects and to evoke people's sense of loss), an analysis of causes that led to these problems (to know about the root causes and stimulate people's sense of justice), an articulation of strategies for change using creativity to stimulate people's sense of mission, and, lastly, identification of visions for the future.

Research results

Associations/Kongsi

Chinese people began to emigrate to Nanyang ('South Sea' or Southeast Asia) from the beginning of the seventeenth century. These immigrants had to unite in order to protect their rights, trades, and the 'territory', and, hence, localized associations and lineage associations, or 'Kongsi', were established, especially at those main ports where many foreign immigrants gathered. At first, the purpose of these associations was to unite immigrants from the same village/place so that they were able to help each other, and this vital role was irreplaceable for many decades. Nevertheless, the need for mutual support faded as these 'immigrants' settled down and increasingly perceived Malaysia as their home country. The role of the associations therefore changed, and some of these associations are now facing challenges in attracting younger generations to join. Although many associations try to attract youth using different strategies, for example, by awarding scholarships, the lineage connections have been lost. Nevertheless, as these associations 'witnessed' the history and the development of a locale's identity, and cohesiveness within the clan is vital for the young to connect to their ancestors, the importance of these associations should not be overlooked.

One of the root causes of the younger generation loosening their connections with their ancestor's hometown is that they do not understand the meaning of the local associations. This 'why' knowledge is important: by providing proper information about their ancestors' history, it is believed it may 'trigger' the youngsters' awareness/consciousness about themselves, such as who they are, and why they are here. However, many youngsters are not aware of their history. An interviewee at Melaka raised a concerning question:

> Why do our younger generations want to leave our country? Our ancestors tried so hard and sacrificed so many things just to stay here. However, many youngsters are not aware or conscious about it. Hence, many are taking it for granted and leaving the country when their financial means can support them to do so.

Knowledge about strategies for change is important to be able to change the current situation. What are the strategies that can be applied to stimulate youths' sense of belonging, and awareness/consciousness of themselves and their culture? The migration of Chinese people was recorded either in official archives or in unofficial documents (Tan and Ooi, 2014). Some Chinese associations or

Kongsi took the initiative to collect these data and publish books to tell the stories to the youth. However, this is not sufficient, as the young may not even be aware of these publications. Hence, creativity becomes an important means of linking life experiences together, and telling a story about the community for itself and others.

For example, many of the buildings used by the associations were built decades or even centuries ago. Some of these buildings are 'heritage buildings' that may impress people if they are able to maintain their 'look' as a heritage building. These heritage buildings may serve as a museum of each clan, to tell the story of its past. Nevertheless, bridging past and present may need more 'assistance', such as the development of interactive apps that can tell the stories of the past and have more interaction with the different layers of life experiences. Apps are a fundamental tool for the younger generations to learn. In other words, by combining the 'hardware' of the museum and the 'software' of interactive apps, it is hoped that younger generations' sense of mission will be stimulated, and their sense of belonging will be evoked for the long term.

Parents/grandparents/neighbourhood

Each generation has their own 'Belle Époque'. Older generations who were born in an era of scarcity are relatively more appreciative of what they have and tend to reuse and recycle materials more readily. For instance, a member of a non-governmental organization states: 'When we were young, we always reused these tins, the tin could be used to make our new toys, such as the lanterns, but nowadays these tins have been thrown away.' As the world keeps changing, the new generations who have grown up with new technology find it hard to understand the world their parents and grandparents lived in. In addition, these new generations have also lost the opportunity to appreciate what they own, as their parents easily satisfy their desires for material things. The gap between grandparents' and parents' generations and the younger generations is growing larger. And, as children seldom engage in outdoor activities, their connections with the neighbourhood are loosening as well.

Each place and each generation has their own traditional 'childhood games', which can create interactions and strengthen family bonds. For the generations without e-gadgets, they played in an outdoor environment, using simple tools such as a chalk or stick to draw the 'outline/square' of the 'chip chip chom' (hopscotch) game. Chip chip chom is a game in which the player has to jump from one square to another. The game was very popular during the 1950s to the 1980s. The younger generations who have grown up with e-gadgets or smartphones may have never known what chip chip chom is.

The founder of the Gohkaki Childhood Museum, Mr Chang, not only established a museum that exhibits traditional childhood games, but also aims to convince all apartment occupants and residential areas to add the traditional childhood games such as hopscotch to their parks (Zhang, 2016). His intention is to stimulate the parents' generations to play the game when they see it at the parks, and when the younger generations pass by, they will be attracted by their curiosity: 'They will stop and ask what you are doing here, and they will also ask you how to play with it.' Curiosity has been used as a tool to stimulate interest in learning. It is hoped that the young will appreciate the resources which have been ignored, but which still exist in our surroundings.

Traditional traders/craftspeople

Different jobs and professions emerge in society over time. The history of why a job was created at a particular time in a particular place is worth recording, as this will tell us the story of that time. For example, the blacksmiths gathered near the port many decades ago, as the carriages needed their work. Years later, the immigrants who settled in a new place liked to tell others about their origin using the 'Tang Hao'[1] and, hence, the signboard engraver emerged. Many craftspeople, such as rattan weavers, bead-shoe makers, and goldsmiths, were needed between the 1900s and the 1970s, and hence these jobs became popular. However, as time passed, the once busy and lively pier/quay/port lost its function as a main business and social hub. How do these traders or craftspeople survive or transform, and how can these traders assist in nurturing creative tourists?

Traditional traders and craftspeople may add value to their previous craftwork by, for example, integrating aesthetic elements into their products. For instance, a signboard engraver in Melaka realized that the traditionally large signboards are not desired by customers nowadays due to their high price and outdated design, so he reduced the plaques' size, invited the masters of calligraphy to write Chinese characters for the plaques, and used different materials in their design. These plaques now serve as gifts to congratulate someone for getting recognitions from the king, opening a new business, or other celebratory events. Nevertheless, in order to create an active participation opportunity, which is vital for creative experience, perhaps the craftspeople could also invite their customers to write and design their own plaque, as people will have strong affective ties with the experience of making something themselves.

On the other hand, the Baba and Nyonya (Peranakan or Straits-born Chinese) culture is unique to these two World Heritage Sites. The broaches people wear, the bead crafts they practise, the costumes they wear – are all products to be consumed. Some craftspeople are still active at these sites, and they are willing to teach others their beading skills. Nevertheless, they did not integrate these skills into their culture. In other words, there is no 'story' connecting the culture with the 'experience'. For traditional craftspeople, such as the signboard engravers, perhaps what is needed is a workshop or activities that can transform their consumer into a 'prosumer', whereas for craftspeople such as the bead-shoe makers, perhaps they may consider telling a story that links the crafts with their cultural background, such as the three-inch lotus shoes that illustrate the story of their 'small feet' female ancestors.

Challenges

Encouraging creative tourists is vital for developing a sustainable tourism eco-system; nevertheless, in order to develop creative tourism at heritage sites, some challenges need to be overcome. Practically, first, although the heritage buildings of some associations/kongsi have been maintained well, many committee members are not experts in heritage conservation. If people are not sensitive to conservation issues, such as simply putting in neon lights for decoration, this will sometimes result in negative impacts rather than attracting people to visit. In addition, these associations/kongsi represent different 'families' or 'clans' from different 'villages', hence more conversations need to be arranged in order to connect them. Second, nurturing the parents' generation is more challenging than nurturing their children, as children are more willing to accept the guidance and opinions of others compared to adults. Third, the attitude of traditional traders may become a problem if they discourage their children and urge them to stay away from jobs such as blacksmiths, silversmiths, rattan weavers, bead-shoe makers, joss-stick makers, signboard engravers, and so on that have been 'categorized' as 'hard work but low pay' jobs. These challenges will not only affect the development of a lively tourism destination, but also the conservation and preservation of a heritage site.

Nevertheless, the main challenge here is the vision of policymakers. While the policymakers are trying their best to attract tourists, they should also be aware that the heritage of a destination should not be sacrificed. This issue raises other questions: Whose and what cultural heritage shall be preserved, especially in a multi-cultural and multi-racial society? Shall we preserve only the heritage of a dominant group? Or should more assistance and support be given to minority groups? If local communities are not supported by the government, what can they do to preserve their heritage? To answer these questions, all stakeholders – especially policymakers – should be invited to join a dialogue to foster better understanding among them.

Conclusion

Although creative tourism has been developed for decades, more research is needed, especially in a developing country such as Malaysia, in order to address the challenges discussed in this chapter.

First, research should be conducted on how to bridge the link between culture and creativity in the context of tourism. We argue that cultural heritage should be the foundation of creative tourism and, from this perspective, knowledge and aware-ness of historic conservation is vital for creative tourism. In turn, creative tourism can provide the 'know-how' strategies that may add value to the cultural heritage. However, many stakeholders have limited knowledge on how to preserve their cultural heritage. Perhaps this is because people take their own culture for granted and only 'copy' ideas from others without really understanding why an idea could be applicable in some places but not in others. Fostering a deeper understanding of cultural heritage and its conservation can be combined with appropriate creative strategies to revitalize these resources for community benefit.

Second, while creative tourism offers cultural activities to directly experience and in which to participate, not all tourists will appreciate what is offered as different tourists have their own 'trigger point' and interests. For example, traditional childhood games may evoke feelings such as nostalgia among middle-age groups, but not for younger generations. However, these younger generations might be attracted by curiosity. Therefore, research could be done to find out the elements that may generate the interest of different generations for cultural heritage-related creative tourism offers.

Third, to sustain creative tourism, the 'strengths' of each stakeholder should be identified, and more should be known about how their interactions may inspire innovations. For example, younger generations may have innovative skills but lack the technical skills to carry out traditional work, whereas some traditional crafts-people may have the technical skills but lack innovative skills. In addition, tour-ists may have a lot of experiences with different creative activities in which they have participated throughout their travel careers, and their ideas may inspire local residents to adapt or transform the artefacts or creative activities that are offered. More research on how different cultures, generations, and stakeholders interact and inspire 'sparks' would help inform innovation processes and strategies in crea-tive tourism and, more broadly, in keeping cultural heritage a vital resource.

Fourth, awareness and creativity are important in developing creative tourism, and the relationships between these two factors require further research. In addition, as creativity can serve as a tool to motivate people to take action, besides curiosity, life experiences, and the demands of society discussed previously, how other 'crea-tivity' elements can be used to nurture creative tourists remains understudied. In particular, the elements of mini-c creativity, which relates to transformative learn-ing, should be identified in order to serve as guidelines for industry practitioners. In addition, processes to foster an affective sense of place towards a heritage site or other historic location could be used to encourage local residents to become crea-tive tourists.

Lastly, some local neighbourhoods are rich in cultural heritage but these resources are deteriorating due to tourism activities. Countering negative impacts and issues of (over)tourism is a pressing issue in some locations. Can creative tourism approaches help devise new approaches and strategies for sharing this heritage with others? Or do we have to wait for the sense of loss and sense of justice to emerge in order to do something to conserve and preserve our heritage? Addressing these pressing issues deserves inquiry as well.

Acknowledgement

Financial support provided by the Ministry of Higher Education (MOHE), Malaysia, under Fundamental Research Grant Scheme (Ref: FRGS/2/2014/SS05/MMU/03/8) is gratefully acknowledged.

NOTE

1 'Tang Hao' represents the origin of a family name and also the alternate name of a family name. Chinese, especially those from Hakka, like to hang their 'Tang Hao' at their front door, so others will know what the family name of that house is.

References

Adams, J.D., S. Ibrahim and M. Lim (2010), 'Invoking the ontological realm of place: a dialogic response', in D.J. Tippins, M.P. Mueller, M. Van Eijck and J.D. Adams (eds), *Cultural Studies and Environmentalism: The Confluence of Ecojustice, Place-based (Science) Education, and Indigenous Knowledge Systems*, London and Dordrecht: Springer, pp. 215–28.

Chapin, F.S. III and C.N. Knapp (2015), 'Sense of place: a process for identifying and negotiating potentially contested visions of sustainability', *Environmental Science and Policy*, **53**, 38–46.

Howell, R.A. and S. Allen (2016), 'Significant life experiences, motivations and values of climate change educators', *Environmental Education Research*, **4622** (September), 1–19.

Jensen, B.B. (2002), 'Knowledge, action and pro-environmental behaviour', *Environmental Education Research*, **8** (3), 325–34.

Kaufman, J.C. and R.A. Beghetto (2009), 'Beyond big and little: the four c model of creativity', *Review of General Psychology*, **13** (1), 1–12.

Raymond, C. (2003), *Case Study – Creative Tourism New Zealand*, Auckland: Creative Tourism New Zealand and Australia Council for the Arts.

Richards, G. (2011), 'Tourism development trajectories – from culture to creativity', *Tourism and Management Studies*, **6**, 9–15.

Richards, G. and J. Wilson (2006), 'Developing creativity in tourist experiences: a solution to the serial reproduction of culture?', *Tourism Management*, **27** (6), 1209–23.

Tan, K.H. and B.K. Ooi (2014), *The Story of Hokkien Kongsi, Penang*, Penang: Hokkien Kongsi.

Tan, S.-K., S.-F. Kung and D.-B. Luh (2013), 'A model of "creative experience" in creative tourism', *Annals of Tourism Research*, **41**, 153–74.

Tan, S.-K., D.-B. Luh and S.-F. Kung (2014), 'A taxonomy of creative tourists in creative tourism', *Tourism Management*, **42**, 248–59.

Tan, S.-K., S.-H. Tan, Y.-S. Kok and S.-W. Choon (2018), 'Sense of place and sustainability of intangible cultural heritage: the case of George Town and Melaka', *Tourism Management*, **67C**, 376–87.

Zhang, P.C. (2016), '那些童玩教我的事' (What I learn from traditional childhood games), *E-Nanyang*, 27 March, accessed 1 January 2018 at http://www.enanyang.my/news/20160327/那些童玩教我的事/.

3 The role of authenticity in rural creative tourism

Manuela Blapp and Ondrej Mitas

Like many popular tourism destinations, the Indonesian island of Bali offers a variety of environments and experiences for mass tourists, many of which are highly standardized for Western sun-seeker expectations and offer little interaction with local culture (Shaw and Shaw, 1999). The profits from this sort of tourism often leak to the cities and off the island altogether (Cole, 2012), while local cultural practices erode in the face of mass employment in low-level service jobs (Hitchcock, 2000; Jenkins and Romanos, 2014). Two models of tourism development have been discussed in the tourism literature as alternatives to mass tourism that interact more respectfully and constructively with local populations: community-based tourism and creative tourism.

Community-based tourism refers to tourism in rural regions based on locally relevant activities with low environmental and sociocultural impact (Goodwin and Santilli, 2009; Hall, 1996; Tolkach et al., 2013). From the supply side, community-based tourism is planned and executed with substantial local involvement from a variety of stakeholders, whose actions and priorities complement rather than implement outside investment (Hall, 1996). The potential of community-based tourism was also recognized in Bali and the Community-Based Tourism Association Bali (CoBTA) was established in 2010 to support its development. The non-profit and non-governmental organization (NGO) aims to distribute tourism more equally by offering cultural and natural attractions in underutilized regions of Bali to international tourists (CoBTA, 2013).

Creative tourism refers to tourism involving expressive or creative activities in which tourists learn artistic, performative, or daily living skills of the culture they are visiting (Landry, 2010; Raymond, 2007; Richards, 2011). It is seen as the successor of cultural tourism, which has become large scale and has drifted towards mass tourism (Fernandes, 2011; Richards and Wilson, 2006). Creative tourism aims to open new possibilities in attracting various visitor segments, developing lesser-known areas of a destination, and benefiting local artists and residents when compared to mass tourism. The Bali CoBTA recommends the use of creative tourism in a similar way in Bali: to differentiate community-based tourism products (Dolezal, 2013). Community-based tourism experiences in Bali are attractive to tourists who are curious about Balinese culture. There is a risk, however, in marketing similar experiences in myriad villages, thus creating wasteful internal competition. The purpose of the present study was to determine the feasibility of creative tourism product development as a tool for distinguishing between community-based tourism products at different villages, so that they complement rather than compete with each other in the market. While the general findings related to this question are published elsewhere (Blapp and Mitas, 2017), this chapter re-examines the context and data collected for a concept absent from the original analysis, which is nevertheless important in current writing on creative and community-based tourism forms: authenticity.

Researchers and sector authorities concerned with creative tourism as well as community-based tourism both use the concept of authenticity extensively, but uncritically. Authenticity is a key element of creative tourism (e.g., Raymond, 2007; Rudan, 2012; UNESCO, 2006) from perspectives of supply and demand. Authenticity is the major motivation for creative tourists (Ohridska-Olson and Ivanov, 2010) and the essential attribute of creative tourism products is creating memorable and authentic visitor experiences (Richards, 2008; Voss, 2004). To develop creative tourism in rural areas and prevent commodification, the theor-etical assumptions and definitions behind authenticity must be considered. Our study analyzes how different theories of authenticity are applied in creative and community-based tourism literature, suggests a synthetic theory of authenticity applicable to creative tourism development in rural areas, and proposes further research needed on this topic.

Authenticity in tourism research

In tourism research, three main theories about authenticity are found: objec-tive, constructive, and existential authenticity. Objective authenticity is based on modernism and interprets authenticity as the original as defined by absolute and objective criteria (e.g., Boorstin, 1964; MacCannell, 1973). Tourism products are authentic if they are made or performed by locals according to their traditions (Boorstin, 1964; MacCannell, 1973). In this case, tourists may still judge an experi-ence as authentic although under the view of objective authenticity it is inauthen-tic, 'false', or 'staged' (MacCannell, 1973). Constructive authenticity is based on constructivism and argues that authenticity is a result of social constructs, such as points of view, beliefs, perspectives, or powers (e.g., Bruner, 1994; Cohen, 1988; Hobsbawm and Ranger, 1983). It can be seen as the projection of stereotypes or expectations of the visited destination (Bruner, 1991; Silver, 1993), as defined by the tourist or supplier. As such, there is no absolute authenticity but rather dif-ferent versions of authenticities for the same objects, and a tourist's view of the same object or ritual as authentic is as legitimate as a local's view of the same object or ritual as 'staged'. Existential authenticity is based on post-modernity. According to Wang (1999), tourists are not interested in the authenticity of objects but rather look for their authentic selves through touristic activities. Thus, 'people feel they themselves are much more authentic and more freely self-expressed than in everyday life, not because they find the tour objects are authentic but simply because they are engaging in non-ordinary activities, free from the constraints of the daily life' (p. 351).

Many tourism researchers, managers, and developers borrow the different concepts behind these theories – whether separately, in combination, or with nuances – to come up with new definitions of authenticity. Community-based tourism and creative tourism literatures also use and interpret concepts of authenticity in different ways. In community-based tourism, tourists are increasingly looking for 'authentic' experiences that bring them closer to locals (Butcher, 2003; MacCannell, 1999; Wang, 1999). Scholars argue that communities need to preserve their traditional way of life to satisfy the interest of the tourist (Boonratana, 2010; Ivanovic, 2008; Taylor, 2001). As an example, Boonratana (2010) states that communities should 'retain a traditional way of life and culture that is of interest to tourists' (p. 284). In this regard, community-based tourism is believed to provide a more authentic experience than other forms of tourism (Mowforth and Munt, 2003) as it goes hand in hand with the idea of objective authenticity as something that 'connotes traditional culture and origin' (Sharpley, 1994, p. 130). However, culture is a dynamic concept (Burns, 2001) that evolves constantly through globalization and foreign influences (van der Duim et al., 2005), among other things. This idea leads to a paradox when using the understanding of objective authenticity in community-based tourism: while community-based tourism is promoted as a tool for development, the culture is expected to remain traditional to appeal to tourists. Thus, in the objective understanding of authenticity, tourist expectations may conflict with the advancement of culture that would have happened without tourists expecting to see traditions.

The literature on creative tourism claims that the meaning of authenticity has changed as a result of the evolution from cultural tourism to creative tourism, giving it a more interactive connotation. 'Authentic' in cultural tourism is interpreted as seeing tangible heritage icons (Richards, 2011; Stipanović and Rudan, 2014), which strongly refers to objective authenticity. In creative tourism, authenticity concerns 'immersing oneself in the culture at large' (Stipanović and Rudan, 2014, p. 508), thus shifting the meaning to the understanding of existential authenticity. More specifically, Richards (2011) refers to the original concept of the performer or maker by Ex and Lengkeek (1996), where authenticity is reached through the co-creation of tourist experiences 'in situ by the host and the tourist, each playing a role as the originator of the experience' (Richards, 2011, p. 1245).

This review shows that understandings of authenticity within community-based tourism and creative tourism are very diverse. On the one hand, community-based tourism often interprets authenticity in its objective understanding, although it has recognized certain limitations when it comes to the dynamism of culture over time. On the other hand, creative tourism builds on the concept of existential authenticity. This study suggests a synthetic theory of authenticity that is built on MacCannell's (1999) model of 'front' and 'back' regions, based on objective authenticity. At the same time, the proposed theory recognizes the paradox put forward by Burns (2001) and aims to address it by integrating culture as a dynamic element of authenticity. According to MacCannell (1999), hosts who are confronted with mass tourism aim to isolate and protect their culture by setting up back regions in which locals can pursue important traditions far away from the tourist's gaze. At the same time, they create front regions where locals stage a limited array of activities for tourists. Hence, the front region is what is shown to the tourist, whereas the back region represents the hosts' private lives (Dolezal, 2011). As such, MacCannell (1999) argues that the back region is the 'authentic' area sought by tourists 'motivated by a desire to see life as it is really lived' (p. 94). Thus, the daily life of locals in the villages, which is lived in the back regions, is interpreted as the authentic way of life in this study. This also conforms to the idea of creative tourism showing the everyday life of locals to tourists (Richards, 2011). Considering culture as dynamic (Burns, 2001), the authentic way of life is not absolute as argued in objective authenticity (MacCannell, 1973) but also changes over time. Thus, changing behaviour, values, beliefs, and traditions of locals change authenticity over time.

This study suggests that the behaviour and traditions lived by the locals, in what they would call their back regions, define what is authentic and how authenticity changes over time. This understanding of authenticity is used because, first, MacCannell's theory is often stated in community-based tourism literature (e.g., Boonratana, 2010; Ivanovic, 2008; Taylor, 2001) and has been used for other studies of community-based tourism (e.g., Dolezal, 2011). Second, the distinction of front and back regions is also applicable to creative tourism, which aims to show the everyday life of locals to tourists (Richards, 2011). In this regard, it is important to consider to which parts of the back regions tourists are granted access, to see what potential creative tourism products can be developed without commercializing everyday life. The limitation of such a definition of authenticity is that it understands authenticity only in this very meaning of MacCannell's (1999) model of 'front' and 'back' regions based on objective authenticity, combined with Burns's (2001) notion of culture being a dynamic element of authenticity. However, this meaning does not correspond to different understandings of authenticity and thus cannot be claimed as authentic from a strictly objective, constructive, or existential point of view.

Methods

The suggested theory was explored in the context of five Balinese villages using a microethnographic approach with participant observation and expert as well as tourist interviews. Ethnographic methods are particularly useful for research on complex experiential services such as tourism products (Botterill and Platenkamp, 2012). Creative tourism is arguably complex, as it involves intangible cultural values and unpredictable expressive processes. Ethnographic approaches have proved useful in various studies on community-based tourism development (e.g., Botterill and Platenkamp, 2012; Konu, 2015).

I (first author) collected primary data during four weeks in July and August 2015 in five Balinese villages. I chose the villages from 30 villages that offer community-based tourism products. In two of the selected villages, tourism had been developed in terms of tourist numbers and income (D1, D2). In three villages, tourism development has only started recently (U1, U2, U3). Moreover, I conducted 11 in-depth interviews with 14 experts as well as interviews with 43 tourists, clusterd in 15 groups in the field. A qualitative content analysis, using a three-step approach with open coding, focused coding, and theoretical synthesis described by Charmaz (2014), was used to ground results in the data and connect it to the literature.

Findings

Activities in locals' front and back regions

I (first author) experienced activities in the front as well as the back region of the locals. For example, in D1 a front region was set up by packaging the activities into a day programme for tourists and conducting them in a Balinese housing complex especially built for tourists. Contrastingly, in U1 there was no special programme for tourists, but we were told to join locals in their everyday life activities, hence their back region activities. I, for example, participated in a Gamelan music practice and a temple cleaning by the locals. Similarly, in U2 I went 'shopping' with my host who took me to the beach to buy fresh fish from his favourite local fisherman. Findings showed that these spontaneous activities of the normal daily routine of locals are perceived as more authentic than planned activities in the front regions conducted just for tourists.

In some cases, a mix of front and back region activities was experienced. In D1, I was an hour too early for the village tour for which I had signed up. While waiting for the other tourists, I could help to prepare snacks for them and remarked that this was actually one of the things I liked the most, as it was not part of the tourist programme but an activity of the locals. In U2, the content of the activity 'rice field trekking' was adapted daily, depending on which tasks were performed by the farmers on that day with which the tourists could help. In contrast, in D1, a field was prepared especially for tourists to ride a cow with a plough and to plant rice.

Limited tourist access to back regions

Findings showed that locals enjoyed sharing many aspects of their everyday life, which tourists would perceive as the back region. For example, in U2 and U3, I was immediately invited into the living room of the family and started a long conversation with my host. During my whole stay in U2, I was integrated in family activities such as helping to prepare dinner or meeting relatives and friends. I had similar experiences in U1, and, after the day tourists had left, in D1. The hosts signalled their willingness to share their everyday life by starting conversations, asking me questions, or encouraging me to participate in their everyday life activities. For example, in U2 the daughter of my host invited me to join her in visiting some friends to help prepare decorations for a dance festival.

Despite the high willingness and enthusiasm to share their everyday life, there were also limitations for three reasons: privacy, gender roles, and culture. One employee in D1 explained that she would not take tourists to the temple for her prayers because she needs time to pray for herself. This example illustrates that some activities are too personal for some locals to be shared with tourists and, in that case, access to back regions is not given to tourists.

The second limitation observed was due to traditional gender roles. In U2, my host explained on the day of a festival that involved a feast at the community hall of the banjar: 'in Balinese banjar women don't cook, the men do the cooking . . . [Women] make offerings, so you go with my wife.' Similarly, women who have their menstruation were not allowed to enter temples; therefore, some female tourists had to take a detour during a trek passing a temple in U2. This shows that tourists are expected by some locals to adhere to local gender roles when entering their back regions.

Another limiting aspect was cultural and traditional beliefs. A tourist in U1 told me that her host and his neighbour got very upset when they noticed that she opened the gate to the ricefields for a few minutes during the night to take pictures of the full moon. According to Balinese belief, bad spirits can enter through open gates during the night and gates should therefore remain closed. This incident shows that some locals get uncomfortable when tourists enter parts of their back regions and do not adhere to their cultural and traditional beliefs.

Desired front regions

While in some instances locals set limits to their back regions, in other cases, tourists were happy with front regions because they did not feel comfortable in the settings of the back regions. Findings showed that different tourists required different levels of adaptations of the back regions. For example, I enjoyed the cooking class in U2, which meant sitting on the floor of a private kitchen of a Balinese family, their back region, and cutting up fish on a tree trunk. I also perceived it as more authentic than the class in D1 where a traditional kitchen was built and adapted for tourists as a front region. Contrastingly, one participant in D1 was glad about the adapted tourist environment: 'The market which we visited on the way here was too dirty . . . so it's too dirty outside here.'

Despite these differences, most villagers believed that the tourists anticipate high standards and thus a high level of adaptation. During the interviews with villagers, one of the most often mentioned challenges was that they are 'not ready' to cater for international guests. This was mainly related to the standards of the homestays, which they rated as insufficient for international visitors. However, for me as well as the interviewed experts of an NGO supporting rural tourism development in Indonesia, the homestays by far exceeded expectations: I often stayed in large rooms including air conditioning, a private bathroom, sometimes a television, shampoo, towels, and so on, which resembled a hotel room more than a homestay. In U3, the different categories were labelled as in hotels, using the terms 'deluxe/ superior/suites'. This indicates that villagers may have a wrong perception about some tourists' expectations or try to cater for the wrong target market. One expert remarked: 'It's actually sad, because it can destroy the whole idea of the concept. What they need to do is not that much, rather being authentic, being what they are and offer what they have.'

Authenticity changing over time

Research has shown that everyday life changes over time due to modernization and that these changes impact tourism products. Changes in everyday life refer to the notion that culture is dynamic (Burns, 2001), a phenomenon which was also incorporated in the understanding of authenticity of this study. Hence, if the everyday life changes over time, the meaning of what is authentic also changes over time.

Many interviewed villagers believed that their culture is so strong that it will be preserved in the future. There were many children and teenagers engaging in traditional dancing, music, and religious observances. However, modernization is experienced in villages, as is illustrated by a local's concern: 'We need to hold the traditional technique . . . because now, everything is already modern.' In all destinations, this issue was raised during interviews and villagers often stated that handicraft, home industries, and farming – currently the main tourist activities offered – are mainly performed by old people. When I asked one villager if they still have enough people who know about their traditions, he said: 'Yes, yes, we still have many old people who know the local traditions.' Villagers often expressed concerns that the younger villagers do not know about some traditions anymore and most young people leave the village and work in hotels or on cruise ships. Hence, although traditions are still alive, this may change in the future and the currently traditional everyday life may become more contemporary and globalized.

Interacting with tourists, especially from countries where traditions are less important than in Bali, could accelerate the process of modernization. One villager in U2 observed: 'Since we have so many foreign surfers on the beach, the locals have changed their habits. They start wearing their pants lower and become more easy-going like the surfers'. Some villages plan to educate local youth more about traditional activities to preserve the culture. In that sense, creative tourism can help to preserve culture, subject to their interest in it. However, some tourists also see preventing modernization as less authentic. For example, one tourist in D2 said: 'It [the village] is not lively or real, they just keep the village like this, just for the tourists . . . it doesn't feel like an authentic experience.' Some villages combined tradition and modernity; for example, in the orphanage in U3 the children showed different traditional and modern dances during a show. In that way, they preserve traditions without negating modernity. This makes the experience seem more authentic as it illustrates the fusion of the tradition and the modern in the locals' everyday life.

Tourists' impacts on back regions

Findings show that if the villagers are too involved in tourism due to high visitor numbers, serving and entertaining tourists becomes their new everyday life. Hence, not many activities interesting to creative tourists will remain in the back regions. For example, I observed in my field notes: 'When you enter a Balinese house, there is always something going on; but in D1, there are only tourist activities. This makes it feel more artificial and less authentic and tourists cannot integrate in the village life.'

Similarly, in D2, which is visited by around 200 tourists each day, some visitors complained that due to the high number of visitors it is not possible to 'mix with the local life and be part of it'. To experience the everyday life of locals, it has to be ensured that tourism remains limited and a side business, which is currently the case in U2, U3, and U1. This was one of the reasons why, in those villages, I felt part of an experience I would describe as authentic. As one tourist in U1 remarked, 'I want this interaction with locals and I'm very happy that I'm most of the time the only one here.'

Discussion

The definition of authenticity used in this study is based on MacCannell's (1999) front and back regions as defined from the host perspective as well as Burns's (2001) notion that culture, and thus authenticity, is dynamic. Findings extend the discussion in the literature review and provide further evidence that this definition of authenticity is reasonable for community-based creative tourism. Data showed that spontaneous activities from the locals' everyday lives are perceived as more authentic by tourists than planned ones. This corresponds to MacCannell's explanation that the back regions, which are the private lives of the hosts, are the authentic way of life in which tourists, such as those studied, are interested. These findings also conform to creative tourism theories, for example, Landry's theory (2010) that activities can be very simple and ordinary and Raymond's (2007) definition that activities are informal and take place at the teachers' home or place of work. Furthermore, results have also confirmed that the everyday life of locals is changing over time (Burns, 2001) and thus also the meaning of authenticity. The notion that the meaning of authenticity changes over time has three implications for creative tourism in rural areas. First, the content of creative tourism products changes over time. Second, the hosts' perspective on authenticity changes over time and does not correspond to every tourist's understanding of authenticity. The term 'authenticity' should therefore be used with care when managing tourists' expectations. Third, tourism influences how authenticity, as defined in this study, changes over time.

Authenticity as a dynamic element

The content of creative tourism products, which is based on the everyday life of locals, changes over time. This means that a less traditional show, where modern and traditional are mixed, represents today's everyday life of locals more accurately than a strictly traditional show and is thus seen as authentic according to the host. This notion also extends Jenkins and Romanos's (2014) conclusion about authenticity in art in Bali: 'Rather than trying to recapture or preserve the past, forwardlooking, hybrid models and strategies seem to be the most artistically and economically beneficial to artists along tourist routes' (p. 303). Our study extends this idea showing that hybrid models fusing the past and advancement are not only desirable in art but in any kind of creative tourism products, such as tourists cooking or engaging in religious observances with their hosts. Thus, the tourist should be taught about the evolution of culture for an authentic experience. By fusing traditional and modern elements of the culture in creative tourism products, authenticity is recognized as dynamic.

Tourists also interpreted authenticity as a dynamic concept in tourism products. For example, about half of the visitors to D2 with whom I interacted commented that the village was not authentic because it was just preserved for tourism and does not represent the way locals currently prefer to live their life. These findings refute the claim that communities have to retain a traditional way of life to be interesting to tourists and to be seen as authentic (Boonratana, 2010; Ivanovic, 2008; Taylor, 2001). However, other tourists liked to see the traditional village, described it as authentic, and therefore seemed to interpret authenticity in its traditional understanding. Hence, tourists have different understandings of what is authentic.

Different expectations about authenticity

When defining authenticity from the locals' point of view only, tourists do not always get to see what they think is authentic. I was surprised to see a lot of people smoking and using their cell phones in the temple or to see locals driving from temple to temple by motorbike. This was not how I imagined the authentic way of life to be. For this reason, it is suggested that the term 'authentic' should not be used in marketing because tourists' expectations, whose understanding of authenticity differs from that of locals, will not be met. As an alternative, 'experiencing the local way of life' could be used.

Furthermore, research findings show that locals are not willing to show every aspect of their everyday life. The 'back region', which may carry creative tourism potential, may itself have a back region where many or most locals truly do not wish tourists to enter (MacCannell, 1973). Thus, tourists' expectations of a completely authentic experience would not be met, which is another reason why it is not advisable for authenticity to be used to promote community-based creative tourism.

Tourism influencing authenticity

Tourism can have a twofold influence on how the everyday life of locals could change in the future – on the one hand, it can help to preserve culture and, on the other hand, it can accelerate modernization. Research findings have shown that a high number of tourists may change a currently traditional everyday life to an everyday life dominated by serving tourists. Many locals stated that they aim to preserve their culture, which they observe eroding due to advancement, and see tourism as a suitable tool to do so. However, tourism is only effective in helping to preserve the culture if two requirements are fulfilled. First, it should remain small scale so that a high level of interaction and traditional everyday life can be incorporated into the tourism experience. Consequently, the cultural identity of locals is reinforced and tourists as well as locals create knowledge about Balinese culture. Second, the priority of strengthening Balinese culture should be weighted higher than the effects of tourists as accelerators of modernity. This again implies a low number of tourists that can be integrated into the Balinese life rather than the tourist lifestyle taking over the village.

Conclusion

The research findings presented in this chapter provide evidence that the definition of authenticity synthesized from the literature is reasonable for community-based creative tourism. This definition implies that the everyday life of locals lived in their back regions (MacCannell, 1999) is seen by them as authentic and that this everyday life, and thus authenticity, changes over time (Burns, 2001). This definition has three implications for creative tourism in rural areas. First, contents of products change over time and should incorporate local cultural change. Second, the meaning of authenticity differs between locals and tourists as well as among tourists; the term 'authenticity' should therefore be replaced with 'local way of life' in marketing. Third, tourism influences how authenticity changes over time and should remain small scale if culture is to be preserved through tourism as desired by locals.

The definition of authenticity proposed in this chapter may develop differently in other cultural contexts. The findings capture a particular place, populated by a people with particular practices and norms, at a particular moment in time. Not only the native delineation of what comprises a 'back region' but the very role that back region plays in daily life is not expected to be the same in any two contexts. The South of Bali, for example, has seen mass tourism developed on a much larger scale for many years. It would be premature to assume that the definition of authenticity proposed here would easily translate to that context. Thus, from a global perspective, it may be more useful to speak of *authenticities* rather than simply authenticity, where regional, temporal, and cultural contexts influence not only what is seen as authentic but also what ontological position the concept of authenticity holds in those contexts.

More research is also needed to classify expectations of authenticity among different types of creative tourists. Substantially different – even opposing – sentiments were expressed by the visitors contacted in this study. It was not recorded, however, how the backgrounds or tourism behaviours of these visitors may have differed. Such differences may be particularly relevant for the marketing of creative tourism and should be explored further.

Finally, future research on the carrying capacity of rural areas is essential for the development of creative tourism there. An important finding of our research was that visitor numbers need to be limited for community-based creative tourism to develop in a way that locals see as both authentic and beneficial. This finding raises an obvious but very difficult question: How many tourists are too many? This question has, not surprisingly, bedevilled tourism researchers for decades but could perhaps be more easily answered when the context of the inquiry is limited. In any case, in practice, policymakers and tourism managers understand how many tourists *were* too many when it is much too late to do anything about it. A serious attempt to plan ahead, including attendant carrying capacity research, is warranted to protect the vernacular cultural treasures researched here.

References

Blapp, M. and O. Mitas (2017), 'Creative tourism in Balinese rural communities', *Current Issues in Tourism*, doi:10.1080/13683500.2017.1358701

Boonratana, R. (2010), 'Community-based tourism in Thailand: the need and justification for an operational definition', *The Kasetsart Journal: Social Science*, **31** (2), 280–9.

Boorstin, D.J. (1964), *The Image: A Guide to Pseudo-events in America*, New York: Atheneum.

Botterill, D. and V. Platenkamp (2012), *Key Concepts in Tourism Research*, London: Sage.

Bruner, E.M. (1991), 'Transformation of self in tourism', *Annals of Tourism Research*, **18**, 238–50.

Bruner, E.M. (1994), 'Abraham Lincoln as authentic reproduction: a critique of postmodernism', *American Anthropologist*, **96** (2), 397–415.

Burns, P.M. (2001), 'Brief encounters: culture, tourism and the local-global nexus', in S. Wahab and C. Cooper (eds), *Tourism in the Age of Globalisation*, London: Routledge, pp. 290–305.

Butcher, J. (2003), *The Moralisation of Tourism: Sun, Sand . . . and Saving the World?*, London: Routledge.

Charmaz, K. (2014), *Constructing Grounded Theory* (2nd edn), London: Sage.

CoBTA (Community-Based Tourism Association Bali) (2013), *Responsible Tourism Forum and Networking Session ITB Asia*, Singapore, 25 October.

Cohen, E. (1988), 'Authenticity and commoditization in tourism', *Annals of Tourism Research*, **15**, 371–86.

Cole, S. (2012), 'A political ecology of water equity and tourism: a case study from Bali', *Annals of Tourism Research*, **29** (2), 1221–41.

Dolezal, C. (2011), 'Community-based tourism in Thailand: (dis-)illusion of authenticity and the necessity for dynamic concepts of culture and power', *ASEAS – Austrian Journal of South-East Asian Studies*, **4** (1), 129–38.

Dolezal, C. (2013), 'Community-based tourism in Bali: on the road towards empowerment? An interview with Djinaldi Gosana', *ASEAS – Austrian Journal of South-East Asian Studies*, **6** (2), 366–73.

Ex, N. and J. Lengkeek (1996), 'Op zoek naar het echte?', *Vrijetijdstudies*, **14**, 21–46.

Fernandes, C. (2011), 'Cultural planning and creative tourism in an emerging tourist destination', *International Journal of Management Cases*, **8** (13), 629–36.

Goodwin, H. and R. Santilli (2009), 'Community-based tourism: a success?', ICRT occasional paper, no. 11, International Centre for Responsible Tourism, Leeds.

Hall, C.M. (1996), *Introduction to Tourism in Australia: Impacts, Planning and Development*, Melbourne: Addison, Wesley and Longman.

Hitchcock, M. (2000), 'Ethnicity and tourism entrepreneurship in Java and Bali', *Current Issues in Tourism*, **3** (3), 204–25.

Hobsbawm, E. and T. Ranger (1983), *The Invention of Tradition*, Cambridge: Cambridge University Press.

Ivanovic, M. (2008), *Cultural Tourism*, Cape Town: Juta and Company.

Jenkins, L.D. and M. Romanos (2014), 'The art of tourism-driven development: economic and artistic well-being of artists in three Balinese communities', *Journal of Tourism and Cultural Change*, **12** (4), 293–306.

Konu, H. (2015), 'Case study: developing a forest-based wellbeing tourism product together with customers – an ethnographic approach', *Tourism Management*, **49**, 1–16.

Landry, C. (2010), 'Experiencing imagination: travel as a creative trigger', in R. Wurzburger, T. Aageson, A. Pattakos and S. Pratt (eds), *Creative Tourism, a Global Conversation: How to Provide Unique Creative Experiences for Travelers Worldwide*, Santa Fe, NM: Sunstone Press, pp. 33–42.

MacCannell, D. (1973), 'Staged authenticity: arrangements of social space in tourist settings', *American Journal of Sociology*, **79**, 589–603.

MacCannell, D. (1999), *The Tourist: A New Theory of the Leisure Class* (2nd edn), Berkeley, CA: University of California Press.

Mowforth, M. and I. Munt (2003), *Tourism and Sustainability: Development and New Tourism in the Third World* (2nd edn), London: Routledge.

Ohridska-Olson, R.V. and S. Ivanov (2010), *Creative Tourism Business Model and its Application in Bulgaria*, Proceedings of the Black Sea Tourism Forum 'Cultural Tourism: The Future of Bulgaria', Varna, Bulgaria.

Raymond, C. (2007), 'Creative tourism New Zealand: the practical challenges of developing creative tourism', in G. Richards and J. Wilson (eds), *Tourism, Creativity and Development*, London: Routledge, pp. 145–57.

Richards, G. (2008), 'Creative tourism and local development', in R. Wurzburger, T. Aageson, A. Pattakos and S. Pratt (eds), *Creative Tourism, a Global Conversation: How to Provide Unique Creative Experiences for Travelers Worldwide*, Santa Fe, NM: Sunstone Press, pp. 78–90.

Richards, G. (2011), 'Creativity and tourism: the state of the art', *Annals of Tourism Research*, **38** (4), 1225–53.

Richards, G. and J. Wilson (2006), 'Developing creativity in tourist experiences: a solution to the serial reproduction of culture?', *Tourism Management*, **27**, 1209–23.

Rudan, E. (2012), 'Razvojne perspektive kretivnoga turizma Hrvatske' (A developmental perspective on creative tourism in Croatia), *Ekonomska misao i praksa (Economic thought and practice)*, **21** (2), 719.

Sharpley, R. (1994), *Tourism, Tourists and Society*, Huntingdon, Cambridgeshire: ELM.

Shaw, B.J. and G. Shaw (1999), '"Sun, sand and sales": enclave tourism and local entrepreneurship in Indonesia', *Current Issues in Tourism*, **2** (1), 68–81.

Silver, I. (1993), 'Marketing authenticity in third world countries', *Annals of Tourism Research*, **20**, 302–18.

Stipanović, C. and E. Rudan (2014), 'Development concept and strategy for creative tourism of the Kvarner destination', in *22nd Biennial International Congress Tourism and Hospitality Industry 2014* (Congress Proceedings), University of Rijeka, pp. 507–17.

Taylor, J.P. (2001), 'Authenticity and sincerity in tourism', *Annals of Tourism Research*, **28** (1), 7–26.

Tolkach, D., B. King and M. Pearlman (2013), 'An attribute-based approach to classifying community-based tourism networks', *Tourism Planning and Development*, **10** (3), 319–37.

UNESCO (2006), *Towards Sustainable Strategies for Creative Tourism*. Discussion report of the planning meeting for the 2008 International Conference on Creative Tourism, Santa Fe, New Mexico, USA, 25–27 October.

van der Duim, R., K. Peters and S. Wearing (2005), 'Planning host and guest interactions: moving beyond the empty meeting ground in African encounters', *Current Issues in Tourism*, **8** (4), 286–305.

Voss, C. (2004), *Trends in the Experience and Service Economy: The Experience Profit Cycle*, London: London School of Economics.

Wang, N. (1999), 'Rethinking authenticity in tourism experience', *Annals of Tourism Research*, **26** (2), 349–70.

4 The value of experience in culture and tourism: the power of emotions

Daniela Angelina Jelinčić and Matea Senkić

In the past decade, cultural tourism has proven to be 'one of the fastest-growing tourism trends . . . This dynamic has been clearly reflected in a rise in cultural activities in recent decades and social longing for culture' (UNWTO, 2015, p. 36). It is estimated that 'cultural tourism accounts for 40% of all European tourism; 4 out of 10 tourists choose their destination based on its cultural offering' (European Commission, 2017, n.p.) and, in financial terms, estimates account for around US$800 billion–1.1 trillion earned by cultural tourism globally. These promising numbers affected a number of places that decided to use their local cultural resources as grounds for cultural and creative tourism development. However, with the exception of a few really innovative cultural tourism attractions, many cultural attractions look alike. While cultural tourism once represented a new tourism type and a niche market segmentation distinguished from mass tourism, in many destinations today it has become a type of mass tourism, commodifying culture and offering poor experiences both for tourists and for local communities. This situation has resulted in the need for more sophisticated products to satisfy ever more demanding tourists with their growing tendency to seek deeper experiences as well as to protect the value of local culture and to offer unique attractions. Creative tourism, as a form of cultural tourism, promised to offer a deeper engagement of tourists, eventually opening doors to authentic experiences for its consumers.

The superficiality of experiences and false values immanent to the times we live in, which are visible in different facets of life (e.g., politics, industry, education, health, precarious work, and so on), have especially affected the tourism industry. While tourism cannot simply be 'undone' since people are constantly seeking new stimuli to give meaning to their lives and thus searching for experiences outside their place of residence, we must seek new sustainable models for tourism development. This calls for the development of deeper experiences that offer value for both the suppliers of tourism products and their consumers. The experience economy has proven to be an appropriate solution for creating meaningful experiences in tourism. A number of definitions of the term have been applied in the existing literature, from the 'design of new goods and the process of coating them with stronger, brighter, more emotion-packed psychological connotations' (Toffler, 1970, p. 233), to the consumption experience seen as a phenomenon directed towards the pursuit of fantasies, feelings, and fun (Holbrook and Hirschman, 1982), to simply 'economic activities related to people's experiences' (Sundbo and Sørensen, 2013, p. 1). But rather than trying to provide an authorized definition, the focus should be on the connection between consumers' emotional experiences and the products/services that this type of economy entails. While previously the economy focused on tangible satisfaction, the experience economy offers psychological gratification (Jelinčić and Senkić, 2017).

The experience economy has been studied primarily in relation to marketing as its principles were promising for increasing the 'consumption of products/services by creating experiences around them' (Jelinčić and Senkić, 2017, p. 114). Although it can be applied in cultural and creative tourism in the same manner, this chapter focuses instead on its application within the very process of experience creation to enhance a cultural asset for consumers' enjoyment of its cultural value, not for any increased consumption as such. This approach may eventually increase the value of the cultural asset itself, offer memorable experiences for tourists, and affect the overall image of a destination, which may then stand out among a number of similar attractions. The aim of this chapter is to provide theoretical tips on how to create memorable cultural and creative tourism experiences and unique cultural attractions that offer deep and valuable impressions for their consumers. It is based also in practice, through a case study of the Museum of Broken Relationships, located in Zagreb, Croatia. In closing, it offers a perspective on possible future development scenarios of cultural/creative tourism, and suggests possible research lines.

Theoretical approaches to experience creation

In order to stand out in comparison with other competitors and to create a memorable experience, it is necessary to employ creativity.[1] However, this prerequisite does not guarantee that deep experiential traces will be left on the consumer. Relatively recent literature (e.g., de Bruin and Jelinčić, 2016; Lanier and Schau, 2007; Prahalad and Ramaswamy, 2004; Russo and Richards, 2016; Walmsley, 2013) popularized the concepts of co-creation and participation, which may contribute to the creation of an experience. Co-creation refers to the free exchange of ideas between an organization and its audience, which sometimes culminates in something new (Govier, 2009; Ind et al., 2012) but not necessarily; it is, rather, 'the art of with' (Leadbeater, 2009). Similarly, participation, according to the Oxford English Dictionary, originates from the Latin *participat*, which denotes 'shared in'. The terms may, in the context of the research presented in this chapter, be viewed as synonymous.[2] Their importance for experience creation is viewed as their power to engage the consumers where they are turned 'from passive recipients into active participants' (Walmsley, 2013, p. 110). Consumer engagement is the principal factor of success in effective and efficient experience creation, allowing for intensified consumer identification with the topic presented.

Pine and Gilmore (1998), the fathers of contemporary experience creation design principles, refer to the following factors as prerequisites for success: (1) attributing a theme to each experience; (2) harmonizing impressions with positive cues; (3) eliminating negative cues; (4) supplying memorabilia as additional experience enhancers; and (5) engaging all five senses in experience creation (pp. 102–5). With a well-defined theme, consumers can organize their impressions around it with more ease if they have clear associations and know what to expect (Jelinčić and Senkić, 2017). If these are paired with positive impressions, it is highly likely that the consumer will develop satisfaction with the attraction, which may eventually have experiential effects. This is additionally enhanced if the attraction is staged in a way that engages all five senses by employing visual and sound representations, scents, flavours, and tactile sensations. In order to extend the experience beyond the actual moment, Pine and Gilmore stress the power of different memorabilia, such as souvenirs. Therefore, staging an experience should focus on the visitor's identification with the attraction, engaging the senses and creating memories. Such attractions, however, although stirring greater interest in consumers than those not employing these principles, do not guarantee a real feeling of a deep experience. According to Pine and Gilmore (1998, p. 102), there are four realms of an experience, which range from absorption to immersion on one axis and from passive to active participation on the other one. They differ in intensity and are 'specified according to . . . consumer connection . . . and the form of participation . . . of the consumer in the experience' (Jelinčić and Senkić, 2017, p. 114). Thus, absorption is less intense than immersion and active participation is more likely to engage the consumer than passive participation. The authors label passive participation and absorption as an *entertainment experience* (e.g., watching a film), active participation and absorption as an *educational experience* (e.g., taking a pottery workshop), passive participation and immersion as an *aesthetic experience* (e.g., visiting an art gallery), and active participation and immersion as an *escapist experience* (e.g., acting in a play). The highest level of engagement is the escapist experience, which is highly likely to produce a deep and memorable experience.

The Latin root of the word *experiential* is *expiriri*, which means 'to try'. Experience creation, therefore, involves the acquisition of knowledge and/or skills, stressing the importance of learning-by-doing activities. This brings in the terms of participation and co-creation, which have the power to engage consumers. Escapist experiences that entail active participation and immersion are the most solid grounds for deep experiences since they provide the highest probability of stirring consumers' affect, feelings, and/or emotions. Psychologists struggle with making a clear distinction among these concepts; so a simple explanation is offered here which suits the needs of this research. An *affect* is a non-conscious experience of intensity and can be labelled as pre-personal (Shouse, 2005); it is 'a generic term that covers a broad range of feelings people experience' (Barsade and Gibson, 2007, cited in Robbins and Judge, 2013, p. 98). A *feeling* is a sensation that has been checked against previous experiences and labelled; it is personal and biographical. An *emotion* is the projection/display of a feeling (Shouse, 2005); 'Emotions are affective states characterized by episodes of intense feelings associated with a specific referent and instigate specific response behaviors' (Cohen and Areni, 1991, cited in Prayag et al., 2017, p. 42). These affective states of consciousness may instigate experiences of joy, sorrow, fear, anger, disgust, and so forth. While it is not easy to clearly differentiate affects, feelings, and emotions, it is possible to create immersive experience independently of the intensity with which consumers perceive it. Emotion is thought to be the deepest feeling since it instigates response behaviours, engaging the consumer participatively. In addition, 'the arousal intensity of an affective experience increases people's immediate and long-term memory for this experience' (Cohen et al., 2008, p. 302), which adds to Pine and Gilmore's design principle of memorabilia as experience enhancers. This can be related with moods, defined as 'less intense feelings than emotions which often ... arise without a specific event acting as a stimulus' (Weiss and Cropanzano, 1996, cited in Robbins and Judge, 2013, p. 98). Many researchers believe that emotions are more fleeting than moods (e.g., Ekman and Davidson, 1994); in other words, although moods are less intense than emotions, they last longer. It may be stated that *an affect* is just an umbrella term for different feelings; *a feeling* is just a label for a certain sensation but incites no action by a person who has it; *an emotion* entails intense feelings in a shorter period of time and incites responses by the person who feels it; and *a mood* is a less intense feeling felt in a longer period of time but without a specific stimulus.

It is generally thought that 'the experiences provided by touristic destinations are emotionally attractive' (Santos et al., 2014, p. 47) and that tourism incites satisfying and positive emotions. Still, it is erroneous to characterize emotions as positive or negative. Two major theoretical approaches to the study of emotions are offered in psychology: dimensional (or valence-based) and categorical. 'Dimensional approaches conceptualize emotions ... as positive and negative' (Watson et al., 1988, cited in Prayag et al., 2017, p. 42) while categorical approaches see them as a set of individual emotions (such as joy, anger, disgust, sadness, fear, and so on). Tourism research in general focuses on the dimensional (valence-based) approach simplifying it to the positive and negative images it creates. Our research advocates for a categorical approach to attribute the relevance of each individual emotion in creating experiences. Thus, certain attractions, to prove their effectiveness, must stir fear, anger, or sadness (e.g., in staging an earthquake, fire, or volcano eruption; creating empathy for war victims; and so forth). If a customer gets engaged in such an experience and actually feels this way, a positive rather than a negative cue has been achieved.

The arts and culture sectors inherently deal with emotions, where the quality and efficiency of an art work or a cultural event can be measured by the emotions it manages to stir. Therefore, culture is a suitable means for an emotional transfer of experiences in tourism. Tourism can also create long-lasting experiences due to its fertile nature for mood enhancement (immanent association with relaxation time). However, it is not easy to perform research that would make clear distinctions between affects, feelings, emotions, and moods as to be able to create cultural experiences ready-made to influence individual tourists on a differentiated affective intensity scale.

Experiential tourism

The diversification of tourism, which started in the 1980s, arrived as a result of the new postmodern tourist who focused on the *interest* of a destination rather than its *attractiveness*, preferred active holidays and experiences, and demonstrated a willingness to learn something new (Simonicca, 1997). The new tourist was no longer satisfied with a standard tourism offer but wanted to experience something new. This resulted in tourism segmentation, with cultural, adventure, sports, rural, urban, and so on tourism products on the rise. Today, segmentation is even more evident and also occurs within individual tourism segments. Thus, cultural tourism no longer satisfies the specific needs of different tourist interests, and we see development towards music, film, literature, and an array of other subsegments of cultural tourism. The greatest change, coming as a response to the rise of the experience economy, is in the development of creative tourism. Tourists seeking experiences increasingly present their need for participation in the life of local communities, which enhances the co-creation of their own holidays, whose nature then becomes extremely individual. Creative tourism was initially defined narrowly, as tourism offering visitors an opportunity to develop their creative potential through active participation in courses and learning experiences that are characteristic of the destination where they are undertaken (Richards and Raymond, 2000), while today its scope has widened considerably including a myriad of different activities whose real *creativity* feature is questionable (de Bruin and Jelinčić, 2016, p. 58). Participation and co-creation, however, have still remained its main feature. Co-creation is also evident on the supply side, with citizens becoming Uber drivers or Airbnb hosts, for example. Such an offer is acceptable to tourists not only due to economic prices but also for the local experience it offers to interact with members of the community.

Besides creative tourism, other, even more segmented types of tourism have developed around the notions of creativity, co-creation, participation, education, engagement, and experience. We can talk about participatory tourism, which entails public participation in tourism planning and development (Haywood, 1988; Tosun, 2000), and a number of socially conscious types of tourism such as ethical and responsible tourism (Goodwin and Francis, 2003), social tourism (Minnaert et al., 2011), volunteer tourism/voluntourism (Wearing and Gard McGehee, 2013), and ecotourism (environmentally aware tourism) (Buckley, 1994). De Bruin and Jelinčić (2016) developed the concept of participatory experience tourism (PET). While the notion of experiential travel/tourism has mainly been used for practical marketing purposes, it is rarely discussed in academia (Smith, n.d.). In recent years, transformational (Reisinger, 2013) or transformative tourism (Kirillova et al., 2017) has come to the fore, dealing with the impacts travel and tourism may have on changing human behaviour and eventually having a positive impact on the world. These various types of tourism have *experience* in common, with transformational tourism going further by discussing not only the experiential effects of tourism during the trip but also those occurring afterwards.

A second central feature common to all these types of tourism is *the value* they entail. According to Ricardo Blaug et al. (2006), value has three meanings: it describes an idea about economics (indicated by the price), about personal expression (satisfaction with a service), and about morality (such as security and integrity). This definition can be applied to any type of tourism since it relates to the price an individual is ready to pay for the service provided which is, at the same time, related to one's own integrity. The value that types of experiential tourism provide is related to value changes in the general society. For example, Ray and Anderson (2000) observed the rise of a new class of so-called *cultural creatives*, the change-makers who place priority on authenticity, engaged action, whole process learning, idealism and activism, globalism and ecology, women's issues, altruism, self-actualization, and spirituality. They are best described with reference to their worldviews and value orientation (Assenza, 2017, p. viii): they have a heightened social conscience and 'the stronger their values and beliefs about altruism, self-actualisation, and spirituality, the more likely they are to be interested in social action and social transformation' (Ray and Anderson, 2000, p. 15). They reject materialism, greed, me-firstism, status display, social inequalities, intolerance, big institutions, and superficiality; their reality includes heart and mind, personal and public, individual and community (Ray and Anderson, 2000, p. 17). All the above-mentioned types of experience-related tourism offer such values: turning away from superficiality and offering deeper cognition. The cultural attraction at the focus of this research is therefore analyzed not solely as bringing economic benefits but also as bringing personal growth and 'other sets of values which help societies to grow' (Jelinčić, 2017, p. 104). For consumers, the benefits seen in co-creative experiences 'have been argued to include self-expression, self-realization, enhanced socialization, confidence and aesthetic insight together with improved creative thinking, communication and problem solving skills' (Arvidsson, 2008; Brown et al., 2011, cited in Walmsley, 2013, p. 111). In potentially alienating environments (such as tourism), co-creative experiences can help people create meaning through direct experience.

Tourist emotional engagement in the case of the Museum of Broken Relationships

In order to ground the conceptual aspects presented, the case study of the Museum of Broken Relationships is analyzed in this chapter. It has been chosen as a successful case study because it focuses on a theme that is likely to stimulate a complex array of emotions that may greatly affect its visitors.[3]

This chapter does not examine whether the chosen case study applies the theoretical principles of experience creation by Pine and Gilmore (1998)[4] but rather goes further and focuses on a new concept, 'tourist emotional engagement' (TEE),[5] to see how this museum concept is experienced by its visitors. In general, the way visitors experience the museum and what they learn is influenced by a wide range of factors, including visitors' prior knowledge, experiences, and motivations; the museum exhibitions and programmes with which they engage; and their reflections, records, and memories shared and co-created after the visit (Russo and Richards, 2016, p. 120). The purpose of this research is to investigate in practice, and to compare, visitors' personal experiences to the tourist emotional engagement concept in order to explore if the museum was successful in engaging its visitors in an emotional way.

The research method used a content analysis of the visitor book at the Museum of Broken Relationships. Although rarely used as a research source, museum visitor books provide valuable insights on visitors' views, experiences, and understandings of museums and exhibitions (MacDonald, 2005). Making an entry in a visitor book is voluntary. Visitors' books are open to the public gaze and are composed of numerous individual comments and expressions. With this method, the researched are not aware that research is being undertaken (MacDonald, 2005). The visitor book of the Museum of Broken Relationships is the central part of the exhibition called 'Confession room', an interactive exhibit in which many visitors participate, either by writing or reading confessions and personal stories. Thus, using the visitor book as a research source on visitors' experiences is especially useful in the case of the Museum of Broken Relationships. The research used texts collected from the museum visitor book as empirical data to investigate and understand the different emotions and experiences expressed through the visitors' comments. The research focused on the visitor book in the museum's high season period (June to August 2017), and selected only English-language visitor comments.

Focusing on emotions and universal experiences of love and loss, the Museum of Broken Relationships enables visitors to identify with the exhibited story and reflect upon it, stimulating different emotions. Visitors' engagement, participation, and co-creation as well as their identification and immersion with the exhibited stories present the core activity of the museum. The comments from the visitor book were divided into two main types: (1) visitors' reflections on the museum stories (showing personal identification with the museum stories) and (2) visitors' personal experience stories (showing their emotional engagement and participation).

Personal connection (identification) with the museum story is desirable in every museum (Jelinčić and Senkić, 2017) because it can generate a meaningful emotional connection with visitors and leave a memorable impact on them. An effective immersive narrative not only shapes the exhibition design, it also provides a bridge between the visitor's own life experiences and the objects that represent another time and place. Perhaps most significantly, this personal connection makes visitors care (Stogner, 2011, p. 19). This is represented by several examples of comments where museum visitors were mostly emotionally affected and connected by the museum story in a positive way:

> This museum makes you appreciate what you have closest to your heart. Cherish every second and make every moment count.

Inspiring, humorous and heart-breaking. This visit has been an emotional journey towards healing.

I'm so sensible, I can feel the sorrow through the objects, I'm almost crying . . . It's difficult . . . I can't breathe . . . Thank you for this feeling. (Visitor book, The Museum of Broken Relationships)

From these comments, it is obvious that this creative museum concept can actually help people to resolve their own issues, to manage their behaviours and feelings, and to improve their physical, mental, and emotional well-being. Although the museum focuses mainly on 'negative' emotions expressed through heart-breaking stories and broken relationships, the comments show how the stories presented generate positive emotions and an optimistic life perspective for visitors.

One way to achieve such emotional reactions and to improve physical, mental, and emotional well-being is to encourage visitors to compose and tell their own personal stories and secrets in the Confession room. Imagining, telling, and discussing personal experience stories can help visitors to deal with challenges that they may be facing in real life and give them a feeling of hope. The majority of comments were related to their own experiences of broken relationships. Analysis of these comments revealed three main relationship types: intimate/romantic relationships, family relationships, and friendships. In their comments, visitors mainly reflected on their past relationships and events, writing from either the position of someone who was being hurt or someone who was hurting someone.

Visitors' personal experience stories mostly focused on still-present 'negative' emotional experiences from broken relationships. Most of these confessions were very painful and hard to read, so in this chapter we decided not to reproduce those quotations directly related to experiences of rape, violence, and incest. Some examples of other personal experience stories are:

Mom, I just want you to know that I forgive you for leaving us. I know how hard it was to live with dad, a man you loved but were not in love with anymore. I know how hard it was to leave your kids behind and return to Ireland. Now, 5 years on, it still hurts. Feelings of separation and abandonment never really go away. However, standing here today, in this museum, I know love is love and that's all that matters. Our relationship will never be broken.

I miss my mom. I'm sorry I wasn't a better daughter. Mom, I love you.

My dad told me he doesn't care about me. Nothing hurts more.

I met her 28 years ago and still love her. Just as much as the first day. Yes, it's possible.

I'm sorry for cheating on you. You gave me your heart and I broke it. I'm an asshole and you deserve better.

I hope we won't end up in this museum.

I never thought that breaking up with a friend can hurt more than breaking up a romantic relationship. It's been years. It still hurts ... (Visitor book, The Museum of Broken Relationships)

Visitors' comments show how the museum's stories stimulated their emotions, creating emotional responses that reflect their personal experience. People react to these personal stories differently, mainly because they also bring their own personal experiences to these narratives. Intimate stories and items from individuals gathered all over the world make people reflect on their own past and current relationships, no matter how intense they are. What was seen from these comments is that the Museum of Broken Relationships not only offers the chance for its donors to overcome an emotional breakdown and loss through creativity, but it also helps visitors deal with their own personal issues and gives a feeling of hope. Tourists/visitors are part of the exhibition process – they are emotionally engaged and involved in it. It is a two-way process: they react to others' stories but also bring in their personal experiences, thus creating the new museum artefact: the visitor book, which, as mentioned, is a part of the exhibition. This all would not be possible without the museum concept based on universal stories of love and loss which is a prerequisite for personal identification. Personal stories are the best way to connect on an emotional level with people – people relate to life stories and then engage in them (Figure 4.1).

Figure 4.1   Tourist emotional engagement process

If tourist emotional engagement is achieved, it will leave a positive impact on an individual and, more importantly, it can help individuals experiencing emotional and psychological challenges to achieve personal well-being. Writing about traumatic, stressful, or emotional events has been found to result in improvements in both physical and emotional health (Baikie and Wilhelm, 2005). Individuals experiencing difficulties discussing or remembering painful experiences may find this museum especially beneficial and therapeutic. The case study analyzed here and its Confession room exhibit proved to be a creative spur which elicited visitors' emotional reactions. Creativity may lead to transformation. Further longitudinal research could be applied to detect whether such transformation of the visitors really occurred. If so, this case of creative tourism would qualify as transformative tourism.

Conclusions

The tourism industry today is characterized by ever-growing segmentation (e.g., from cultural to creative) and more demanding tourists in search of experiences and meaning. While creative tourism is an extension of cultural tourism, to keep up with contemporary demands it needs further enhancements. Tourists increasingly seek experiences that reflect their own personal stories, and successful experience creation must include this personal identification with the attraction. To stir visitors' emotions, attractions are further enhanced if designed to use all five senses, and if appropriate memorabilia are supplied, the experience can be further enhanced even after the tourist visit.

This research shows that the Museum of Broken Relationships is successful in developing tourist emotional engagement by offering immersion and enabling the active participation of visitors. It engages its visitors in an escapist experience, which is confirmed by their active engagement in writing their personal experiences in the museum's visitor book. Since emotions instigate response behaviours, this activity offers not only a participative experience but also a chance for self-healing and, eventually, transformation. Thus, a greater role for cultural/creative tourism is observed: it becomes a means for solving personal problems. Although the museum's theme mainly stirs emotions that would, in a dimensional approach, be seen as negative (e.g., anger, disgust, fear, hatred), we advocate a categorical approach, which means that all the emotions are seen as equally important, not as having a positive/negative label. Thus, 'negative' emotions are, from this perspective, 'positive' since they offer personal relief – this is a sound example of creativity applied in a healing context.

Such participative and experiential creative tourism activities offer values revealing that, in the future, (creative) tourism will need to: (1) create attractions which are able to relate to individual personal experiences; (2) use creativity in art therapy tourism programmes; and (3) offer experiences that have the power to transform the visitor, thus leaving memorable traces. Research studies that cover these topics are very scarce. Although the supply of individual personal experiences is common in practice, few studies dig deep into the human psyche to explore how to trigger each individual's emotions. Gaining knowledge about know-how to access these triggers would not only benefit tailor-made cultural and creative tourism experiences but could easily expand into psychology- and medicine-related cultural/creative tourism research topics. In the last two decades, art therapy has become an increasingly popular research topic (see, e.g., Gilroy, 2007; Gussak and Rosal, 2016; Kapitan, 2010; Neilsen et al., 2016), but this line of research is practically non-existent in tourism – presenting a significant research gap to fill. Related to this are potential research lines concerned with transformative tourism experiences (e.g., Dwyer et al., 2017; Kirillova et al., 2017; Reisinger, 2013), which have been detected as 'on the rise' and trendy. Both culture and tourism have transformational powers, as indicated by the case study presented in this chapter, but in-depth research into this subject in the area of cultural and creative tourism is still needed. In order to provide memorable experiences, future research on creative tourism should pay greater attention to the creation of personal programmes that correspond to highly individualized interests. This calls for a transdisciplinary research approach grounded in culture, arts, and neuroscience that focuses on the stimulation of the senses by way of different cultural/creative visual, aural, olfactory, gustative, and tactile stimuli that can eventually stir emotions. Results of this research could provide general data on the types of stimuli that correspond to certain emotions, which could be used in creating memorable experiences in creative tourism. Once detected, they could also act as a solid ground for art therapy as well as for trans-formative/transformational tourism.

NOTES

1 In the context of this research, 'creativity' is defined as the formulation of new ideas and their application to produce original cultural tourism attractions. As defined by the United Nations Conference on Trade and Development (UNCTAD), there is 'an economic aspect to creativity, which is observable in the way it contributes to entrepreneurship, fosters innovation, enhances productivity, and promotes economic growth' (UNCTAD, 2008) but also a developmental aspect since it can have impacts on a balanced development . . . or increased quality of life in general (Jelinčić, 2017, p. 24).

2 Although nuances exist between the terms 'co-creation' and 'participation', they are not relevant for this research.

3 The Museum of Broken Relationships (https://brokenships.com) includes a permanent exhibition of donated items and stories, travelling exhibitions, and a virtual web museum. The project first started as a travelling collection of items donated by members of the public. In 2010, the project founders opened Zagreb's first privately owned museum dedicated to heartbreak love stories and broken relationships. The whole project is based on collecting, preserving, and presenting the tangible and intangible heritage of broken relationships from all over the world, connecting different people through universal experiences of love and loss, thus creating emotion-driven museum experiences. The museum received the Kenneth Hudson Award for Europe's most innovative museum in 2011, and opened its first franchise in Los Angeles in 2016. At its core, the museum has a constantly growing collection of items, offering people the chance to overcome an emotional breakdown through direct personal action and creativity – by contributing to its universal collection.

4 For more on the process of museum experience creation in the case of the Museum of Broken Relationships, see Jelinčić and Senkić (2017).

5 Tourist emotional engagement (TEE) can be defined in two ways: (1) as a general term used to describe various techniques used by cultural institutions in presenting their cultural attractions to stir the emotions of their visitors, and (2) as an emotional engagement of tourists towards individual cultural attractions.

References

Arvidsson, A. (2008), 'The ethical economy of customer coproduction', *Journal of Macromarketing*, **28** (4), 326–38. doi:0.1177/0276146708326077

Assenza, G. (2017), 'Foreword', in D.A. Jelinčić (ed.), *Innovations in Culture and Development: The Culturinno Effect in Public Policy*, Cham: Palgrave Macmillan, pp. vii–xv.

Baikie, K. and K. Wilhelm (2005), 'Emotional and physical health benefits of expressive writing', *Advances in Psychiatric Treatment*, **11** (5), 338–46.

Barsade, S.G. and D.E. Gibson (2007), 'Why does affect matter in organizations?', *Perspectives*, February, 36–59.

Blaug, R., L. Homer and R. Lekhi (2006), *Public Value, Citizen Expectations and User Commitment: A Literature Review*, London: The Work Foundation.

Buckley, R. (1994), 'A framework for ecotourism', *Annals of Tourism Research*, **21** (3), 661–5.

Cohen, J.B. and C.S. Areni (1991), 'Affect and consumer behavior', in T.S. Robertson and H.H. Kassarjian (eds), *Handbook of Consumer Behavior*, Englewood Cliffs, NJ: Prentice Hall, pp. 188–240.

Cohen, J.B., M.T. Pham and E.D. Andrade (2008), 'The nature and role of affect in consumer behavior', in C.P. Haugtvedt, P.M. Herr and F.R. Kardes (eds), *Handbook of Consumer Psychology*, New York: Erlbaum, pp. 297–348.

de Bruin, A. and D.A. Jelinčić (2016), 'Toward extending creative tourism: participatory experience tourism', *Tourism Review*, **71** (1), 57–66.

Dwyer, L., I. Ateljević and R. Tomljenović (2017), 'Tourism future: towards transformational tourism', in L. Dwyer, R. Tomljenović and S. Čorak (eds), *Evolution of Destination Planning and Strategy*, Cham: Palgrave Macmillan, pp. 279–94. doi:10.1007/978-3-319-42246-6_14

Ekman, P. and R.J. Davidson (eds) (1994), *The Nature of Emotions: Fundamental Questions*, Oxford: Oxford University Press.

European Commission (2017), *Cultural Tourism*, accessed 28 July 2017 at https://ec.europa.eu/growth/sectors/tourism/offer/cultural_en.

Gilroy, A. (2007), *Art Therapy, Research and Evidence-based Practice*, Thousand Oaks, CA: Sage.

Goodwin, H. and J. Francis (2003), 'Ethical and responsible tourism: consumer trends in the UK', *Journal of Vacation Marketing*, **9** (3), 271–84.

Govier, L. (2009), 'Leaders in co-creation: why and how museums could develop their co-creative practice with the public, building on ideas from the performing arts and other non-museum organisations', accessed 31 July 2017 at https://www2.le.ac.uk/departments/museumstudies/rcmg/projects/leaders-in-co-creation/Louise%20Govier%20-%20Clore%20Research%20-%20Leaders%20in%20Co-Creation.pdf.

Gussak, D.E. and M.L. Rosal (2016), *The Wiley Handbook of Art Therapy*, Hoboken, NJ: John Wiley and Sons. doi:10.1002/9781118306543.ch0

Haywood, K.M. (1988), 'Responsible and responsive tourism planning in the community', *Tourism Management*, **9** (2), 105–18.

Holbrook, M.B. and E.C. Hirschman (1982), 'The experiential aspects of consumption: consumer fantasies, feelings, and fun', *Journal of Consumer Research*, **9** (2), 132–40. doi:10.1086/208906

Ind, N., C. Fuller and C. Trevail (2012), *Brand Together: How Co-creation Generates Innovation and Re-energizes Brands*, London: Kogan Page.

Jelinčić, D.A. (2017), *Innovations in Culture and Development: The Culturinno Effect in Public Policy*, Cham: Palgrave Macmillan.

Jelinčić, D.A. and M. Senkić (2017), 'Creating a heritage tourism experience: the power of the senses', *Etnološka tribina: Journal of Croatian Ethnological Society*, **47** (40), 109–26. doi:10.15378/1848-9540.2017.40.03

Kapitan, L. (2010), *Introduction to Art Therapy Research*, Abingdon: Routledge.

Kirillova, K., X. Lehto and L. Cai (2017), 'What triggers transformative tourism experiences?', *Tourism Recreation Research*, **42** (4), 1–14.

Lanier, C.D. and H.J. Schau (2007), 'Culture and co-creation: exploring consumers' inspirations and aspirations for writing and posting on-line fan fiction', in R.W. Belk and J.F. Sherry (eds), *Consumer Culture Theory (Research in Consumer Behavior, Volume 11)*, Bingley: Emerald Group Publishing, pp. 321–42.

Leadbeater, C. (2009), *The Art of With*, Manchester: Cornerhouse.

MacDonald, S. (2005), 'Accessing audiences: visiting visitor books', *Museum and Society*, **3** (3), 119–36.

Minnaert, L., R. Maitland and G. Miller (2011), 'What is social tourism?', *Current Issues in Tourism*, **14** (5), 403–15.

Neilsen, P., R. King and F. Baker (2016), *Creative Arts in Counseling and Mental Health*, Thousand Oaks, CA: Sage.

Pine, B.J. II and J.H. Gilmore (1998), 'Welcome to the experience economy', *Harvard Business Review*, July–August, 97–105.

Prahalad, C.K. and V. Ramaswamy (2004), 'Co-creation experiences: the next practice in value creation', *Journal of Interactive Marketing*, **18** (3), 5–14.

Prayag, G., S. Hosany, B. Muskat and G. Del Chiappa (2017), 'Understanding the relationships between tourists' emotional experiences, perceived overall image, satisfaction, and intention to recommend', *Journal of Travel Research*, **56** (1), 41–54.

Ray, P.H. and S.R. Anderson (2000), *The Cultural Creatives: How 50 Million People are Changing the World*, New York: Harmony.

Reisinger, Y. (2013), *Transformational Tourism: Tourist Perspectives*, Wallingford, Oxfordshire: CABI.

Richards, G. and C. Raymond (2000), 'Creative tourism', *ATLAS News*, **23**, 16–20.

Robbins, S.P. and T. Judge (2013), *Organizational Behavior*, Boston, MA: Pearson.

Russo, A.P. and G. Richards (2016), *Reinventing the Local in Tourism: Producing, Consuming and Negotiating Place*, Bristol, Tonawanda and North York: Channel View Publications.

Santos, V., P. Ramos and N. Almeida (2014), 'Consumer behaviour in tourism: a content analysis of relationships between involvement and emotions', *Journal of Tourism Research*, **9**, 28–64.

Shouse, E. (2005), 'Feeling, emotion, affect', *M/C Journal*, **8** (6), accessed 31 July 2017 at http://journal. media-culture.org.au/0512/03-shouse.php.

Simonicca, A. (1997), 'Il turismo fra esperienza e cultura' (Tourism between experience and culture), in Enzo Nocifora (ed.), *Turismatica: Turismo, cultura, nuove imprenditorialità e globalizzazione dei mercati*, Milano: Franco Agnelli s.r.l., pp. 130–40.

Smith, W.L. (n.d.), 'Experiential tourism around the world and at home: definitions and standards', accessed 1 August 2017 at https://www.emporia.edu/dotAsset/1565fddf-5141-48f8-9aee-24aaad00781d.pdf.

Stogner, M.B. (2011), 'The immersive cultural museum experience: creating context and story with new media technology', *The International Journal of the Inclusive Museum*, **3** (3), 117–30.

Sundbo, J. and F. Sørensen (2013), 'Introduction to the experience economy', in J. Sundbo and F. Sørensen (eds), *Handbook on the Experience Economy*, Cheltenham, UK and Northampton, MA, USA: Edward Elgar, pp. 1–17.

Toffler, A. (1970), *The Future Shock*, New York: Random House.

Tosun, C. (2000), 'Limits to community participation in the tourism development process in developing countries', *Tourism Management*, **21** (6), 613–63.

UNCTAD (2008), *Creative Economy Report*, Geneva: UNCTAD, accessed 31 July 2017 at http://unctad. org/en/Docs/ditc20082cer_en.pdf.

UNWTO (2015), *Affiliate Members Global Reports, Volume Twelve – Cultural Routes and Itineraries*, Madrid: UNWTO.

Walmsley, B. (2013), 'Co-creating theatre: authentic engagement or inter-legitimation?', *Cultural Trends*, **22** (2), 108–18.

Wearing, S. and N. Gard McGehee (2013), 'Volunteer tourism: a review', *Tourism Management*, **38**, 120–30.

PART II

Forms of creative tourism destinations

5   Creative tourism in creative outposts

Patrick Brouder

In our twenty-first century urbanized world, there is a tendency to reserve words like 'creative' and 'innovative' for the most geographically central places with high population growth and high-technology sectors. This is reflected in studies which tend to focus on the low-hanging fruit of creativity in central places that have a lot of creativity to be studied. However, through tourism studies, we have a window on another kind of creativity in another kind of place. The CREATOUR project in Portugal is leading the way in developing and showcasing creative tourism in small cities and rural areas (see www.creatour.pt). This chapter builds on the research on creative tourism led by CREATOUR, Greg Richards, and others and takes it to the next geographical level of the rural peripheral places – creative outposts.

Many rural peripheral communities have a strong tradition of innovation as they thrived on entrepreneurial activity to develop their natural resources and agricultural land and managed to carve out a place to live in an often unforgiving environment. Other peripheral communities have been home to Indigenous peoples for countless generations and these groups have lived with the land by displaying incredible resourcefulness. Such communities have something in common – a seemingly inexhaustible ability to innovate in and adapt to their local environment. However, recently these groups have been suffering multiple blows to their social cohesion. Challenges include an ageing population, a lack of employment opportunities, and declining local government revenues, among other factors.

Tourism development is one way in which rural peripheral regions can stem the tide of their decline and prosper once more. There is a growing body of research on tourism and regional development in rural peripheral places and it has examined many of the opportunities and challenges facing such communities (for example, Brouder and Eriksson, 2013; Giaoutzi and Nijkamp, 2006; Hall et al., 2009; Mose, 2007; Müller and Jansson, 2007). While some researchers wisely caution against a new mono-crop of tourism (Schmallegger and Carson, 2010), this is not a significant issue for most peripheral regions due to a combination of distance decay and intervening opportunities restricting any major growth in demand (Lew et al., 2004). Put simply, there are huge barriers to rapid growth for most rural peripheral places. In addition, government agencies, from local to supra-national, endorse tourism as a way to advance rural peripheral economic development (European Commission, 2002; OECD, 2010).

What is a 'creative outpost'?

A 'creative outpost' is a rural peripheral community that faces a challenging socio-economic environment but meets its challenges by deploying endogenous creative capital, resulting in a palpable shift towards a more sustainable socio-economic environment. Such a shift is led by a measurable increase in local innovation and ultimately acts as a community coping strategy (Brouder, 2012a, 2013). Some common characteristics of creative outposts include: a history of economic dependence on outside capital often existing alongside a local subsistence economy, a socio-economic trajectory perceived as being in perpetual decline with a negative outlook for the future, and a noticeable presence of persistent local attempts at community coping and resilience. Creative outposts are further characterized by their geographical distance from the core and often from other rural peripheral communities. This 'island-like' status opens the possibility for (and the challenge of!) increased local interaction and cooperation. Creative outposts can overcome their distance deficits by acting as local centres and banding together following a similar approach to their traditional past roles as market towns or trading posts.

Tourism is one form of development that has proven to be resilient in a rural setting (Brouder and Fullerton, 2015; Fullerton and Brouder, 2019) and, as such, it contributes to community coping strategies (Bærenholdt, 2007; Brouder, 2017a) as well as the more promoted economic opportunities it presents (Löffler, 2007). Moreover, 'there is a creative effervescence brought on by community-based tourism development and that tourism acts as a catalyst to enable local social capital to be utilised for the benefit of the community' (Brouder, 2013, p. 184). Other studies of creativity in tourism have quite rightly examined creative industries and creative clusters (Petrov, 2007; Richards and Wilson, 2007a) but in this chapter I focus on the subtle, yet palpable, role of the creative processes that contribute to rural peripheral tourism innovation.

Creativity in tourism

Richards and Wilson (2007b) have listed the indicators of creative development, including:

- increased creativity and creative activities among locals
- growth in tolerance towards those from outside the locale
- greater social cohesion in the local community.

While each of these is a legitimate indicator, they are also desirable outcomes in their own right and tourism is one sector which allows such development to occur.

The development of this positive social capital acts as a conduit for a culture of support to flourish (Putnam, 2000). Importantly, many rural communities see such indicators as optimal outcomes and more important than economic development. This ties into the pursuit of 'quality of life' for individuals and 'quality of place' for communities and remains a pertinent goal for rural peripheral communities. The contribution of tourism to local social capital development in rural peripheral areas has been well studied (Macbeth et al., 2004; Schmallegger and Carson, 2010; Schmallegger et al., 2011). A persistent theme has been a lack of innovation on the production side and a latent demand for innovative tourism products on the consumption side (cf. Hjalager et al., 2018), yet this general pattern breaks down when examining creative and cultural tourism at a more localized scale where innovation is palpable, even if it remains difficult to quantify and is not present in all places to the same degree. The main long-term trend at the grassroots level is best summarized by Ateljevic (2009), who writes: 'opportunities have been created worldwide for a wider array of specialized small-scale tourism firms' (p. 154) and such opportunities have needed a great deal of tourism innovation (by the entrepreneurs themselves as well as by the attendant planning and destination management organizations) (Brouder, 2012a). The overall tenacity of tourism in rural areas is testament to its innovation and resilience in an environment not expected to be so creative (Brouder, 2012b).

Creativity in place

Creativity in place is best thought of as a process of spillover and diffusion of knowledge (Jacobs, 1969) and in the twenty-first century such creativity has been positioned as the means by which regions can gain competitive advantage over other places (Florida, 2002). While these leading theories have focused on urban areas and growth in cities, others have moved the discussion to mid-sized cities and tourism destinations (Hjalager, 2010; Richards and Wilson, 2007a). Such studies have opened new avenues of research specific to these regional and sectoral contexts. For instance, there is a clear need to move away from studies of creative industries and related product development towards creative processes, for example, 'co-creation' in tourism (Richards, 2011).

In this chapter, the focus is on creative processes in regional development. The operational term 'innovation' is also used to represent the innovative processes communities engage in. Previous studies of creativity in rural peripheral places have included scientists, leaders, bohemians, and entrepreneurs as four important groups (Petrov, 2007) although it must be noted that such definitions are not exhaustive categories of all innovators in rural peripheral places. It is thus necessary to conceptualize the local processes of innovation in a more inclusive manner starting from the position that all places and all community members have a latent creative energy. In studying creativity in rural peripheral places, we must first recognize the existence of this latent creativity in order to design studies capable of capturing 'innovation' in such places.

From coping to creating

Rural peripheral places have often been (unfairly) characterized as only having marginal economic activities and only being relevant for their role in supporting the core (Anderson, 2000). While it is true that primary sector activities such as agriculture, forestry, and mining are an important part of the story of rural peripheral places, they do not tell the whole story. In fact, Anderson labelled the innovation of entrepreneurs, who created novel worth out of seemingly low-value resources, as the 'paradox in the periphery' (Anderson, 2000). This 'paradox' is ever more prevalent as local creativity is coupled with the growing tourism sector in communities latching on to the development potential of tourism by innovating in ways never considered before. In spite of the multiple pressures rural peripheral communities face (for example, declining public sector job opportunities and a reduction in the labour requirements of primary industries) (Brouder et al., 2015; Lundmark, 2005), many places manage to cope and some even thrive.

'Coping' is a regionally specific form of resilience as it more accurately relates the challenging environment which rural peripheral communities have been facing over the years (cf. Bærenholdt, 2007) and also better captures the ongoing processes of dealing with that environment. The alignment of an increasing number of tourists seeking out the 'last wilderness' (Müller, 2011) or some distant cultural heritage (Brouder, 2017b) alongside locals seeking new endogenous development opportunities (Carson et al., 2017) has created new ways of coping. Many rural peripheral communities are building community capacity through local tourism development and even though this does not necessarily have a great impact on the labour market, it does create opportunities for entrepreneurship (Müller and Brouder, 2014) and drives the reproduction and enhancement of positive social capital (Macbeth et al., 2004).

From inertia to innovation

'Tourism innovation is not the preserve of elite places and elite individuals' (Hall and Williams, 2008, p. 3) and, even in rural peripheral places, is easily identified by a set of local characteristics:

- multitude of actors (with a few key actors)
- diversity and density of relations (with a strong public sector)
- keen competition (driven by demand-led innovation)
- global outreach (driven by technology)
- cross-sectoral outreach (driven by individual entrepreneurship)
- resistance (from local elites as well as other locals who fear change)
- natural resources (forming the basis of local tourism development)
- economic resources (adding a local market for tourism development)
- social capital (forming the basis for creative processes to flourish)

- cultural capital (adding a local rationale for tourism development) (based on Hall and Williams, 2008; Huijbens et al., 2009).

The challenge in rural peripheral communities is to identify the available local characteristics which may form a local innovation system and develop those accordingly. This is, of course, easier said than done but is possible due to the nature of creative outposts – the local social networks are often geographically concentrated with an oasis of creative energy present. This community-led development embeds adaptive management in the local tourism innovation system (George et al., 2009) and leads to 'co-evolution' (Brouder and Fullerton, 2017).

Co-evolution in creative outposts

In rural peripheral communities, the institutional environment is often perceived as stagnant. However, as tourism emerges locally, institutional innovation becomes central to the dynamic process of tourism evolution (Brouder et al., 2017). In this context, institutions are the norms and behaviours of local tourism stakeholders and these local 'ways of doing things' often co-evolve with the emergent entrepreneurial spirit arising in the community. When tourism innovation is conceptualized as a process, institutions are central to understanding the positive development taking place as they set the framing conditions for local development. The institutions that are central to rural peripheral tourism development are most often region-specific (rural peripheral) and not necessarily sector-specific (tourism) because in such locales there is most often an 'all-hands-on-deck' approach to development opportunities. This allows an environment of support to develop for the relatively new sector of creative tourism. It is also important to note that such developments must be examined in a long-term perspective as change comes slowly but is quite palpable in the communities where it is emerging.

Canadian creativity: cases from British Columbia

In order to illustrate the challenge of, and the necessity for, understanding the potential of creative tourism in creative outposts, this chapter presents three cases from British Columbia (BC). BC is the westernmost province in Canada bordered by the Pacific Ocean in the west and the Rocky Mountains in the east. With a population of just under 5 million and an area of just under 1 million square kilometres, BC receives over 5 million overnight visitors each year (Destination BC, 2018). Destinations such as Vancouver and Whistler are well known internationally but the province is also a major destination for tourism in rural peripheral areas.

The three selected cases offer research vignettes of creative tourism and are purposively chosen to represent a diverse range of creative outposts which may be comparable with other regions. The selected cases are Ashcroft, Fernie, and Salt Spring Island and are typical of rural peripheral tourism in BC. The research vignettes are based on six expert interviews conducted in 2017 as part of a larger, long-term research programme on tourism and sustainable rural development.

Ashcroft: community creativity in an undiscovered heritage town

Located just off the Trans-Canada Highway in central BC, the village of Ashcroft, with a population of approximately 1,600, can be said to have met the definition of an outpost twice in its history. First, it was a vital trading post for the Cariboo Gold Rush in the mid-1800s. The Trans-Canada Highway brought some business near Ashcroft throughout the second half of the twentieth century but the opening of an alternative, faster route through the mountains meant Ashcroft has returned to being an outpost as nearby traffic volumes have decreased significantly. However, the community has shown tremendous resilience in utilizing its local assets to develop alternate economic possibilities. Leading the way is a subtle but significant turn towards tourism – building on the historic legacy of the Gold Rush and the development of a small cluster of wellness tourism operators. Yet the strongest evidence of creative tourism in the community has been the leveraging of the skills and collaborative spirit of local artists to create a unique niche:

> Ashcroft has a vibrant and diverse Arts community. However, one artform in particular is becoming a draw for many visitors to our community – glass mosaics. This visually stunning artform is proudly displayed throughout the community . . . Don't be surprised to find other mosaics that are not located on the map, the collection is growing every year. (Village of Ashcroft, 2018, n.p.)

Of particular note is that the main focus of the mosaics is the drive to collaborate among the local artists rather than creating a tourism product per se, and the result is a community resource that acts as both a tourism draw and an ongoing and evolving community cohesion endeavour. For example, the recent installation of a mosaic commemorating the Chinese labourers who died during the construction of the Canadian Pacific Railway was seen as a way to honour a previously forgotten group as well as a way to highlight the location of their graves for visitors (Figure 5.1). Such efforts raise the tourism profile of the village while honouring its unique cultural heritage.

Fernie: a nature-based resort town with a penchant for creativity

Fernie is a village in southeast BC with a population of just over 5,000 and surrounded by an abundance of natural resources (that is, the Canadian Rocky Mountains), helping it overcome its economic outpost position to become a regional centre of nature-based tourism. A high level of amenities (as a direct result of a strong tourism sector) has made Fernie an attractive locale for one-time tourists to become second-home residents and, in quite a few cases, permanent residents (Williams et al., 2016). One noticeable sub-sector in Fernie which blurs the lines between tourism and local living is the arts and culture sector. As well as a great selection of public artwork spread around the town, the village has two important resources creating space for collaboration and community development.

Source: Photo taken by author.

Figure 5.1 Glass mosaic commemorating deceased Chinese railway labourers in Ashcroft, BC

First, the Fernie Arts Co-op is a volunteer organization sharing the work of over 30 local artists and artisans. Second, The Arts Station is the heart of the cultural and creative sectors in Fernie with a theatre, art gallery, and studios, and space available for community workshops. Importantly, The Arts Station functions primarily as a community resource but one that is made viable by the additional audiences, participants, and revenue brought by creative tourism. Moreover, the ability of Fernie to leverage its nature-based tourism market to develop its arts and culture sector has seen some novel cooperation on diverse events such as the Wapiti indie music festival and the GillBilly old time music festival. In Fernie, tourism development and community cultural development are clearly complementary.

Salt Spring Island: island community with a renowned arts cluster

As the largest of BC's southern Gulf islands with a population of over 10,000 and a very healthy tourism sector due to its proximity to the provincial capital of Victoria on Vancouver Island, Salt Spring is the most central (close to population centres) yet most natural (island) of the outposts presented in this chapter. In this case, 'outpost' only truly applies in the economic sense as the island has been a central place for the Coast Salish peoples before colonial settlers arrived to engage in primary industries (for example, logging and agriculture) in the mid-nineteenth century, thus making the area an economic outpost serving the core of the colony of Vancouver Island. Its proximity to Victoria saw it become one of the earliest major regional rural tourism destinations:

> By the 1930s the island's reputation grew and the word got out to vacationers and resorts were opened to welcome these early tourists. By the 1960s, artists such as potters, paint-ers, stained-glass and basket makers, woodworkers, quilters and paper makers began arriving on the island and started what is now the heart of island culture. (Salt Spring Island Chamber of Commerce, 2018, n.p.)

Over time, this eclectic mix of new residents has evolved and Salt Spring is now full of creatives:

> Artists and young neo-hippies, retired millionaires and restaurateurs, trades people and boot-clad farmers, writers and musicians all happily co-exist on what the *Washington Post* once called 'the coolest island in Canada.' (Destination BC, 2018, n.p.)

However, the long-term sustainability of Salt Spring's heritage-scape has been called into question as growth-focused initiatives within the tourism economy may alter the institutional environment with only the response of sustainability minded locals countervailing this (Halpern and Mitchell, 2011). The local creative tourism sector is at the forefront of the sustainability drive with its community-first focus and remains a powerful counterbalance to growth-centric plans while still providing meaningful community economic development opportunities for many.

Towards a research agenda for creative tourism in creative outposts

> Whereas economic capital is in people's bank accounts and human capital is inside their heads, social capital inheres in the structure of their relationships. (Portes, 1998, p. 7)

The extant literature on creativity in rural peripheral areas (Cloke, 2007; Gibson, 2010; Petrov, 2007) is now being linked with the literature on creative tourism (Richards, 2011). The cases presented in this chapter show that a focus on com-munity relationships, rather than tourism relationships per se, is needed in order to open new avenues of research in places which are not creative tourism centres yet still have ongoing creative processes related to tourism innovation.

In the case of Ashcroft, the local artists collaborate with clear community goals in mind and their outcomes also have a clear tourism dividend. This raises an impor-tant question as to how we measure (and value) softer goals of community develop-ment as opposed to the harder goals of economic development (cf. Brouder, 2018) since in Ashcroft the direct economic impact of the glass mosaics is minimal yet the community cohesion is developing in a virtuous spiral and, ultimately, the glass mosaics add to the cultural heritage platform of the village for the future.

Turning to Fernie, it is clear that the confluence of tourists, second-home owners, and locals all engaging in creative tourism activities is an important coping opportunity (Bærenholdt, 2007). Tourism's interaction with, and support of, the creative industries adds to the positive spiral of creative development by creating a 'local breeding ground' for new ideas (Karlsson, 2005). While tourism-focused communities such as Fernie are very outward-looking in terms of sourcing customers and investment (for example, second homes), they must also be inward-looking and continue to activate and support the local social capital which makes them more liveable places.

Finally, Salt Spring Island is a long-established creative outpost with a long history of creative tourism as well. There has been a creative effervescence on the island since at least the 1960s. The tourism economy of the island is a model of community-based development and yet even here there is the continuing challenge of pro-growth models of development (Halpern and Mitchell, 2011) threatening local sustainability (cf. Brouder, 2017a, 2018). The challenge for Salt Spring Island is how to allow for economic development that does not cause the long-term creative effervescence to fizzle out in a region with massive pro-growth pressures.

What the research vignettes presented above show is that tourism has proven to be tenacious in rural peripheral areas and that it has a clear role in the long-term resilience of rural communities. The three cases have very different profiles but all three have one thing in common – community groups engaged in creative processes which are aimed, to varying degrees, at the creative tourism sector. The main role of the creative processes in these three creative outposts is to add to the local quality of life in order to develop more resilient communities over the long term.

Based on these cases, there are a number of clear research paths for creative tourism in creative outposts going forward. First, the concentration of tourism supply in rural peripheral places is expected to consolidate further (Müller, 2011) in future creative outposts. Thus, studies of the early stages of what seems like a subtle process may turn into long-term studies of the virtuous spiral of creative tourism evolution. Second, the metrics we use to measure 'innovation' need to be further developed. The focus should be on the community relationships and processes of interaction in creative outposts – places where the isolation from the regional core is offset by strong in situ cooperation and interaction (Brouder, 2012a). Any measures also need to be refined enough to fully value the local gains made in creative processes even when immediate outcomes are less noticeable in the short term since creative tourism development is a long-term process. Third, new path development in creative outposts is a precarious process. Formulaic developments are far less common than idiosyncratic, place-dependent developments and many nascent successes are undone over time. Thus, research needs to better assess what is actually accomplished in any given creative tourism development. This also means looking beyond product and/or project 'failures' to the learning and increased community cohesion which comes from the process of creative tourism development since the knowledge gained becomes a resource for future development regardless of the present outcomes.

Such research on the processes of creative tourism development in creative outposts will also add to the growing literature on creative tourism in general (Richards, 2011) because many creative outposts face significant challenges to their social cohesion and yet creative tourism is proving to be one endogenous development path through which rural peripheral areas increase their local resilience.

References

Anderson, A. (2000), 'Paradox in the periphery: an entrepreneurial reconstruction?', *Entrepreneurship and Regional Development*, **12**, 91–109.

Ateljevic, J. (2009), 'Tourism entrepreneurship and regional development', in J. Ateljevic and S.J. Page (eds), *Tourism and Entrepreneurship: International Perspectives*, Oxford: Butterworth-Heinemann, pp. 149–71.

Bærenholdt, O.J. (2007), *Coping with Distances: Producing Nordic Atlantic Societies*, Oxford: Berghahn Books.

Brouder, P. (2012a), 'Creative outposts: tourism's place in rural innovation', *Tourism Planning and Development*, **9** (4), 383–96.

Brouder, P. (2012b), 'Tourism development against the odds: the tenacity of tourism in rural areas', *Tourism Planning and Development*, **9** (4), 333–7.

Brouder, P. (2013), 'Embedding Arctic tourism innovation in "creative outposts"', in R.H. Lemelin, P. Maher and D. Liggett (eds), *From Talk to Action: How Tourism is Changing the Polar Regions*, Thunder Bay, ON: Centre for Northern Studies Press, pp. 183–93.

Brouder, P. (2017a), 'Evolutionary economic geography: reflections from a sustainable tourism perspective', *Tourism Geographies*, **19** (3), 438–47.

Brouder, P. (2017b), 'Post-inscription challenges: renegotiating world heritage management in the Laponia area in Sweden', in L. Bourdeau, M. Gravari-Barbas and M. Robinson (eds), *World Heritage Sites and Tourism: Global and Local Relations*, Oxon, UK: Routledge, pp. 117–28.

Brouder, P. (2018), 'The end of tourism? A Gibson-Graham inspired reflection on the tourism economy', *Tourism Geographies*, **20** (5) (in press).

Brouder, P. and R.H. Eriksson (2013), 'Staying power: what influences micro-firm survival in tourism?', *Tourism Geographies*, **15** (1), 124–43.

Brouder, P. and C. Fullerton (2015), 'Exploring heterogeneous tourism development paths: cascade effect or co-evolution in Niagara?', *Scandinavian Journal of Hospitality and Tourism*, **15** (1–2), 152–66.

Brouder, P. and C. Fullerton (2017), 'Co-evolution and sustainable tourism development: from old institutional inertia to new institutional imperatives in Niagara', in P. Brouder, S. Anton Clavé, A. Gill and D. Ioannides (eds), *Tourism Destination Evolution*, Oxon, UK: Routledge, pp. 149–64.

Brouder, P., S. Karlsson and L. Lundmark (2015), 'Hyper-production: a new metric of multifunctionality', *European Countryside*, **7** (3), 134–43.

Brouder, P., S. Anton Clavé, A. Gill and D. Ioannides (2017), 'Why is tourism not an evolutionary science? Understanding the past, present and future of destination evolution', in P. Brouder, S. Anton Clavé, A. Gil and D. Ioannides (eds), *Tourism Destination Evolution*, Oxon, UK: Routledge, pp. 1–18.

Carson, D.A., P. Brouder and S. de la Barre (2017), 'Communities and new development paths in the sparsely populated north', *Journal of Rural and Community Development*, **12** (2–3), i–xi.

Cloke, P. (2007), 'Creativity and tourism in rural environments', in G. Richards and J. Wilson (eds), *Tourism, Creativity and Development*, Oxon, UK: Routledge, pp. 37–47.

Destination BC (2018), DestinationBC.ca, accessed on 15 February 2018.

European Commission (2002), *Using Natural and Cultural Heritage for the Development of Sustainable Tourism in Non-traditional Tourism Destinations*, Brussels EC Reports.

Florida, R. (2002), *The Rise of the Creative Class: And How It's Transforming Work, Leisure, Community and Everyday Life*, New York: Basic Books.

Fullerton, C. and P. Brouder (2019), 'Rural tourism in a metropolitan hinterland: co-evolving towards a resilient rural fringe', in R. Koster and D.A. Carson (eds), *Perspectives on Rural Tourism Geographies: Case Studies from Developed Nations on the Exotic, the Fringe and the Boring Bits in Between*, Dodrecht: Springer.

George, E.W., H. Mair and D.G. Reid (2009), *Rural Tourism Development: Localism and Cultural Change*, Bristol: Channel View.

Giaoutzi, M. and P. Nijkamp (2006), *Tourism and Regional Development: New Pathways*, Burlington, VT: Ashgate.

Gibson, C. (2010), 'Creative geographies: tales from the "margins"', *Australian Geographer*, **41** (1), 1–10.

Hall, C.M. and A. Williams (2008), *Tourism and Innovation*, Oxon, UK: Routledge.

Hall, C.M., D.K. Müller and J. Saarinen (2009), *Nordic Tourism: Issues and Cases*, Bristol: Channel View.

Halpern, C. and C.J. Mitchell (2011), 'Can a preservationist ideology halt the process of creative destruction? Evidence from Salt Spring Island, British Columbia', *The Canadian Geographer/Le Géographe Canadien*, **55** (2), 208–25.

Hjalager, A.M. (2010), 'A review of innovation in tourism', *Tourism Management*, **31** (1), 1–12.

Hjalager, A.M., G. Kwiatkowski and M. Østervig Larsen (2018), 'Innovation gaps in Scandinavian rural tourism', *Scandinavian Journal of Hospitality and Tourism*, **18** (1), 1–17.

Huijbens, E.H., A.M. Hjalager, P. Björk, S. Nordin and A. Flagestad (2009), 'Sustaining creative entrepreneurship: the role of innovation systems', in J. Ateljevic and S.J. Page (eds), *Tourism and Entrepreneurship: International Perspectives*, Oxford: Butterworth-Heinemann, pp. 55–74.

Jacobs, J. (1969). *The Economy of Cities*, New York: Random House.

Karlsson, S.E. (2005), 'The social and the cultural capital of a place and their influence on the production of tourism – a theoretical reflection based on an illustrative case study', *Scandinavian Journal of Hospitality and Tourism*, **5** (2), 102–15.

Lew, A., C.M. Hall and A. Williams (eds) (2004), *A Companion to Tourism*, Oxford: Blackwell.

Löffler, G. (2007), 'The impact of tourism on the local supply structure of goods and services in peripheral areas', in D.K. Müller and B. Jansson (eds), *Tourism in Peripheries: Perspectives from the Far North and South*, Wallingford, UK: CABI, pp. 69–84.

Lundmark, L. (2005), 'Economic restructuring into tourism in the Swedish mountain range', *Scandinavian Journal of Hospitality and Tourism*, **5** (1), 23–45.

Macbeth, J., D. Carson and J. Northcote (2004), 'Social capital, tourism and regional development: SPCC as a basis for innovation and sustainability', *Current Issues in Tourism*, **7** (6), 502–22.

Mose, I. (ed.) (2007), *Protected Areas and Regional Development in Europe: Towards a New Model for the 21st Century*, Burlington, VT: Ashgate.

Müller, D.K. (2011), 'Tourism development in Europe's "last wilderness": an assessment of nature-based tourism in Swedish Lapland', in A.A. Grenier and D.K. Müller (eds), *Polar Tourism: A Tool for Regional Development*, Québec: Presses de l'Université du Québec, pp. 129–53.

Müller, D.K. and P. Brouder (2014), 'Dynamic development or destined to decline? The case of Arctic tourism businesses and local labour markets in Jokkmokk, Sweden', in A. Viken and B. Granås (eds), *Tourism Destination Development: Turns and Tactics*, Farnham, UK: Ashgate, pp. 227–44.

Müller, D.K. and B. Jansson (eds) (2007), *Tourism in Peripheries: Perspectives from the Far North and South*, Wallingford, UK: CABI.

OECD (2010), *OECD Tourism Trends and Policies 2010. Industry and Entrepreneurship Report*, Paris: OECD.

Petrov, A.N. (2007), 'A look beyond metropolis: exploring creative class in the Canadian periphery', *Canadian Journal of Regional Science*, **30** (3), 451–74.

Portes, A. (1998), 'Social capital: its origins and applications in modern sociology', *Annual Review of Sociology*, **24** (1), 1–24.

Putnam, R.D. (2000), *Bowling Alone: The Collapse and Revival of American Community*, New York: Simon and Schuster.

Richards, G. (2011), 'Creativity and tourism: the state of the art', *Annals of Tourism Research*, **38** (4), 1225–53.

Richards, G. and J. Wilson (eds) (2007a), *Tourism, Creativity and Development*, Oxon, UK: Routledge.

Richards, G. and J. Wilson (2007b), 'Creativities in tourism development', in G. Richards and J. Wilson (eds), *Tourism, Creativity and Development*, Oxon, UK: Routledge, pp. 255–88.

Salt Spring Island Chamber of Commerce (2018), SaltSpringTourism.com, accessed 19 February 2018.

Schmallegger, D. and D. Carson (2010), 'Is tourism just another staple? A new perspective on tourism in remote regions', *Current Issues in Tourism*, **13** (3), 201–21.

Schmallegger, D., S. Harwood, L. Cerveny and D. Müller (2011), 'Tourist populations and local capital', in D. Carson, R.O. Rasmussen, P. Ensign, L. Huskey and A. Taylor (eds), *Demography at the Edge*, Burlington, VT: Ashgate, pp. 271–88.

Village of Ashcroft (2018), AshcroftBC.ca, accessed 17 February 2018.

Williams, P.W., A.M. Gill and J.M. Zukiwsky (2016), 'Tourism-led amenity migration in a mountain community: quality of life implications for Fernie, British Columbia', in H. Richins and J.S. Hull (eds), *Mountain Tourism: Experiences, Communities, Environments and Sustainable Futures*, Wallingford, UK: CABI, pp. 97–110.

6   Stories of design, snow, and silence: creative tourism landscape in Lapland

Satu Miettinen, Jaana Erkkilä-Hill, Salla-Mari Koistinen, Timo Jokela, and Mirja Hiltunen

This chapter discusses the creative tourism landscape in Lapland and its transformation into a topography of artistic collaboration, walking, and gazing. Three case studies are presented that outline the characteristics of creative participation in tourism activities in the arctic context and introduce a polyphonic discussion of the tourism landscape in Lapland which expands the landscape into a multidimensional and spatial topography. This chapter asks: How is the creative tourism landscape in Lapland constructed? and How is the topography of creative tourism constructed? Arctic design and artistic production are introduced as creative contexts that allow people to both participate in and develop a cluster of events aimed at increasing art, creativity, and innovation in the arctic. The first case study, 'Lapland Snow Art and Design', represents snow and ice forming the landscape and location for artistic production and tourist activity. The second case study, 'Travelling Laboratories for Artistic Thinking', studies the artist's way of producing a tourism experience through performance and mediation in silence and walking. The third case study, 'Master's degree programme of Applied Visual Arts and Nature Photography', introduces a contemporary discussion on creating the tourist gaze in the arctic through photography.

As an outcome, this chapter introduces a thematic framework, 'the topography of creative tourism in Lapland'. Topography is used as metaphor that introduces boundedness (Kearns, 1997), which enables the shift from passive to active role in learning through creative engagement. Further, topography introduces the spatial dimensions (Levine, 2008) of the creative landscape where people walk, engage in creative activities, and even shape and change the landscape through snow design. The three case studies are analyzed using art education as an embodied practice (Hiltunen, 2007, 2008) and as a collaborative design process for creative tourism (Miettinen, 2007). The chapter discusses active engagement and ways of introducing creative and cultural activities as tools for collaboration between tourists and local communities, and even the positioning of the community members as visitors in their own topography. In closing, the chapter suggests future directions for research.

State of the art: creative tourism as an embodied, collaborative, and spatial experience

Creative tourism has introduced participation as a means for cultural learning experience in tourism (Miettinen, 2007; Richards and Wilson, 2006). In this chapter, we discuss and expand the idea of creative tourism into the embodied practice of walking as a way of studying and researching the landscape (Macpherson, 2016). Walking is a way to self-reflect, think, and move in the landscape. Further, creative tourism places the self in the landscape through selfies – photographed self-representations – among other possible modes of self-expression. This shifts the attention from managing the landscape into addressing one's expression and the flow of the travel experience into more strategic and aesthetic presentation of one's travel experience (Lyu, 2016). The addition of collaboration with local communities suggests new roles for both tourists and community members through embodied activities in and with snow and ice. Both construct and change the landscape using snow and ice as material for sculpturing. This kind of collaboration can also enable communities to discuss their goals (Richardson, 2010). In these ways, creative tourism can reposition both the communities and oneself. This creates a research gap in the creative tourism discourse. In the creative tourism experience examined here, the qualities of learning about local culture, such as artistic or design skills, and the tourist experience meet. Both the host and the guest possess artistic and creative skills; processing these skills and artistic learning becomes a shared experience where the two parties encounter each other. In Finnish Lapland, the landscape itself becomes the arena for the creative tourism. It allows the tourist to immerse himself or herself in creative activity through winter art, walking in silence, and working with local communities.

Creative tourism experience typically enables tourists to actively participate in local creative activities such as arts and crafts production, participating in a cultural performance, or learning to paint during a workshop. It is a multi-sensory experience where the feel of materials, smells, and the relationship with local crafts or cultural people become important parts of the experience. The creative tourism experience is not only the cultural workshop encounter with local craftspeople or other cultural producers but an experience that commits the tourists to a deeper understanding of the local culture, history, and tradition (Miettinen, 2007). In-depth understanding is created through sharing narratives in social contact while being engaged in creative activities. The narratives work as a vehicle for both sharing empathy and creating understanding about the local context. Thus, the creative tourism process is not only about consuming, but it also concerns becoming more aware of the society and local ways of living. It shifts the role of the tourist from being an outsider into an active process of learning and becoming aware – this is the core of creative tourism in Lapland. Collaborative working with ice and snow changes the position not only of the tourist but also of the community member. Community members reposition themselves and evaluate their community from a development perspective as snow and ice design can give them a means for income generation.

Narratives are central to our lives as humans. Stories have the ability to form and shape parts into meaningful wholes as they are entangled in personal and community histories and environments (Ricoeur, 2004). Narrative is a basic human strategy, or practical wisdom, to assist individuals in dealing with and making sense of their experiences (Ricoeur, 1992). Stories are a medium for the shaping of the self; individuals continually attempt to hold themselves together through the narrative ability of stringing events, reflections, and experiences together. Narratives' rationality is about explaining, expressing, understanding, and constituting human life as a whole (Ricoeur, 2004), and this is the value and role of story in human life. Narratives are a tool for communicating about the local culture. The narrative practice keeps local tradition alive. The arctic creative tourism landscape is both generating new stories and providing a platform to learn about existing skills.

Dewey (1934 [1980]) writes that in an experience, flow is from something to something. We have an experience when the material experienced runs its course to fulfilment. Because of continuous merging, we have an experience. Experience is always subjective. It is often defined as a multi-sensory event that is positive, remembered, emotional, and individual. Experiences cannot be produced, but different services and service concepts can offer various possibilities from which experiences can emerge. The meaning of an experience cannot be discovered immediately, and it can change over time. Meanings can be based on cognitions, emotions, beliefs, and intuitions. Through asking questions and trying to find new solutions, the learner changes his or her old ways of experiencing. When experiencing the creative tourism experience in Lapland, the arctic landscape is a frame for the selfie and becomes a more strategic and managed part of the creative tourism experience. Further, the tourist becomes actively engaged in the production of experience and the flow.

Case 1: Lapland Snow Art and Design

The use of snow and ice for tourism has a long history in Lapland in its many shapes, starting from snow-related sports and more recently snow and ice sculpting events and constructions for different tourism purposes such as hotels, bars, restaurants, chapels, and other designs. Snow covers the landscape in northern Scandinavia eight months a year and northern forms of culture have emerged and developed in a close relationship with nature and harsh winter conditions. The snowy landscape still plays an important role in local customs and traditions, identities and culture in the North and Arctic region. Snow, ice, polar culture, and northern lights have developed into a nature- and culture-based service ecosystem. These natural conditions and phenomena are exploited in a sustainable way in creative tourism activities inspired by winter art.

The concept of 'winter art' was introduced in 2003 to describe artistic features and phenomena related to winter aesthetics. Creative tourism activities inspired by winter art are considered cultural changes and opportunities in Lapland in terms of winter. As Jokela (2003) notes, 'One manifestation of this change is the brisk increase in winter festivals, winter theatres, snow and ice sculpting events and snow archi-tecture. At their best these phenomena can be called winter art' (p. 7). Since those days, the University of Lapland has developed strong expertise in winter art-related research, art production, and winter art development projects where the artistic use of snow and ice has been introduced and established within the tourism industry. These activities have developed into applied visual art (Jokela et al., 2013), winter art (Jokela, 2007a, 2014), and further merged with community-based art (Hiltunen, 2008, 2010). Art-based action research has worked as the main methodology to pro-duce this paradigm and applications for creative tourism (Jokela et al., 2015).

Three examples demonstrate how winter art has inspired creative tourism services in Lapland. The first example is formed around curated snow and ice art events for visitors to watch and enjoy. The Snow Show was a curated snow and ice art event that took place in Finnish Lapland in the winters of 2003 and 2004. The event brought together some of the world's best-known contemporary artists and archi-tects. These professionals paired up to design snow and ice art and architecture (Jokela, 2007a, 2007b). These snow and ice art and architecture constructions were produced using local resources in Rovaniemi and Kemi. This was an enormous challenge that increased snow- and ice-related know-how and expertise in Lapland.

These winter art events and their impact cannot be only evaluated from the lens of a contemporary art critic, but should also inspire discussions in which art is seen as a part of the tourism industry. The creative tourism services inspired by winter art should be offered in similar ways as other tourism service products in Lapland. According to Saarinen (2004), the weaknesses of these winter art events were in their non-recurrent nature and in the case of The Snow Show (Figure 6.1), its image as an international and largely 'high-brow' event aimed mainly at serving global and mostly 'unknown' objectives of the 'art world'. Saarinen (2004) advises the organ-izers of similar events to carefully consider the event's relationship with the locality and interaction with communities.

The second example of winter art as creative tourism service offers artistic snow and ice sculpting activities for visitors. During The Snow Show event, the University of Lapland realized a winter art education project for local artists, designers, and art educators to work as facilitators for creative tourism. One of the aims was to learn how to offer ice and snow sculpting experiences as tourism services in an active and inspiring way. Through guided experiences, visitors came to better understand snow and ice as natural material, they learned to use exotic tools, and they took photos and selfies. These kinds of activities are now a part of a tourism series involving, for example, an Ice Sculpting School in the Ice Hotel Jukkasjärvi in Sweden and the Arctic Snow Hotel in Finland.

The third example of creative tourism service offers culturally sensitive learning experiences for visitors through participatory winter art events and performances with local actors and facilitators. The participatory dialogue between community-based art education and tourism companies has opened up new perspectives

Source: Photo by Timo Jokela.

Figure 6.1 Ice and snow installation of The Snow Show event and the beauty of a winter day as attraction

for creative tourism in Lapland. The art projects carried out by the University of Lapland's art education department attempt to influence people through art; the aim is often to strive for social change, environmental responsibility, participatory thinking, and enhanced communality. These are highlighted in responsible tourism as well. Good examples of the University of Lapland's long-term community-based art education and co-design projects, where participation is the core element, are the *Utsjoen Tulikettu* project (2004–06) and development work done in the context of the *Tunturin taidepaja* workshop in the Pyhä Ski Resort, Pelkosenniemi (2000–06), located in the eastern region of Finnish Lapland.

In Pelkosenniemi art education students, local unemployed youth, local schools, and the hotels of the Pyhä Ski Resort worked together to construct events for tourists. Community-based art education and co-design projects offer a variety of possibilities to work with different sectors of society, the art world, local people, and the tourism industry. The aim was to develop art education practices with tourism and to use community art as a method for creative tourism activities. The motivation for creative tourism is often educational or, more specifically, engaging oneself in a creative production process.

Through co-design and art-based action research, we were exploring the possibilities and ways the tourist should not be just a spectator, but also a participant. In the events, the presence of the silence, forest and fjell area, and lantern-carrying audience, the tourists were a major factor in creating the magical atmosphere. Here, the winter environment plays the central role and the old fairy tales and beliefs concerning the place constructed the basis and content for the events. That is experience co-creation.

In these projects, art is a tool for socio-cultural inspiration but, at the same time, the events have strong connections to creative tourism too. Very often the final productions, such as the Forest Theatres or other performances outdoors, are performances for and with the tourist. The process of constructing an art event can offer an open space for conversation and collaboration between the locals and visitors, and performative art in the northern environment can open the senses and lead one towards embodied experiences. This becomes a possibility for change by offering a space for interaction, participation, and dialogue. The basis for the activity is the empowering impact of art on communities that respects the northern cultural identity. Art is considered as a potential agent of fostering, sustaining, developing, and regenerating communities, especially in remote northern areas (Hiltunen, 2007, 2008, 2010).

The Firefox project was an educational art event carried out by several people and organizations in the northernmost municipality of Finland, Utsjoki (Hiltunen, 2005). The project was funded by the European Social Fund and consisted of science and art events with the common theme of the Northern Lights and research into that phenomenon. The main goal of the project was to educate people to produce events that would touch and unite all of the villagers and visitors, from the Finnish to the Sámi, and from the children to the elderly. Other goals included increasing people's skills and knowledge of winter arts, and developing ways in which science and art could support each other. In the project, art acts as an open space that invites people into action. The public art works that were created, such as large snow and ice sculptures, are an indication of the many kinds of skills the villagers possess, and they also speak of a desire to cooperate. When working together as a group, and when observing the work of others, unique opportunities for learning open up (Hiltunen, 2008, 2010).

Creative tourism and artistic work offer a framework that 'mixes up' the roles of the tourists, who move from spectator to participant, and of the hosts, who become guests experiencing new things in their local context. Roles, meanings, and needs of the local community members and tourists are changing. 'Post-tourists' are aware of the postmodern 'game' where cultural encounters and environments are not authentic, but they can still play along. Encountering the local community through a creative activity enables both parties to increase the value of this encounter and look at the meanings of the production processes from another point of view. This process contextualizes again the value system of crafts production. The product itself is less meaningful than the learning process (Miettinen, 2007).

Source: Photo by Mirja Hiltunen.

Figure 6.2   Utsjoki, The Fire Fox. Festivities after the winter art week, making visible the strength and rich culture of the community, 2005

The activities in Utsjoki (Figure 6.2) are created as an experimental performance springing from the locality that supports the local culture but also invites visitors to take part. In local schools, they are instruments for integrating school subjects and for the eventuality that culminates in thematic work. The project has made visible and celebrated the strengths of the unique multicultural community and the splendid local nature (Hiltunen, 2005, 2008).

Joseph Pine and James H. Gilmore have explored today's consumer expectations. According to them, staging experience is not about entertaining customers, it is about engaging them. A person who takes part in an experience production wants to accomplish something more permanent than just a memory, something more desirable and valuable than the experience as such. These customers want to experience a change; they desire new, permanent qualities (Pine and Gilmore, 1999). Soile Veijola (2002) deliberates on the idea and asks how the transformers themselves are transformed during the process, who exercises power in it, and how the power is used.

It is important to assess the extent to which the tourist can act as an active learner, not only as a passive receiver. If we perceive the tourist as a learner, it opens up new perspectives on the experience industry and could offer work opportunities for art educators and other professionals. At best, Lappish creative tourism products are designed with cultural, social, economic, and ethical aspects in mind.

Case 2: Travelling Laboratories for Artistic Thinking

Walking has been used as a medium by several artists in the past and also in the field of contemporary art. There is also a long list of writers who have praised the benefits of walking throughout the centuries. Walking has enabled artists to articulate ideas about time and space. Walking gives freedom of movement and expression, it creates a personal engagement with one's environment, and it feeds imagination. A journey can be seen as a work of art. Cynthia Morrison-Bell (2013, p. 1) asks, what else is needed to make art than time, space, and the artist's own body?

The Travelling Laboratory for Artistic Thinking serves sustainable tourism with an emphasis on sustainable living and creative well-being. It is more about new ways of looking at everyday life and your familiar environment than actually travelling in the sense of tourism as we recognize it in the world of industry and traditional livelihood. Like service design has brought new understanding of how we see design not only as the production of objects, the Travelling Laboratories for Artistic Thinking project looks at tourism not only as concrete travelling, but as a concept of tourism that takes place outside traditional travelling.

Walking as an act of art puts the focus on awareness and presence. In the Travelling Laboratories for Artistic Thinking, an artistic way of being present is combined with walking. A journey can have a break and stop for sketching, documenting, writing, or working on land art using natural materials that happen to be available, or the stop can take place just for quiet observation. Through artistic thinking while walking we learn about observing and seeing what is around us and how to possibly use that awareness for making something out of it.

A simple act of walking seen in the context of the contemporary art world takes us into the realm of imagination and re-thinking what could be art. Artistic thinking can be understood as an abstract construction of imaginative worlds, but equally it can take the form of visual expression or a literal narrative that is based either on fact or on fiction. What shifts/transforms our thinking and the act of walking from ordinary to artistic is the framework and purpose of the action. In the realms of art, we deal with aims and goals that do not have to have anything to do with what so-called reality is about, even if the art work itself is a document of what can be seen and observed.

Artists could be called the nomads of contemporary times, travellers who find home where their work takes them. Artists do travel between countries and continents, but also between identities and ways of making their everyday living. Artists travel between personal and common, from individual to community-based exist-ence; they rise from ashes over and over again like the phoenix. Artistic nomadism means flexibility, being present where you are, and being free to take an unexpected route and change your plans when your intuition tells you so.

You can travel in your own environment without going anywhere further than walking distance. Gertrude Emily Benham (1867–1938) was called 'a very quiet and harmless traveler' (Howgego, 2011, n.p.) although she walked extensively on every continent. Most of us could be described as very quiet and harmless travellers like her, and it is meaningful to introduce such a traveller who goes nowhere to rec-ognize that even after extensive travels, one may still be 'very quiet and harmless'. You can travel even in your own room, through your imagination, and enter the universe of other people's imaginative worlds through works of art.

You might ask what good is it for tourism to encourage people not to travel and what kind of traveller is the one who never goes anywhere? We have to change our ideas about travelling. We will have soon, if not already, exploited every corner of the world: small islands, distant mountains, jungles, deserts, every continent. We have succeeded in destroying Indigenous cultures and ways of living in the name of tourism and livelihood.

We could once again become quiet and harmless travellers who do not need an intercontinental flight in order to experience something out of the ordinary. Through artistic thinking we can transform the ordinary to the extraordinary. If we are seriously concerned about cultural and ecological sustainability, we should not encourage building new touristic resorts or routes for transportation. Walking and cycling or 'mind travelling' at home should be made such a fashionable brand that people would hesitate before booking a holiday anywhere further than walking distance! Art can reach millions of people all around the world through contempo-rary digital technology that makes travelling available to all, regardless of economic barriers or physical disabilities. Even reading an old-fashioned printed book about distant and imaginative worlds is more sustainable than transporting millions of people on touristic journeys to places where nature and local culture are in danger of being destroyed.

Art is about immaterial ideas expressed in forms that can be approached through senses or just ideas and concepts that never need to become objects, sounds, or even smells. The magic is to see the invisible and to believe that it is enough. There is no need to go anywhere. A moment in the present is all we need.

Case 3: Master's degree programme of Applied Visual Arts and Nature Photography

The master's degree programme of Applied Visual Arts and Nature Photography is a two-year programme that is ongoing until 2019.[1] Research findings of engagement with place, materials, and local nature photographers, as well as work-ing with local bear and bird watchers in meaningful creative tourism experiences, have been a vital part of the curriculum design for the new programme. The educa-tional foundation for the programme is in Visual Arts Education in the University of Lapland as well as the long-term development work on nature photography of Kuusamo College. Both institutes are located in northern Finland. The programme is organized in Kuusamo as the region provides an inspirational setting for the practices of the programme, which considers the landscape as a stage or an arena for creative tourism. The location provides environments for experiences that are at the core of creative tourism, enabling students as well as companies and their customers to create solutions and services that are dealing with the locality's sense of place and people. Contextual and place-specific contemporary environmental and community art has become a way for the university to meet the northern environment in practice (Jokela et al., 2013).

Photographs in tourism have been studied from different viewpoints. Studies of travel photos (Haldrup and Larsen, 2012; Pan et al., 2014), the tourist gaze (Urry and Larsen, 2011), online sharing of travel photos (Lo et al., 2011), and social media and selfies in tourism (Gretzel, 2017) are providing information for under-standing the tourist's experiences in places. It is recognized that photographs both document and shape the travel experience, and enable travellers to share their experiences with others and craft the memories into narratives and stories (Lo et al., 2011). In their study of tourist photographs, Michael Haldrup and Jonas Larsen (2012) noticed that the classical tourist image of rural landscapes or cultural sights, the image typically reproduced in postcards and brochures, is only approximately a quarter of all the photos in their study. Photos of familiar people and loved ones are taken more often and in focus even when the loca-tion is a spectacular site with views. This led Haldrup and Larsen (2012) to think about 'how photographs are made, used, kept and stored' (p. 162). When study-ing tourist photographs and travel photos in the context of creative tourism, a stronger emphasis could be placed on *how* the photographs are made, continuing from Jonas Larsen's (2005) suggestion that tourist photography is a performed activity that is an embodied production of place myths, social roles, and social relationships.

John Urry and Jonas Larsen (2011) state that photography has been crucial in devel-oping the tourist gaze and digital photography has led to shallow glancing and to 'seeing and clicking' instead of picture-making. The tourist gaze is dependent on the experience in contrast with the 'normal' of the tourist's everyday life. The 'gaze' has evolved from emphasizing vision to understanding the tourist gaze as a performa-tive, embodied practice and interaction between tourists, tourism workers, and locals. Professional images script the gazes of tourists by framing the sceneries and creating ideas of the destinations. Locals and tourists, however, bend the media-scapes and scripts by reproducing the received imagery by their unpredictable, creative, and embodied behaviour (Urry and Larsen, 2011). In the master's degree programme of Applied Visual Arts and Nature Photography, the interactions and embodied experience of the tourist gaze that is producing unpredictable, creative, and embodied behaviour is also very much affected by the natural environment and conditions of Finnish Lapland.

In relation to travel photos, we must also discuss the travel selfies. Ulrike Gretzel (2017) suggests that the tourist gaze is increasingly directed towards the self in the process of producing content for social media instead of focusing on the destinations and attractions. Travel selfies include different genres, such as mundane travel selfies, aesthetic/artistic selfies, animal selfies, sunglass selfies, panoramic selfies, drink selfies, ironic selfies, and contemplative selfies. Travel selfies are often part of a larger travel narrative and even though the location or the destination are often serving as background, interesting angles and perspectives, and only parts of the self, are extensively used in travel selfies. In travel selfies, the aim to produce different photos that stand out from the photo stream of social media encourages travellers to observe the iconic destinations from different angles and add a 'twist' to their photos. A common aim in selfies is to regenerate and transform our online and offline identities (Gretzel, 2017). In the field of creative tourism, there is a need for research into the role of travel selfies in creative interaction and learning experiences. In the case of the master's degree programme of Applied Visual Arts and Nature Photography, the concept of selfie is expanded to include, for example, the Global Positioning System (GPS)-tracking routes the students have strolled in nature when in hunt for the photo.

In the programme, creative nature photography is applied to tourism, well-being, and research. In addition to the focus areas noted above, empowering photography (e.g., Savolainen, 2009) and photo elicitation (e.g., Griebling et al., 2013; Scarles, 2012) are used as methods to work with local actors, communities, and places as well as with tourists and tourism companies. In Caroline Scarles's (2012) article, the notion of contemporary digital photography being a tool for an encounter between locals and tourists is especially fruitful for creative tourism and a point of inspiration to continue further research on tourist photography experiences.

Findings on creating the tourism landscape

The creative tourism landscape is formed around the natural arctic landscape that is covered with snow eight months a year. This landscape frames the activities taking place in it. Creative tourism in Lapland shifts the passive role of spectating into the more active role of learning and participating in activities and into a dialogue with local communities. Narratives of the local history and creative experiences are shared with visitors through active engagement, walking in the landscape, and becoming aware of the tourist gaze in the landscape through hearing the narratives and browsing the imageries in social media. Embodied practices (Hiltunen, 2007, 2008) are present not only in activities with snow and ice but also in walking and studying the landscape through mundane practices. Creative tourism (Miettinen,

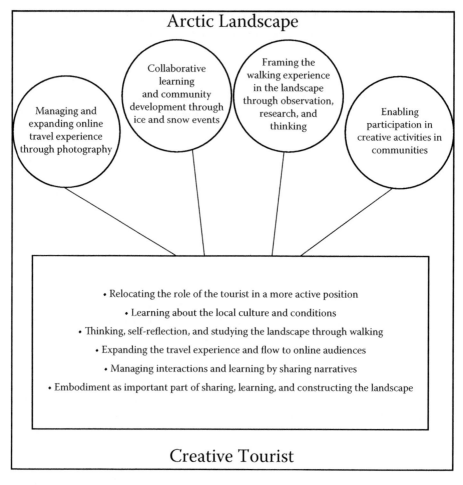

Figure 6.3   The topography of creative tourism in Lapland

2007) expands into topography where local community members as well as tourists are engaged in active creative activities of sharing narratives, learning about the local culture through the production of snow and ice events, and even redefining and developing their communities (Figure 6.3). In the creative tourism topography in Lapland, embodied practice is as important as the mental practice of using imagination and mental travel through the landscape. This manifests itself especially in the Travelling Laboratories for Artistic Thinking. The topography is dynamic and changes with the practices of shaping and sculpting the landscape. Even the traditional practice of documenting the landscape through a camera has taken a creative and postmodern turn by repositioning the photographing self within the picture. The selfie practice, as well as other social media practices, has become part of extending the ongoing travel experience with larger audiences.

Discussion

The topography of creative tourism in Lapland has an important role in both the arctic and tourism landscapes of Lapland. It enables negotiation about the roles of tourists and hosts, changing these roles into something new and not yet defined. A discussion about this transformation in the hosts' positioning (Turner and Tomer, 2013) is needed in small Lappish communities as tourism enables livelihoods but also has effects on traditions and local culture. The main outcomes of the topography include the transformation and expansion of the landscape into spatial, online, and mental dimensions. Embodied experience incorporates all the sensorial levels (Carreira et al., 2013), from seeing, smelling, touching, and hearing in the landscape through to thinking and self-reflective processes. The main contribution of this chapter is in opening a discussion about the concept of topography and its role in the arctic tourism landscape of Lapland.

Three ideas for further research lines

Based on our research to date on creative tourism in the arctic context, we propose three lines for further research:

1. How can we develop applied research and tourism products around the creative tourism topography in Lapland? How can we better use the opportunities of culture and creativity to support livelihoods in sustainable ways in geographically marginalized or extremely remote locations?
2. How can we support local communities' position, and participation in, and even manage their resistance to, tourism by using a creative tourism approach? How can local communities participate in the co-design of tourism products to have greater influence on the way they are presented and visualized? How can we improve dialogue, communication, and collaboration between the tourism industry and local communities, especially in the Arctic regions?
3. How can we research sensorial and mental tourism experiences through the creative tourism topography in Lapland? How can we develop and utilize new technologies to create competitive and sustainable new tourism products in areas that are environmentally or culturally fragile? How can we benefit from all senses when designing tourism experiences, even when they are not embodied but more mental 'armchair' experiences?

NOTE

1 The master's degree programme of Applied Visual Arts and Nature Photography (2017–19) is funded by the European Social Fund granted by the Centre for Economic Development, Transport and the Environment and city of Kuusamo, University of Lapland and Kuusamo College.

References

Carreira, R., L. Patrício, R.N. Jorge, C. Magee and Q.V.E. Hommes (2013), 'Towards a holistic approach to the travel experience: a qualitative study of bus transportation', *Transport Policy*, **25**, 233–43.

Dewey, J. (1934), *Art as Experience*, reprinted in 1980, New York: Perigee Books.

Gretzel, U. (2017), '#travelselfie: a netnographic study of travel identity communicated via Instagram', in S. Carson and M. Pennings (eds), *Performing Cultural Tourism: Communities, Tourists and Creative Practices*, London and New York: Routledge, pp. 115–27.

Griebling, S., L.M. Vaughn, B. Howell, C. Ramstetter and D. Dole (2013), 'From passive to active voice: using photography as catalyst for social action', *International Journal of Humanities and Social Science*, **3** (2), 16–28.

Haldrup, M. and J. Larsen (2012), 'Readings of tourist photographs', in T. Rakić and D. Chambers (eds), *An Introduction to Visual Research Methods in Tourism*, London and New York: Routledge, pp. 153–68.

Hiltunen, M. (2005), 'The Fire Fox: multisensory approach to art education in Lapland', *International Journal of Education through Art*, **1** (2), 161–77.

Hiltunen, M. (2007), 'Embodied experiences: constructing a collaborative art event in northern environment', in M. Kylänen and A. Häkkinen (eds), *Articles on Experiences 5 – Arts and Experience, Lapland Centre of Expertise for the Experience Industry 2007*, Rovaniemi: University of Lapland Printing Centre, pp. 62–90.

Hiltunen, M. (2008), 'Community-based art education in the north – a space for agency?', in G. Coutts and T. Jokela (eds), *Art Community and Environment: Educational Perspectives*, Bristol: Intellect Books, pp. 91–112.

Hiltunen, M. (2010), 'Slow activism: art in progress in the North', in A. Linjakumpu and S. Wallenius-Korkalo (eds), *Progress or Perish: Northern Perspectives on Social Change*, Farnham, Surrey: Ashgate, pp. 119–38.

Howgego, R.J. (2011), 'Gertrude Emily Benham (1867–1938) – English mountaineer, traveller and collector', accessed 15 May 2018 at https://ilab.org/fr/node/56943.

Jokela, T. (2003), 'Johdant' (Introduction), in M. Huhmarniemi, T. Jokela and S. Vuorjoki (eds), *Talven taidetta. Puheenvuoroja talven kulttuurista, talvitaiteesta ja lumirakentamisesta (Winter Art. Statement on Winter Art and Snow Construction)*, trans. R. Foley, Lapin yliopiston taiteiden tiedekunnan julkaisuja D 6, Rovaniemi: Sevenprint, pp. 6–11.

Jokela, T. (2007a), 'Winter art project', *The International Journal of Art and Design Education*, **26** (3), 238–50.

Jokela, T. (2007b), 'Winter art as an experience: Teoksessa arts and experiences', in M. Kylänen and A. Häkkinen (eds), *Articles on Experiences 5*, Rovaniemi: University of Lapland Printing Centre, pp. 114–35.

Jokela, T. (2014), 'Snow and ice design innovation in Lapland', in E. Härkönen, T. Jokela and A.-J. Yliharju (eds), *Snow Design in Lapland – Initiating Cooperation*, Rovaniemi: Rovaniemen painatuskeskus, pp. 180–1.

Jokela, T., G. Coutts, M. Huhmarniemi and E. Härkönen (2013), *COOL: Applied Visual Arts in the North*, Rovaniemi: University of Lapland.

Jokela, T., M. Hiltunen and E. Härkönen (2015), 'Art-based action research: participatory art for the north', *International Journal of Education through Art*, **11** (3), 433–48.

Kearns, R.A. (1997), 'Narrative and metaphor in health geographies', *Progress in Human Geography*, **21** (2), 269–77.

Larsen, J. (2005), 'Families seen sightseeing: performativity of tourist photography', *Space and Culture*, **8** (4), 416–34.

Levine, A.J.M. (2008), 'Mapping Beur cinema in the new millennium', *Journal of Film and Video*, **60** (3–4), 42–59.

Lo, I.S., B. McKercher, A. Lo, C. Cheung and R. Law (2011), 'Tourism and online photography', *Tourism Management*, **32**, 725–31.

Lyu, S.O. (2016), 'Travel selfies on social media as objectified self-presentation', *Tourism Management*, **54**, 185–95.

Macpherson, H. (2016), 'Walking methods in landscape research: moving bodies, spaces of disclosure and rapport', *Landscape Research*, **41** (4), 425–32.

Miettinen, S. (2007), 'Designing the creative tourism experience. a service design process with Namibian craftspeople', Doctoral dissertation, Gummerus Publishing oy, Jyväskylä, publication series of University of Art and Design Helsinki A, 81.

Morrison-Bell, C. (2013), 'Foreword', in C. Morrison-Bell, M. Collar and A. Robinson (eds), *Walk On: From Richard Long to Janet Cardiff – 40 Years of Art Walking*, Manchester: Cornerhouse Publications, pp. 1–3.

Pan, S., J. Lee and H. Tsai (2014), 'Travel photos: motivations, image dimensions, and affective qualities of places', *Tourism Management*, **40**, 59–69.

Pine, B.J. and J.H. Gilmore (1999), *The Experience Economy: Work is Theatre and Every Business a Stage*, Boston, MA: Harvard Business School Press.

Richards, G. and J. Wilson (2006), 'Developing creativity in tourist experiences: a solution to the serial reproduction of culture?', *Tourism Management*, **27** (6), 1209–23.

Richardson, J. (2010), 'Interventionist art education: contingent communities, social dialogue, and public collaboration', *Studies in Art Education*, **52** (1), 18–33.

Ricoeur, P. (1992), *Oneself as Another*, Chicago, IL: University of Chicago Press.

Ricoeur, P. (2004), *Memory, History, Forgetting*, trans. K. Blamey and D. Pellauer, Chicago, IL and London: University of Chicago Press.

Saarinen, J. (2004), 'Talvitapahtumien matkailullinen merkitys: esimerkkinä The Snow Show – talvitaidetapahtuma' (The importance of winter events for tourism: The Snow Show winter art event as an example), in M. Huhmarniemi, T. Jokela and S. Vuorjoki (eds), *Talven tuntemus. Puheenvuoroja talvesta ja talvitaiteesta* (*Sense of Winter. Statements on Winter and Winter and Art*), trans. V. Välimaa-Hill, Lapin yliopiston taiteiden tiedekunnan julkaisuja D 9, Rovaniemi: Sevenprint, pp. 150–9.

Savolainen, M. (2009), 'Voimauttava valokuva' (Empowering photography), in U. Halkola, L. Mannermaa, T. Koffert and L. Kolu (eds), *Valokuvan terapeuttinen voima* (*Therapeutical Power of Photography*), Helsinki: Duodecim, pp. 210–27.

Scarles, C. (2012), 'The photographed other: interplays of agency in tourist photography in Cusco, Peru', *Annals of Tourism Research*, **39** (2), 928–50.

Turner, M. and T. Tomer (2013), 'Community participation and the tangible and intangible values of urban heritage', *Heritage and Society*, **6** (2), 185–98.

Urry, J. and J. Larsen (2011), *The Tourist Gaze 3.0*, London: Sage.

Veijola, S. (2002), 'Aitojen elämyksiä näyttämöllä: matkailun elä-mysteollisuuden sosiaalisesta ja taloudellisesta logiikasta' (Genuine experience on the stage: about the social and economic logic of the experience economy of tourism), in J. Saarinen (ed.), *Elämys, teollisuutta, taloutta vai jotain muuta?* (*Experience, Industry, Economy or Something Else?*), Lapin yliopiston menetelmätieteellisiä tutkimuksia 2, Yhteiskunta. Rovaniemi: Lapin yliopistopaino, pp. 91–113 (in Finnish).

7   Coffee tourism as creative tourism: implications from Gangneung's experiences

U-Seok Seo

A report on coffee tourism in Korea often causes a feeling of mild astonishment because Korea is neither a coffee-producing country nor is it expected to have developed a café culture. Nevertheless, Gangneung, an east-coast city located 220 kilometres away from Seoul with a population of about 200,000, has become established as a destination for coffee tourism. With about 500 cafés, it is now regarded as 'coffee city', at least in Korea. Numerous articles in the Korean media show 'Coffee City Gangneung' is established as a city brand. At the same time, tourism policy agencies have recognized the significance of coffee tourism in Gangneung. For instance, in 2016 Gangneung Coffee Streets was awarded a 'Star of Korean Tourism' by the Korean Tourism Organization. In addition, the number of visitors to the coffee festival, launched in 2009, reached more than 400,000 for the four-day event in 2016.[1]

The emergence of Gangneung as a coffee city is immensely significant because it occurred at a time when Gangneung had declined from its earlier position as an outstanding historic tourist city (Kim et al., 2012). During the Chosun Dynasty period, from the fifteenth to the nineteenth century, Gangneung was the centre of local administration as well as a transportation hub on the east coast. This remarkable location generated many noteworthy heritage sites, among them Ojukheon, a residence of Yi Yi and Saimdang as son and mother, both of whom are on the Korean banknotes in recognition of their academic and artistic excellence in the sixteenth century, has been one of the most famous tourist destinations for student trips. Moreover, Gangneung has been well known as a summer holiday destination with Kyungpodae Beach. However, Gangneung had lost its attractiveness gradually, as many new tourist attractions have been developed in Korea in recent decades and increasing numbers of Koreans are now making outbound trips for their vacation. At the same time, the image of Gangneung's beach deteriorated thanks to deviant youth behaviour at night.[2] Now, the rise of coffee tourism is enabling a tourism revival in Gangneung.

Although coffee tourism in Gangneung does not present itself as being creative, its success is deeply indebted to the elements of creative tourism. In the context of the diverse relationships between creativity and coffee tourism in Gangneung, and considering coffee tourism as one kind of food and drink tourism, this chapter reviews how previous research has related food and drink tourism with creativity. It then outlines how the rise of coffee tourism has been possible in such a small city as Gangneung and how the city's use of creativity contributed to this achievement. The last section provides suggestions for further research on creative tourism in general as well as with respect to food and drink tourism.

Research on creativity in food and drink tourism

Creativity in food and drink tourism

The last decade witnessed a rise in discussions on the relationships between creativity and food and drink tourism. Gastronomy is viewed as 'a fertile breeding ground for "creative tourism"' (Richards and Raymond, 2000), providing a variety of opportunities for tourists to actively participate in various ways; for example, 'tourists can learn to cook, can learn about the ingredients used, the way in which they are grown and appreciate how culinary traditions have come into existence' (Richards, 2002, pp. 16–17). The significance of food and drink tourism as creative tourism has been underpinned by a broad understanding of creativity, which extends beyond artistic creativity into the intangible everyday culture. The perception of food and drink tourism as creative tourism reveals itself most evidently in the designations of the United Nations Educational, Scientific and Cultural Organization (UNESCO) Creative Cities Network, which acknowledges gastronomy as one of seven creative fields, alongside crafts and folk art, design, film, literature, music, and media arts (Wurzburger et al., 2010). In 2018, 180 cities from 72 countries are members of the Network and, among them, 26 cities are designated in the field of gastronomy.[3]

There are several ways to examine the diverse elements of creativity in food and drink tourism. First of all, cooking itself is a creative process. Throughout the history of cuisine, numerous great chefs have made continuous attempts to achieve a variety of innovations, such as Nouvelle Cuisine and then molecular gastronomy (Cousins et al., 2010). Even though culinary art is centred on its basic practicality, it also has a creative side, as a creative art that entails a series of creative culinary processes (Horng and Hu, 2009) and needs to be built up 'from fundamentals and principles of cooking which include knife skills, food science and knowledge, sanitation and hygiene, and cooking methods and history' (Peng et al., 2013, p. 2695). Remarkably, not just its products but also its spaces, like restaurants, are connected with culinary creativity since the design of these spaces tends to substantially influence dining experiences (Horng et al., 2013). Furthermore, food and drink tourism is arguably seen as having more creative elements than the conventional types of creative industries 'since it deals not just with abstract creative processes, but with the creative articulation between landscape, the peoples who inhabit them, the food they produce, the customs they have developed and the staging of meals for residents and visitors alike' (Richards, 2014, p. 7).

From the standpoint of creative tourism, it is of great importance that the creative features of food and drink tourism are closely related with the participation of ordinary people, since activities of eating and cooking constitute basic parts of everyday life. This trait corresponds to the trend that the distinction between production and consumption in tourism has become blurred (Richards, 2002; Everett, 2016). Research on the phases of food tourism, with attention to the pre-travel and post-travel periods, shows that food experiences at the destination are related with eating at home and eating out (Mitchell and Hall, 2003). Cooking schools illustrate how production and consumption is intermingled around food tourism. The 'learning' element on a cooking holiday gains special significance since there is 'a desire to return home with a package of new or improved culinary skills, which can be used to impress their family and dinner guests' (Sharples, 2003, pp. 108–9). Also, food and drink tourism involves tourists as producers as well as consumers (Everett, 2016). Co-creation activities of tourists, such as butchery, fish filleting, and cake decorating, display a close affinity of food and drink tourism with creative tourism.

Furthermore, the relationship between food and drink tourism and creative tourism is strengthened by the fact that 'gastronomic tourists are looking after the origin of the gastronomic food, legends and stories about food' (Martins, 2016, p. 33). These kinds of features are reflected in various types of coffee tourism attractions, from natural attractions such as coffee plantations to human-made attractions like coffee museums and festivals (Kleidas and Jolliffe, 2010). Visits to coffee production places, usually located in developing countries, provide opportunities for tourists to increase their knowledge of coffee production. Coffee-related events and coffee festivals also provide opportunities to 'taste hundreds of different coffees brewed with different methods (both traditional and new), learn how coffee is marketed, and attend coffee seminars about coffee's tasting, roasting, cultivation, health benefits and coffee shops' management' (Kleidas and Jolliffe, 2010, p. 63). Through coffee tourism, the resulting increase in knowledge on the fine differences among coffee tastes helps to enhance one's consumption skills in coffee drinking.

Another impetus for learning coffee knowledge and refining one's taste buds is given by quality innovations in coffee which have been facilitated with the emergence of specialty coffee and especially with the expansion of Starbucks. Unlike the previous conglomerates mainly concerned with price and consistency, the specialty coffee industry concentrates on a variety of aspects that influence the quality of coffee, such as the cultivation methods of the bean, in what might be coined as the 'relative decommodification of coffee' (Luttinger and Dicum, 2011, p. 156). As coffee culture has evolved in terms of its quality, at the same time speculation about the next new version of specialty coffee has become a popular subject of conversation on the coffee market and among coffee enthusiasts (Halford, 2011). A visit to significant spots in the evolution of coffee quality could be inspiring not only for entrepreneurs who are involved in the coffee business, but also for coffee lovers who are eager to show off their elaborated coffee taste. This endeavour, related with the symbolic struggle around cultural capital (Bourdieu, 1984), leads to a 'high-level interest for tourists seeking coffee education' (Kleidas and Jolliffe, 2010, p. 66) and enables tourism suppliers to magnify creative elements in coffee tourism.

Creativity and space in food and drink tourism

Creative tourism and food and drink tourism have stimulated considerable amounts of discussion on their relation with local development. While creative tourism has been discussed in relation with creative space making and creative city, food and drink tourism is often discussed in terms of its contribution to local development (Hall et al., 2003; OECD, 2012). Compared with these extensive separate discourses, the intersection of the two spheres has produced much fewer discussions on local development, which are, however, significant for understanding food and drink tourism from the perspective of creativity.

In a rural context, the importance of creativity in food and drink tourism is associated with local development. Unlike the previous discussions on creativity, which regard urban settings as an effective background for nurturing and valorizing creativity, emerging discourses critique the exclusive attachment of creativity with urban environments (Stolarick et al., 2010). Rural development gains momentum from creative food clusters, which comprise food clusters combined with creative activities by artists (Lee et al., 2015). Creative tourism based on a creative food cluster has a prominent significance since tourism might have more importance in a rural area than in a city given a lack of other economic opportunities.

In urban settings, the relationship of creativity in food and drink tourism with local development is postulated in a direct manner. A creative urban food economy, as a combination of ethnic foods cuisine and local restaurants, is capable of attracting urban elites, including tourists (Donald and Blay-Palmer, 2006). The relationship between creativity in food and drink tourism and local development is, however, in most cases, less a single causality than part of complex urban dynamics. In many cities across the world, a landscape of consumption related to eating and drinking plays a crucial role for the development of a creative economy. Café culture and restaurants have great meaning for urban creative professions and bohemians (Zukin et al., 2009; Lloyd, 2010). These changing consumption environments also tend to provide service sector jobs for creative people who possess the required performative competence for this labour and regard them as 'temporary stops on the way to something else' (Lloyd, 2010, p. 182). This landscape of consumption is destined at first for the residents of the city but later is very likely to be utilized for the food and drink tourism of creative professionals from other places, as urban tourism tends to blur the distinction between tourists and residents. In addition, there is a tendency in creative tourism to enter more into the realm of everyday life, as the cases of Venice (Russo and Sans, 2009) and the South Bank of London (Maitland, 2010) show.

This possibility of strengthening creative elements in food and drink tourism is particularly evident in the case of coffee tourism. It is worth noting the peculiarity of coffee consumption in terms of its spatial fixity in the café where people meet and socialize with each other. The idea of cafés as spaces of social interaction has appealed to social thinkers historically and today. Habermas (1989) acknowledges the historical significance of the flourishing coffeehouses in eighteenth-century England, which played a role as sites for public discourses in forming the public sphere. Oldenburg and Brissett (1982) view the café and coffeehouse as examples of third places where 'spontaneous and free-wheeling social experience' may take place (p. 277). To understand creativity in coffee tourism it is important to recognize that the café has played a crucial role for artistic creativity as meeting places or as workspaces. The former is, among many cases, pertinent to Café Guerbois in Paris, where regular meetings among artists, art dealers, and art lovers contributed to the birth of Impressionism (White and White, 1993). The latter comprises those cafés where famous writers have worked on their masterpieces, such as the Elephant House for J.K. Rowling in Edinburgh (McKenzie, 2017) and the Grand Café for Henrik Ibsen in Oslo (Stenseth, 2013). It is debatable whether a visit to such cafés can be understood as creative tourism. But in the case of reading, the relationship with creative tourism is much evident. Since a café is good for reading, suggestions for cafés fit to read books in major European cities like Porto, Paris, and Rome are no less than a guide to creative coffee tourism (Hoskins, 2007). With this background, cafés play an important role in establishing a city as an international tourist destination contributing to forming a place image linked with a creative city (Frost et al., 2010; Weaver, 2010).

Coffee tourism of Gangneung

The rise of Gangneung as a coffee city

Coffee tourism in Gangneung is quite exceptional and unexpected. Given the fact that coffee drinking is associated with the rise of modernism in Korea (Jin, 1999; Han, 2014) just like in western countries (Manning, 2013), Gangneung, which is of relatively small size by Korean standards and is located far away from Seoul, has hardly been regarded as a forerunner of modern culture in Korea. Food and drink tourism in small cities or rural areas is usually based on traditional local food and drink. Gangneung was not expected to be a birthplace for refined coffee culture.

More detailed information on the history of coffee culture in Korea helps to establish the significance of the coffee tourism of Gangneung (Jin, 1999). Since its introduction to Korea in the late nineteenth century, coffee had remained a favourite drink of the royal family, until the mass consumption of instant coffee, called 'Dabang' coffee, beginning after the Korean War. 'Dabang' coffee is made of coffee powder, cream, and sugar; a portable mixture came to the market with 'coffee mix', which led to the popularization of coffee consumption. The dominance of instant coffee consumption was challenged with the introduction of espresso coffee in 1999 with the arrival of Starbucks and then hand-drip coffee in the late 2000s. The introduction of high quality coffee has increased the size of Korea's coffee market and, at the same time, led to the spread of cafés around the country (Han, 2014).

During this transition period of the Korean coffee market, there were some celebrity baristas and café owners working in Gangneung, some even calling them 'Coffee Maestros' and symbolizing high quality coffee. To date, there is no comprehensive explanation about why the proficient pioneers of specialty coffee concentrated in Gangneung (GCF, 2012; Kim et al., 2012). Some were born in Gangneung, others moved to Gangneung. Compared with larger cities, there are some advantages to living in Gangneung, particularly in terms of living costs and rents as well as its natural environment. In this regard, it is significant that many well-known café owners in Gangneung have the features of lifestyle entrepreneurs who tend to work not just for economic gain, but also value living conditions such as natural environments and a leisurely life (Seo, 2017). The traits of lifestyle entrepreneurs are especially evident in those who moved to Gangneung from large cities. For instance, the café owner of Judith's Garden, a German philosopher who came to Korea with her Korean husband, explains that she was lured to Gangneung's nature when she was tired of megacity-life stresses teaching at the Korean universities. In addition to coffee quality improvement, these sorts of stories from lifestyle entrepreneurs have attracted the interest of mass media as well as social media, altogether enabling the beginning of coffee tourism in Gangneung.

Two types of efforts are particularly remarkable for strengthening the location as a coffee tourism destination. First, the Gangneung Coffee Festival has been held every year since 2009, hosted by the Gangneung Culture Foundation. The festival programme includes barista performances, barista awards, coffee seminars, workshops, participative events, and music performances. The Gangneung Coffee Festival has contributed to the formulation of the local identity as a 'coffee city' with an increase in visitor numbers from 80,000 at the first festival to 265,000 at the sixth festival (Yu, 2014).

Second, spaces for coffee tourism have formed and expanded in Gangneung as its popularity as a 'coffee city' has grown (GCF, 2012). Anmok Beach, a previously unknown beach with just some coffee vending machines, has evolved into 'Coffee Street' with a variety of cafés, including large coffee chain stores, resulting in a steep increase in real estate prices (Bae, 2015). In addition, coffee-related facilities, such a coffee farm and a coffee museum, have been built in the surrounding area of Gangneung to provide coffee plantation experiences and knowledge on coffee history (GCF, 2012). This expansion of the coffee tourism destination along with its inherent tourism resources has led to 'economies of scope' that provide a range of product choice in tourism in a small area, which can also be understood as 'diagonal clustering' (Michael, 2006).

Furthermore, coffee culture has become an important part of local identity (GCF, 2012). Drinking high quality coffee has become prevalent in Gangneung, regardless of socio-demographic status. Home roasting is widespread and sharing the experiences of newly opened coffee shops becomes a daily practice in Gangneung. A reinvention of local identity has taken place connecting the rise of 'coffee city' with its inherent tea culture, which implies a high quality of waters in Gangneung, and also pointing out the resemblance of preparing for tea with making a hand-drip coffee (Shim, 2010). Correspondingly, tea clubs play an active role in spreading hand-drip coffee and residents have a strong sense of pride as a home country of literary figures suited for developing a high level of taste culture (GCF, 2012). Consequently, as high quality coffee is regarded as the factor distinguishing the city from others, the demand for an even greater coffee supply is increasing, forming the basis for the growth of a coffee industry in Gangneung.

Creativity and spaces in Gangneung's coffee tourism

Creativity in Gangneung's coffee tourism must be discussed in terms of creative experience as well as creative space. As for creative experience, it is worth noting that the emergence of coffee tourism was preceded by an awakening to varying levels of coffee quality through research abroad. Given the lack of formal coffee education in Korea, pioneers share some common features in their personal stories of how they strived to acquire the knowledge and skills to improve coffee quality in Japan or in Europe, and opened their eyes to the wide world of coffee. For instance, Yoon Seon Lee (2011), a 'coffee cupper' working for Tera Rosa, one of the leading cafés in Gangneung, became aware of the various tastes and flavours of coffee when she attended a coffee-tasting seminar hosted by a Japanese coffee bean company Wataru in 2007. She reminisced, 'I was totally amazed when I experienced coffee tasting for the first time.' After this realization, she made continuous efforts to build a successful career in coffee tasting. This kind of realization constitutes the basis of coffee tourism in Gangneung. Creative experiences in Gangneung's coffee tourism are no more than varying forms of the diffusion of these awakening experiences. While a few coffee academies and coffee workshops in Gangneung deliver educational programmes on coffee mainly for those who are preparing to open a café, the most eminent and popular experiences for tourists are the DIY opportunities for roasting, extraction, hand-drip coffee making, and coffee craft. These kinds of DIY experiences are available to tourists during the Coffee Festival. Through these opportunities, tourists are able to obtain knowledge about a variety of coffee-making methods, as they start to learn about coffee-making processes as much as the products. The emphasis on the process of coffee making is reflected in the design of some of the prominent cafés in Gangneung, which expose their coffee bean factory intentionally at the entrance or create the atmosphere of a roasting factory in the café. This feature of café design further generates interest in the processes of coffee making as well as evoking a feeling of authenticity.

Creative spaces are made either in cafés or in urban spaces in relation to coffee tourism. As for cafés, some are remarkable for functioning as cultural spaces. Café Tera Rosa has been using its coffee roasting factory to host cultural events of local artists and more recently for the performance of a world-renowned pianist awarded by the International Tchaikovsky Competition. A different style of cultural space is found at Café Bon Bon Mill, which is run by independent filmmakers. They re-use a closed mill in the inner city as a café where exhibitions of local artists and residents take place and a place for local community meetings is provided.

Creative spaces with a relationship to coffee tourism are also being pursued for urban regeneration purposes. Gangneung City is currently trying to induce coffee tourists from Anmok Beach to Myungju-dong to propel the urban regeneration of this inner city area. Myungju-dong used to belong to the central commercial area and also was a middle-class residential area, which has slowly decayed during the last decades largely due to an ageing population. Currently, various attempts are being made to develop creative spaces in Myungju-dong. For example, Myungju Arts Center is the result of the adaptive re-use of a church into a concert hall, and mural painting is encouraged, aiming for a transformative impact on place image. In addition, a craft village is planned to initiate craft tourism. A closed school in this area near the Gangneung Culture Foundation is intended to be re-used to provide working places for young artists and baristas. In this attempt, Myungju Salon, run by the Gangneung Culture Foundation, plays a central role as a landmark, even if not great in size, which houses a coffee library and provides opportunities to learn diverse ways of coffee making, such as the practice of hand-drip coffee. In addition, Café Bon Bon Mill and other trendy cafés in this area are expected to contribute to place branding and lead to further tourist attractions forming.

Suggestions for further research

Following from this review and research, three main directions for future research are suggested:

1.   A more differentiated typology for understanding the variety of types of creative tourism

In previous discussions on creative tourism, a number of possibilities are proffered to understand its diversity. Richards and Wilson (2006) suggest three different types of creative tourism experiences: creative spectacles, creative spaces, and creative tourism. Tan and his colleagues suggest another typology of creative experience based on a distinction between 'inner reflection' and 'outer interaction' and provide a categorization of creative tourists as 'novelty seekers', 'knowledge and skills learners', 'aware of travel partners' growth', 'aware of green issues', and 'relax and leisure type' (Tan et al., 2014). Yet, a more differentiated understanding of creative tourism is still needed to understand a variety of 'creative tourism' developments, as creative tourism evolves in more diverse ways.

Based on the diverse types of creative experiences in Gangneung's coffee tourism, it is worthwhile to consider applying a distinction between serious leisure and casual leisure (Stebbins, 1982) to various forms of creative elements. Creative experiences in creative tourism often share many features with serious leisure as they involve skill acquisition, a need for perseverance, and personal identity. The common features of creative tourism with serious leisure are particularly evident, when participating in educational events in an academy, workshops, and seminars during creative tourism. However, there are also different types of creative tourism that have fewer features in common with serious leisure. One such case found in Gangneung's coffee tourism is the coffee-making experience programme, which includes many arts of coffee making, such as hand-drip coffee and siphon coffee. Participation in the coffee-making experience programme takes usually less than an hour for the entire course from roasting to hand-drip coffee making. For a limited time, this programme offers an opportunity for active participation in coffee making guided by an expert on coffee. The coffee-making experience programme has been so popular that it has become a standard (core) content offer in the Coffee Festival as well as in many other events in Gangneung.

Compared with serious leisure, this sort of experience programme can be coined as 'snack culture' for active participation. In 2007, *Wired* magazine proclaimed the 'attack' of snack culture and a New Age for 'Bite-Size Entertainment' stating that 'pop culture now comes packaged like cookies or chips in bite-size bits for high-speed munching' (Miller, 2007, n.p.). The emergence of snack culture is deeply related with the attention economy. Attention can be regarded as a scarce resource (Davenport and Beck, 2001) with attention spans getting shorter, particularly when adapted to portable new media devices (Newman, 2010). The coffee-making experience programme can be viewed as snack culture since it promises to offer a DIY-type experience in a tailored time setting adapted to short attention spans. Thus, the coffee-making programme is viewed as lying at the intersection of the attention economy and the experience economy.

It is worthwhile to compare snack culture with McDonaldization (Ritzer, 2011). Snack culture has many features in common with McDonaldization, such as an emphasis on efficiency and control. In terms of predictability, however, there are similarities in terms of time management as well as differences with respect to its outcomes. When someone takes part in a siphon coffee-making programme for the first time, they may be aware of the time required, but have no idea what kind of experience they will be making. Such participation in a coffee-making programme brings new experiences to the tourist and a new stimulus for coffee drinking, even if the time available for participation is relatively short. This kind of participation is increasingly popular in many diverse tourist destinations in Korea. Given the expanding relevance of the attention economy across the globe, a snack culture type of creative tourism is expected to become more popular.

2.   Evolving creative convergence

The development of coffee tourism in Gangneung shows how creative elements have been evolving as it has gained increasing attention and induced more investments. The impetus for this evolution of coffee tourism is, above all, to maintain sustainability through product diversity. In the face of tourists who always want to have new, creative, and authentic experiences, the challenges for coffee tourism suppliers are growing: 'how to supply a heterogeneous product when gastronomic tourism is slowly becoming homogeneous, and here the supply of creative experiences that explore the "real authenticity" can play a key role' (Martins, 2016,

p. 36). In this regard, there are numerous efforts to maintain sustainability through diversification based on creative convergence. For instance, mixtures of coffee and food have been developed as creative products such as coffee bread and coffee rice wine. The development of coffee craft has become an important component in the diversification of coffee tourism, including not just the coffee mug, but also coffee candles, coffee aromatic products, and coffee dyeing. The hybridization of coffee and other activities has given birth to an exhibition of postcards on coffee subjects as well as coffee powder painting.

Another drive for creative convergence came from the perspective of local development to maximize the positive impacts of coffee tourism. Besides the Coffee Festival, there are attempts to launch more creative events such as the Anmok Coffee Street Film Festival, which was launched in 2015 using a café as a small cinema, a small concert hall, and a small coffee museum during the two-day festival. Whereas this festival is a May spin-off of the Coffee Festival in October, the Beach Design Festival, started in 2017, is held during the same period as the Coffee Festival. The Beach Design Festival aims to induce visitors of the Coffee Festival into the newly launched festival and into a beach that has been, so far, relatively less influenced by coffee tourism.

Creative convergence is also evident when cafés and cultural spaces have increasingly intermingled with each other. While cafés play a role as creative places, more and more cultural spaces have begun to sell specialty coffee. The craft village project conducted by the Gangneung City government is a representative case for this convergence, where most stores will function as cafés and cultural places (e.g., a gallery or craft shop) at the same time. Beyond this project, creative convergence is becoming more common as the number of gallery cafés, book cafés, and craft shop cafés grows.

In contrast to these cases where creative convergence has been developed strategically, it sometimes occurred accidently and unexpectedly. Café Bon Bon Mill, as mentioned earlier, is run by local independent filmmakers with a community orientation. The film director, Hong Sang-soo, visited this café often when he visited Gangneung, and the café was represented in a film *On the Beach at Night Alone*, which was awarded a Silver Bear for Best Actress at the Berlin International Film Festival in 2017. Café Bon Bon Mill provides not just a filming location, but also plays a crucial role in the storytelling on film. And thus, Café Bon Bon Mill, whether intentionally or not, will remain a significant part of Korean film history without any big capital investment to induce top-level artists. Gangneung's experiences show that creative convergence is occurring in a greater variety of ways than had been expected and needs to be studied more thoroughly.

3.   Media and celebrities

So far, discussions of creative tourism have barely addressed promotion and marketing strategies, nor its relation with media. Regarding food and drink tourism, the role of media is discussed in forming a foodscape 'in the particular guise of food celebrities' with research regarding 'what contemporary foodscapes consist of, how they "perform" and function and the socio-material means by which they are produced' (Johnston and Goodman, 2015, p. 205). As shown earlier, the media has played a crucial role in establishing Gangneung as a coffee tourism destination. Both mass media and social media have substantially contributed to forming its place identity as a 'coffee city'. In particular, celebrities in Gangneung have made significant media impacts on the rise of coffee tourism. Creative achievement is seldom attributed to an individual alone, as certain networks and social conventions contribute to the birth of creative work (Becker, 1982). Nevertheless, tourists are highly interested in a person who takes a great part in creative production processes. Thus, a celebrity in a specific field, even with very limited awareness, is of great importance for media and tourists. The phenomenon of more enthusiasm over a creative person than over creativity itself is not new in the modern era, as the emergence of the artist as a genius in the Age of Renaissance indicated (Hauser, 1999). However, the interest in celebrities and their influences is growing with the increasing usage of social media. Thus, we cannot exclude the strategic option that creative tourism can be connected with some public figures who symbolize creativity in specific fields. In particular, a celebrity gets more media attention when their personal history provides effective content for the storytelling processes of tourist destinations. When celebrities take a certain role in the development of creative tourism, their influence might be complex. Whereas the influence of celebrities could bring superficial interest in less meaningful elements, certain fandoms may have more interest in person-specific processes, which may enable a deeper understanding of creativity. In the context of such variations and issues, the relation of celebrities and media with creative tourism deserves more elaborated research.

NOTES

1 See the Gangneung Coffee Festival website homepage: http://www.coffeefestival.net/contents.asp?page=36&kind=2 &IDX=4098 (accessed 27 May 2017).

2 This problem led the Gangneung city government to prohibit alcohol drinking at Gyeongpodae Beach in 2012, but the ban was lifted because of the protests of visitors and merchants ('Drinking in public places to be banned', 2015).

3 See the UNESCO Creative Cities Network website homepage: https://en.unesco.org/creative-cities/events/47-cities-join-unesco-creative-cities-network (accessed 25 December 2017).

References

Bae, J. (2015), 'Going to Gangneung: coffee city by the sea', *Urban Problem*, **50** (554), 36–41 (in Korean).

Becker, H.S. (1982), *Art Worlds*, Berkeley, CA: University of California Press.

Bourdieu, P. (1984), *Distinction: A Social Critique of the Judgement of Taste*, trans. R. Nice, Cambridge, MA: Harvard University Press.

Cousins, J., K.D. O'Gorman and M. Stierand (2010), 'Molecular gastronomy: basis for a new culinary movement or modern day alchemy?', *International Journal of Contemporary Hospitality Management*, **22** (3), 399–415.

Davenport, T.H. and J.C. Beck (2001), *The Attention Economy: Understanding the New Currency of Business*, Cambridge, MA: Harvard Business Press.

Donald, B. and A. Blay-Palmer (2006), 'The urban creative-food economy: producing food for the urban elite or social inclusion opportunity?', *Environment and Planning A*, **38** (10), 1901–20.

'Drinking in public places to be banned' (2015, 14 January), *The Korea Times*.

Everett, S. (2016), *Food and Drink Tourism: Principles and Practice*, London: Sage.

Frost, W., J. Laing, F. Wheeler and K. Reeves (2010), 'Coffee culture, heritage and destination image: Melbourne and the Italian model', *Coffee Culture, Destinations and Tourism*, **24**, 99.

GCF (Gangneung Culture Foundation) (2012), *Gangneung Coffee Story*, Gangneung: GCF (in Korean).

Habermas, J. (1989), *The Structural Transformation of the Public Sphere: An Inquiry into a Category of Bourgeois Society*, trans. T. Burger, Cambridge, UK: Polity Press.

Halford, M. (2011, 30 June), 'The coming of coffee's fourth wave?', *The New Yorker*.

Hall, C.M., L. Sharples, R. Mitchell, N. Macionis and B. Cambourne (eds) (2003), *Food Tourism Around the World: Development, Management and Markets*, Oxford: Butterwort-Heinemann/Elsevier.

Han, S. (2014), 'South Korea's coffee market development course reflections and business environment analysis', *Korean Academy of Foodservice Industry and Management*, **10** (1), 115–43 (in Korean).

Hauser, A. (1999), *The Social History of Art, Vol. 4: Naturalism, Impressionism, the Film Age*, New York: Psychology Press.

Horng, J.S. and M.L. Hu (2009), 'The creative culinary process: constructing and extending a four-component model', *Creativity Research Journal*, **21** (4), 376–83.

Horng, J.S., C.H. Liu, S.F. Chou and C.Y. Tsai (2013), 'Professional conceptions of creativity in restaurant space planning', *International Journal of Hospitality Management*, **34**, 73–80.

Hoskins, N. (2007, 13 June), 'Café culture: the best places to read', *Guardian*.

Jin, Y. (1999), 'A study on the present condition of the coffee and vision of 21c in Korea', *Culinary Science and Hospitality Research*, **5** (2), 3–23 (in Korean).

Johnston, J. and M.K. Goodman (2015), 'Spectacular foodscapes: food celebrities and the politics of lifestyle mediation in an age of inequality', *Food, Culture and Society*, **18** (2), 205–22.

Kim, J., Y. Lee and J. Kim (2012), *A Critical Review on the East Coastal Tourism*, Research Institute for Gangwon (in Korean).

Kleidas, M. and L. Jolliffe (2010), 'Coffee attraction experiences: a narrative study', *Turizam: znanstveno-stručni časopis*, **58** (1), 61–73.

Lee, A.H., G. Wall and J.F. Kovacs (2015), 'Creative food clusters and rural development through place branding: culinary tourism initiatives in Stratford and Muskoka, Ontario, Canada', *Journal of Rural Studies*, **39**, 133–44.

Lee, Y. (2011), *Coffee, Specialty Coffee, Special People*, Seoul: Book House Ann (in Korean).

Lloyd, R. (2010), *Neo-bohemia: Art and Commerce in the Postindustrial City*, New York and Abingdon: Routledge.

Luttinger, N. and G. Dicum (2011), *The Coffee Book: Anatomy of an Industry from Crop to the Last Drop*, New York: The New Press.

Maitland, R. (2010), 'Everyday life as a creative experience in cities', *International Journal of Culture, Tourism and Hospitality Research*, **4** (3), 176–85.

Manning, P. (2013), 'The theory of the café central and the practice of the café peripheral: aspirational and abject infrastructures of sociability on the European periphery', in A. Tjora and G. Scambler (eds), *Café Society*, New York: Palgrave Macmillan, pp. 43–65.

Martins, M. (2016), 'Gastronomic tourism and the creative economy', *Journal of Tourism, Heritage and Services Marketing*, **2** (2), 33–7.

McKenzie, A. (2017), 'City of books', *Everythingzoomer.com*.

Michael, E. (2006), *Micro-clusters and Networks*, London: Routledge.

Miller, N. (2007, March), 'Snack attack!', *Wired*, accessed 18 November 2017 at https://www.wired.com/2007/03/snackattack/.

Mitchell, R. and C.M. Hall (2003), 'Consuming tourists: food tourism consumer behaviour', in C.M. Hall, L. Sharples, R. Mitchell, N. Macionis and B. Cambourne (eds), *Food Tourism Around the*

World: Development, Management and Markets, Oxford: Butterworth-Heinemann/Elsevier, pp. 60–80.

Newman, M.Z. (2010), 'New media, young audiences and discourses of attention: from Sesame Street to "snack culture"', *Media, Culture and Society*, **32** (4), 581–96.

OECD (2012), *Food and the Tourism Experience: The OECD-Korea Workshop*, OECD Studies on Tourism, OECD Publishing. doi:10.1787/9789264171923-en.

Oldenburg, R. and D. Brissett (1982), 'The third place', *Qualitative Sociology*, **5** (4), 265–84.

Peng, K.L., M.C. Lin and T. Baum (2013), 'The constructing model of culinary creativity: an approach of mixed methods', *Quality and Quantity*, **47** (5), 2687–707.

Richards, G. (2002), 'Gastronomy: an essential ingredient in tourism production and consumption', *Tourism and Gastronomy*, **11**, 2–20.

Richards, G. (2014), 'The role of gastronomy in tourism development', Presentation to the Fourth International Congress on Noble Houses: A Heritage for the Future, Arcos de Valdevez, 27–29 November.

Richards, G. and C. Raymond (2000), 'Creative tourism', *ATLAS News*, **23**, 16–20.

Richards, G. and J. Wilson (2006), 'Developing creativity in tourist experiences: a solution to the serial reproduction of culture?', *Tourism Management*, **27** (6), 1209–23.

Ritzer, G. (2011), *The McDonaldization of Society 6*, Thousand Oaks, CA: Pine Forge Press.

Russo, P.A. and A.A. Sans (2009), 'Student communities and landscapes of creativity: how Venice – "the world's most touristed city" – is changing', *European Urban and Regional Studies*, **16** (2), 161–75.

Seo, U. (2017), 'Lifestyle entrepreneur and tourism based local development', in M. Koo (ed.), *Success Model of Creative Rural Economy*, Seongnam: Book Korea, pp. 295–327 (in Korean).

Sharples, L. (2003), 'The world of cookery-school holidays', in C.M. Hall, L. Sharples, R. Mitchell, N. Macionis and B. Cambourne (eds), *Food Tourism Around the World: Development, Management and Markets*, Oxford: Butterworth-Heinemann/Elsevier, pp. 102–20.

Shim, K. (2010, 19 April), 'Coffee, another tea ceremony of Gangneung', *Kangwon News* (in Korean).

Stebbins, R.A. (1982), 'Serious leisure: a conceptual statement', *Pacific Sociological Review*, **25** (2), 251–72.

Stenseth, B. (2013). 'Heart of urbanism. The café: a chapter of cultural history', in A. Tjora and G. Scambler (eds), *Café Society*, New York: Palgrave Macmillan, pp. 23–42.

Stolarick, K.M., M. Denstedt, B. Donald and G.M. Spencer (2010), 'Creativity, tourism and economic development in a rural context: the case of Prince Edward County', *Journal of Rural and Community Development*, **5** (1), 238–54.

Tan, S.K., D.B. Luh and S.F. Kung (2014), 'A taxonomy of creative tourists in creative tourism', *Tourism Management*, **42**, 248–59.

Weaver, A. (2010), 'Cafe culture and conversation: tourism and urban(e) experiences in Wellington, New Zealand', in L. Jolliffe (ed.), *Coffee Culture, Destinations and Tourism*, Bristol: Channel View Publications, pp. 41–52.

White, H.C. and C.A. White (1993), *Canvases and Careers: Institutional Change in the French Painting World*, Chicago, IL: University of Chicago Press.

Wurzburger, R., T. Aageson, A. Pattakos and S. Pratt (eds) (2010), *Creative Tourism, a Global Conversation*, Santa Fe: Sunstone Press.

Yu, Y. (2014), *Evaluation Research on Gangneung Coffee Festival and Analysis of Visitors*, Chuncheon: Gangwon Development Institute (in Korean).

Zukin, S., V. Trujillo, P. Frase, D. Jackson, T. Recuber and A. Walker (2009), 'New retail capital and neighborhood change: boutiques and gentrification in New York City', *City and Community*, **8** (1), 47–64.

8 Montréal: a creative tourism destination?

Marie-Andrée Delisle

As a member of the United Nations Educational, Scientific and Cultural Organization (UNESCO) Creative Cities Network as a City of Design since 2006, Montréal is famous for its significant multimedia creative industries. It hosted the first World Design Summit in October 2017, which issued a Montréal Design Declaration to be followed by a ten-year design-driven international action plan. Considered a smart and creative city, Montréal's creativity and innovation are mainly underlined by the strong presence of the multimedia and artificial intelligence creative industries. So far, Montréal has not embraced the concept of creative tourism and its related activities. This chapter examines the creative aspects of the city's reputation and achievements while exploring why those activities are not yet part of its tourism offer, and aiming to find the circumstances that prevent it from becoming a true city of creative tourism.

Branded as a cultural destination with its panoply of festivals in all seasons, its pleasant ambience and 'joie de vivre', the city is also known for its socio-cultural diversity and its culture of innovation – Google, Microsoft, and Facebook have recently opened research centres in the city. It has been working on a Smart and Digital City Action Plan since 2014,[1] while its territory is still at a human scale and reputed for its quality of life. Singularly, in the midst of a sea of English speakers, Montréal's cultural and creative background is largely inspired by the preservation of its language. It is politically recognized as the metropolis of the French-speaking province of Québec. It is considered as having a European feel in a definite North American context, with a lifestyle '*À la Montréal . . . !*'

Internationally known artists such as Leonard Cohen and Céline Dion, Moment Factory immersive multimedia producer, Cirque du Soleil, and Ubisoft Montréal's video games successes (see Cohendet et al., 2010) contribute as ambassadors to bring an attractive set of assets coupled with a dynamic sense of innovation throughout the business community. The city has also been attracting visionaries from all over the world with its yearly C2-Montréal (C2 for Commerce + Creativity) three-day immersive and global innovation event, held since 2012, where the international business community gathers to brainstorm and network in a collaborative and creative environment. Additionally, in operation since 2013, the *Quartier de l'innovation* has become an ecosystem 'hub' located in the recently redeveloped area of Griffintown, where four universities co-exist and collaborate to stimulate innovation and entrepreneurship and promote local start-ups to an international level.

Mass cultural performances are also part of the creative scene. The downtown *Quartier des spectacles* hosts multiple performing arts and venues; its mission is to offer innovative initiatives, performances, and concerts where creativity is constantly stimulated and shared. Many of the year-round outdoor events gather a large attendance with numerous free shows and lively public spaces that are inclusive and accessible to all.

2017 was a very special year, with Montréal celebrating the city's 375th anniversary, Expo 67's 50th anniversary, and Canada's 150th anniversary. Apart from its renowned festivals such as the *Festival International de Jazz, Just for Laughs*, outdoor winter *Igloofest*, and winter gourmet and show *Montréal en Lumières*, the city witnessed more than 100 special events in the summer of 2017 with a contagious enthusiasm from resident Montréalers. Furthermore, the rich gastronomic scene, audacious and plentiful, has local restaurants, locavore bistros, and bars attracting foodies from all over.

Montréalers: curious and involved

It all started with Expo '67, which could have been called a six-month 'wonder' party 50 years ago, opening its population to the world and launching the beginning of Montréal's international radiance. Such an important political, social, and cultural legacy piqued the curiosity of Montréalers for arts, food, and cultural exchanges. This has remained an ongoing trend that culminated with the 375th anniversary programming.

Eager to illustrate its vibrant personality, citizens, elected officials, and the business community got together to keep up with the love and care for the city, their openness to diversity, and its appeal for artistic and cultural expressions. To commemorate Montréal's 375th heritage and historic recollections, over 100 small and big events were programmed with an emphasis on public art, neighbourhood participation, and artistic expressions of all kinds. This array of programming rested on the idea that the more exposed to public art and to diverse cultural expressions in their own environment, the more residents maintain a dialogue with their neighbourhood artists.

The community was eager to participate, influence, and embellish its living environment for this 375th special year. In 2014, civil society organizations were invited to propose their vision of Montréal along with projects they would like to support to revitalize the city. *Je vois Montréal* was born. A year later, some 180 projects were adopted, and the project became *Je fais Montréal*,[2] with the full support of the city's mayor. These initiatives demonstrated the citizens' capacity to participate in imaging and placemaking projections.

Alongside this mobilization and under the support of the Society for the Celebration of Montréal's 375th Anniversary, *La Grande Tournée* became one of the summer 2017 signature events, with each of the 19 boroughs invited to take turns hosting local festivities over 19 weekends and exhibit the richness of their history and their people. Here again, the level of community involvement, creativity, and appreciation, along with local artists, was spectacular. In a sense, they revisited their own neighbourhood narrative, inviting visitors to share their environment (Maitland, 2010), just 'like a local' (Russo and Richards, 2016, p. 18).

Many neighbourhoods annually celebrate a sense of place with the contribution of artists' talents:

- The *Marché des Possibles*: a public open-air space for Mile-End neighbours and artists, and a summer festive 'market of possibilities' featuring free socio-cultural events, food, and local artists' products.
- The *Chasse-Balcon*: a unique summer musical concept where fiddlers use balconies around the city, inviting neighbours to gather for traditional Quebec tunes, accompanied by a dance and foot-tapping show.
- *Chat de ruelles* (back alley cat): a neighbourhood party moving around every weekend to one of the 19 boroughs; they feature emerging music artists, circus performances and workshops, and urban agriculture workshops, thus illustrating and promoting the environmental, cultural, and urban heritage of the back alleys. (More than 30 back alleys have been converted in recent years into green alleys, a great example of citizens' appropriation of these spaces, thanks to the collaboration of street neighbours and the support of the City of Montréal's Environmental Action programme. Guided tours of the green alleys are quite popular with tourists.)
- The *Fenêtres qui parlent* ('talking windows', adapted from a French initiative): another *La Grande Tournée* festive event in the 19 boroughs, where citizens lend their windows to artists who exhibit a work of art, thereby encouraging passers-by to discover local artists.

Most of these small events are free and easily accessible by public transportation. Their festive atmosphere stresses the fact that these events are lived and produced by the people in what could be called a 'tourism of proximity' approach, enabling guests to get closer to their hosts!

Since 2007, a non-profit organization, MU, has created murals in the city, provoking emotions in neighbourhoods and prompting social transformation as an open-air museum of street art. MU also offers mosaic workshops to residents and mural art workshops in local schools. A sister artistic organization, the Mural Festival, also aims to democratize urban art, bringing together artists, musicians, creators, residents, and visiting art enthusiasts in a festival context. The geotagged murals also lead to guided visits on summer weekends.

Various collectives, such as La Pépinière, are dedicated to fostering the use of emblematic or underexploited sites for cultural, social, and economically viable activities, favouring the involvement of local communities. One successful site is the former 'ephemeral village', which occupies a vacant spot under the Jacques-Cartier Bridge. This *Village au Pied-du-Courant* is reinvented each summer, thanks to the collaboration of young designers and community involvement, as 'an urban living lab for the experimentation and development of new practices in design, entrepreneurship and art' (https://www.aupieducourant.ca/english/).

Moment Factory's works of art have familiarized Montréalers with its digital creativity to illustrate the city's landscape and architectural heritage, and more recently with Jacques-Cartier Bridge's illumination. A legacy from the 375th anniversary, this digital multimedia performance changes colours according to each day, to each season, and to different types of light animation provoked by the weather, the traffic, and the pulse of the city via several Montréal-related hashtags such as #MTLMoments, responding in real time to tweets from the population.

These examples show that for a visitor, resident, or tourist, these innovations bring an immersive experience larger than just attending, by sharing a cultural celebration within a powerful artistic environment. Hence, the tourists live the spirit of a mobilized community around its enthusiasm for its neighbourhood or city: 'it seems that many creative experiences are closely linked to the idea of "living like a local". Local people are framed as the gateway to local culture and experience, and they can show visitors how to creatively navigate the city, supposedly finding those places where only locals go' (Richards, 2014, p. 131). Local people become 'the' attraction and the local vibe is being felt, which brings about the *genius loci* of the city (Maitland, 2013, p. 16). This is where the tourism experience is co-created by the resident and the visitor, and where pleasure becomes memorable (Campos et al., 2015).

Montréal and creative tourism

All this being said, the promotion of the 375th anniversary events, meant to attract tourists and increase residents' pride, has consecrated Montréal as a creative tourism city, fulfilling tourists' desire as '[t]hey search for local identity and the atmosphere of a city. In this context, a particular creativity for developing local, locally-related identities, specific for the place and its people, plays an important role for the city visitors . . . Place matters!' (Frey, 2009, p. 141).

The *Guide to Creative Montréal*, published in 2013, presents ten self-guided trails to discover various neighbourhoods, indicating artistic urban spaces, events, visits to artists' workshops, with cafés, restaurants, and shops along the way, promoting the art of living *à la montréalaise*! Tourisme Montréal also projects this image through its website, which includes blogs and Instagram #MTLMoments pics from visitors.

In this sense, the search for authenticity takes places in a natural environment of life as it is lived and not staged by the locals, so that the 'backstage' aspect becomes accessible (Korstanje, 2015; MacCannell, 1999; Maitland, 2013). Since its inception, the creative tourism portrait has expanded, including creativity as background (Richards and Marques, 2012), with these authors stating that '[t]he local community is vital in [the] process [of co-creation]' (p. 8).

Local workshops

There are many workshops that artists and artisans offer to residents, from durations of a few days to a few months. A brief survey shows that artists are generally not familiar with the concept of creative tourism and even less with creative workshops for visitors. Nevertheless, some neighbourhoods offer short workshops that could add the niche market of creative tourists to their programme. For example, Griffintown Art School offers Friday night open classes of wine and painting/drawing, while Les Ateliers C presents Sunday afternoon visual arts workshops. Other short workshops include creative writing, culinary specialties (some as short as one-hour at lunch time), and travel photography and video, to name a few. International networks such as community Art Hives and Urban Sketchers are also active.

To develop creative workshops further, artists and artisans must become aware of the possibility of offering them to visitors, and if enough of them demonstrate an interest in putting up creative workshops, there would be a need to coordinate, structure, programme, and promote them, while some cultural actors such as Culture Montréal could contribute.

Culture Montréal is a non-profit organization supported by municipal and provincial public agencies and private organizations. Its main objective is to anchor culture in Montréal's city and neighbourhood development plans and projects and to ensure cultural accessibility to its citizens. Another significant stakeholder for creative artists is the Ateliers Créatifs, a non-profit real estate developer whose mission is to develop and protect working and creative places in order to make them affordable, adequate, and sustainable. At its heart, the organization values the importance of offering a context of security and longevity to maintain the presence of the artists who contribute to revitalizing their neighbourhood.

One more arts and culture input comes from the city's *Maisons de la culture*, present in 12 boroughs, with free exhibitions, artist performances, and cultural activities of local creators on a weekly basis, and widely attended by local residents. As Klein and Tremblay (2016) note, 'Cultural creation can only serve as a basis for a cohesive urban development strategy if the various populations are enabled to participate and engage actively in the cultural and creative activities themselves rather than being passive observers, or worse, totally excluded from the activities' (p. 457).

Putting Montréal into context

What about creative tourism workshops elsewhere? Since there are so many, I have chosen to describe some aspects related to Loulé, a small town in Portugal, where I recently experienced two different workshops. I am bringing this forward in order to emphasize some important differences.

Although Montréal is much greater in population (city about 2 million and Greater Montréal 4 million versus the town of Loulé at 23,000 and the broader municipality at over 70,000), Loulé has been very active in promoting its creative tourism activities for some time. It offers many workshops and artists to choose from, on a weekly or a monthly basis, with specific ones during special events. Most of its promotion and reservations procedures are covered by Loulé Criativo, the municipal umbrella organization, while its international visibility is ensured by its membership in the Creative Tourism Network. The Loulé Criativo website targets local and national visitors as well as tourists, and many workshops are offered in English. The old city attracts a good number of tourists visiting the well-known sea destination of Algarve and the weather is fair all year round. There are low-cost fares from all over Europe to nearby Faro airport as well as train connections throughout the country, two major assets that Montréal does not possess. As Montréal is not connected to large short-haul markets there are few of the repeat visits or weekend breaks common in European cities. Montréal must also deal with extreme seasonal variations, an important factor that is not as suitable or conducive to attract visitors in the low season Canadian cold months, even though lots of events take place inside and out. Also, since Montréal's history only dates back 375 years, there is not as much historical *savoir-faire* as one could find in a European or Asian city.

Seeds for the implementation of creative tourism workshops

While researching this chapter, I conducted three interviews with officials from organizations that promote culture and tourism activities: Culture Montréal, Regroupement Arts et Culture Rosemont-Petite-Patrie, and Tourisme Montréal. This section presents a synthesis of the key ideas and perspectives on creative tourism development in Montréal gathered through these conversations.

At Culture Montréal, the Executive Director mentioned that the idea of extending an artist's activity into a creative tourism workshop has never been proposed. Although this idea is favourably received, the organization's objective is to work towards improving the quality of life in boroughs through the diffusion of culture, more than developing new business models with the artists and their communities. We discussed the fact that some artists want to concentrate solely on creating while others, such as teachers or creators, are open to plural activities; they might welcome a new source of income since their creative work is often intermittent, temporary, and under fixed-term contracts (Markusen, 2006; Vivant and Tremblay, 2010). Agreeing that artists need to innovate to survive, and although they are at times exhausted, Culture Montréal believes that some of them would be open to this adventure if it were facilitated.

The relevant questions are how to embody such an offer and with whom. What would be the initial step? An inventory of artists? A non-profit organization that could set up a call for applications? Starting with a few artists who show interest in the venture? Meanwhile, the artists presently offering short-duration workshops for residents are only promoted locally, although they could extend their activities to visitors.

Art and culture are also vectors of development in certain boroughs. In the case of Regroupement Arts et Culture Rosemont-Petite-Patrie (RACRPP), the organization's mission is to bring together individuals and professional organizations involved in arts and culture in the neighbourhood, while contributing to the development of local culture and facilitating networking and interactions between artists and their community. Its Project Coordinator was quite interested in examining the possibility of developing creative tourism workshops with local artists, for three main reasons. First, he saw the relevance of such an initiative with the organization's goals. Second, he thought that artists would be receptive. Third, he felt that the project could also benefit from the City of Montréal's cultural mediation programme (Ville de Montréal, n.d.), which provides various ways of supporting projects of this kind.

The cultural mediation programme has been integrated into the city's cultural policy since 2005, aiming to change or improve the well-being of communities on a personal, collective, or social level. It centres on interactions and inclusive encounters between citizens and cultural and artistic circles. It relies on financial assistance programmes jointly offered with the provincial Ministry of Culture and Communications and is orchestrated at the borough level, thanks to decentralized municipal decision-making structures. This facilitates local implementation in line with the needs of its collectivity, which, in turn, helps establish local projects more efficiently. Along with Agenda 21 for Culture, the programme represents a key dimension of Montréal's urban policies and a tool for neighbourhood cultural development and collective democratization. However, both RACRPP and Culture Montréal mentioned that a creative tourism project would need to identify a project leader; a kind of platform would need to be created and financially supported while building a cluster of artists with creative activities.

At Tourisme Montréal, the Cultural Tourism Manager describes the city as radiating a social vibe, where cultural expressions are seen everywhere. From her point of view, a creative tourism initiative sounds promising and there is a noticeable interest in supporting its development. However, although the organization has done some research a few years back, there is no current knowledge about active creators involved in offering creative tourism workshops. She also wondered whether there is a sufficient tourism market at this time for such a product. Thus, in her opinion, the first step would be to study the feasibility of the project, starting with building an inventory and knowledge base, organizing focus groups, identifying an umbrella organization that could initiate a platform to coordinate and accompany the artists while gathering a collection of workshops, and then promoting and commercializing their creative activities.

Furthering my research, I came across a document about new trends related to amateur artistic practices, identified by Montréal's cultural department (Ville de Montréal – Service de la Culture, 2015). These show that more and more residents attend short workshops to practise their hobby freely, while also participating in cultural mediation projects. As Jelinčić (2009) states:

> Creative and hobby tourism can be considered as even more specialized forms of cultural tourism involving narrower target markets . . . Still, as creative/hobby tourism programmes are conceived as a main product and therefore marketed towards travellers which incline to these activities, they have strength as a small but major tourism product for destinations. (p. 264)

These trends could foster the programming of participative workshops to offer to visitors. A good starting point might be to entice already programmed festivals to expand their activities. Artists could produce and propose creative workshops in sync with the theme of a festival. The idea could then percolate among artists and inspire them to jump on the bandwagon of a creative tourism cluster. This could foster new interactions within the framework of innovation and artistic relational initiatives.

Furthermore, those kinds of initiatives could benefit from the proliferation of start-ups that could help market these workshops by putting together a website to gather information about the activities, the dates, the times, and the locations and be able to sell registrations online. Montréal recently partnered with the Paris Welcome City Lab, an urban tourism incubator of start-ups, and took the name of MT Lab. This innovation linchpin dedicated to help these digital businesses could become an important cornerstone to this process.

With the support of major financial partners, the Université du Québec à Montréal, and Tourisme Montréal, MT Lab concentrates on the tourism, culture, and entertainment sectors. The programme includes training, mentoring, and co-working spaces to help promote business solutions to the partners and to consumers. The quite fashionable trend of start-ups brings another element into the equation by offering new ways to collate the information and diffuse it through a much larger international audience as well as specific target markets. Could the new MT Lab start-ups be used as a catalyst for the diffusion of creative artists offering workshops?

Gaps in the research

To date, there have been gaps in the research concerning the subject of creative tourism and more specifically about creative workshops, as defined by Richards and

Raymond (2000) and by the Creative Tourism Network. Indeed, much of the literature concerns the visitors' needs, wants, motivations, and search for self-actualization, whereas little is being written about the 'supply side' – the creative producers, such as artists, artisans, specialists, tutors, suppliers, service providers, and so forth. Little appears to be known about the profile of these individuals and organizations.

Are there some criteria that describe pre-requisites for offering such activities, whether part of the creative producer (micro) or the umbrella organization (meso) that coordinates and/or promotes local, regional, or national creative workshops? From the perspective of these micro and meso levels of intervention and interrelation, it appears no portrait exists, or empirical data about successes and pitfalls. Although these activities provide a foundation for sustainable development, the viability of such activities is seldom addressed. Research should also shed more light on the role of creative producers in local tourism development, including their impact on the sense of place and on the destination image. Is the creative producer an innovative entrepreneur? Does he or she keep a dialogue with the community in order to remain a cultural mediator? And if so, how? Finally, what is the input needed by the creative producer as a host compared to the one expected by the visitor? In other words, where do they meet in terms of adequacy between the supply and demand? What age, sex, and origin are the participants and the workshop locations (large city, small city, rural, and so on) around the world and what is their target market?

Answering these questions, although they would need to be adapted depending on the destination, would certainly help market the workshops strategically. As we know, Airbnb now provides experiences on its website and has recently added some for Montréal. How would creative tourism workshops fare in this context?

Conclusion

Over the last decade or more, creative cities have followed Florida's definition of the creative class and the creative economy (Florida, 2012). Tolerance, Technology, and Talent, the three T's, have depicted the urban creative class, but to what extent does this framework play into creative tourism development in large cities? Is a city leaning towards an extended neoliberal movement? Or is it that creative industries, artists, and municipal governance bring about jobs, better living conditions, and enhanced well-being for the population?

By becoming very attractive to hipster lifestyles, neighbourhoods open up opportunities for gentrification often due to a lack of traditional accommodation, which would signify negative impacts of Airbnb and Sonder's sharing economy. Once costs get high, artists leave, trendy restaurants move on, galleries close, then comes a point of no return unless the borough's governance works upstream to protect the community with restraining laws, mainly for land tenure but also for the preservation of the collective identity and sense of place. In a way, artists could be at the forefront of eventual disruptions of the neighbourhood they themselves created.

Interestingly, Florida's last publication (Florida, 2017) acknowledges that his creative class theory has provoked a 'new urban crisis' in terms of gentrification and class inequalities.

Do creative workshops target a narrow niche market or do they, instead, attract creative individuals who want another kind of relationship with the local community through an artistic learning process? As per Tan et al.'s (2014) taxonomy of creative tourists, it appears that they 'should be seen as a heterogeneous group of consumers who perceive the creative experiences differently' (p. 257). Thus, artists (and participating visitors) may have little to do with the 'creative class' (Markusen, 2006, p. 1937).

Rather, creative visitors seek an authentic exchange, an experience that they create with the contribution of the artist's creative workshop. Is there co-creation involved, or simply the opportunity of doing something they do not take time to do at home? Does the theory of co-creation still apply in the case of creative workshops, or is it more a search by visitors for a small-scale, non-elitist, recreational, or edutaining encounter? Where exercising their creativity within a more inclusive atmosphere stemming from a local initiative, could one call this a culture of proximity? By looking at one another's creativity at work, discussing, and exchanging ideas, participants get influenced by others, by the tutor, and by the ambience (Tan et al., 2014). They may just need a workshop ambience, where pleasure counts more than the result, where the process is central, not the search for fine arts or a transformative experience.

Does Montréal attract Florida's 'creative class'? Yes, it does attract creative industry workers, for it is known for its spirit, its public and private investments in creativity and innovation, its influx of foreign students, its artificial intelligence research centres, its quality of life, its openness to diversity, and the friendliness of its population. One cannot suppress the fact that Montréal is attracting investors, students, and tourists and consequently entering the competitive race among global cities (Harvey, 2008). However, there is no real iconic architecture or outstanding attraction here; Old Montréal cannot compete with the lustre of European historic centres. There is also a language barrier in some cases, where culture is predominantly expressed in French. Tourism is heavily seasonal, and there are still no low-cost airlines, but gentrification is on the way in the most sought-out neighbourhoods such as Plateau Mont-Royal, Griffintown, Rosemont-Petite-Patrie, Mile-End, and Mile-Ex. Creating a touristy environment with galleries, state-of-the-art restaurants and bars, small boutiques, galleries, co-working places, and artists' working spaces does add to the coolness of the city's reputation. However, creative tourism workshops would contribute to local sustainability by using local resources, preserving cultural identities, creating alternatives to serial reproductions, adding value to the host–guest encounter (Musikyan, 2016; Richards and Wilson, 2006; Tan et al., 2014), and providing direct economic benefits for local communities.

Montréal may not be ready yet for a creative tourism network although the interest might just need to be kindled, bolstering the considerable existing activity amongst local workshops. At this time, maybe local residents are more in a search of community strengthening or building via a better use of culture as a means for urban development than to meet the visitors' needs and wants. Reinforcing the cultural identities of citizens and small businesses will help local cultural creativity and innovation remain a contribution to competitiveness and to the development of art with a small *a*. Most importantly, creative tourism activities represent a relevant means of achieving a sustainable cultural development at the local level, in this disruptive era of the sharing economy. Why not think of creative tourism as a community-based tourism development (Delisle and Jolin, 2007) where a bottom-up approach among local community members would design what it finds suitable for its well-being?

NOTES

1 See 'Montréal, Smart City' at http://villeintelligente.montreal.ca/en.
2 A list of website URLs for various events and projects follows the References.

References

Campos, A.C., J. Mendes, P.O. do Valle et al. (2015), 'Co-creation of tourist experiences: a literature review', *Current Issues in Tourism*, **21** (4), 1–32. doi:10.1080/13683500.2015.1081158

Cohendet, P., D. Grandadam and L. Simon (2010), 'The anatomy of the creative city', *Industry and Innovation*, **17** (1), 91–111. doi:10.1080/13662710903573869

Delisle, M.-A. and L. Jolin (2007), *Un autre tourisme est-il possible? Éthique, acteurs, concepts, contraintes, bonnes pratiques, ressources*, Québec: Presses de l'Université du Québec.

Florida, R. (2012), *The Rise of the Creative Class Revisited*, New York: Basic Books.

Florida, R. (2017), *The New Urban Crisis: How Our Cities are Increasing Inequality, Deepening Segregation, and Failing the Middle Class – and What We Can Do About It*, New York: Basic Books.

Frey, O. (2009), 'Creativity of places as a resource for cultural tourism', in G. Maciocco and S. Serreli (eds), *Enhancing the City*, Dordrecht: Springer Netherlands, pp. 135–54. doi:10.1007/978-90-481-2419-0_7

Harvey, D. (2008), 'The right to the city', *New Left Review*, **53**, 23–40, accessed 9 October 2018 at https://newleftreview.org/II/53/david-harvey-the-right-to-the-city.

Jelinčić, D.A. (2009), 'Splintering of tourism market: new appearing forms of cultural tourism as a consequence of changes in everyday lives', *Collegium Antropologicum*, **33** (1), 259–66, accessed 9 October 2018 at http://www.ncbi.nlm.nih.gov/pubmed/19408635.

Klein, J.-L. and D.-G. Tremblay (2016), 'Cultural creation and social innovation as the basis for building a cohesive city', in D.D. Shearmu and R.C. Carrincazeaux (eds), *Handbook on the Geographies of Innovation*, Cheltenham, UK and Northampton, MA, USA: Edward Elgar Publishing, pp. 447–62. doi:10.4337/9781784710774

Korstanje, M.E. (2015), 'The portrait of Dean MacCannell – towards an understanding of capitalism', *Anatolia, An International Journal of Tourism and Hospitality Research*, **27** (2), 1–7. doi:10.1080/13032917.2015.1063283

MacCannell, D. (1999), *The Tourist: A New Theory of the Leisure Class*, Berkeley, CA: University of California Press.

Maitland, R. (2010), 'Everyday life as a creative experience in cities', *International Journal of Culture, Tourism and Hospitality Research*, **4** (3), 176–85. doi:10.1108/17506181011067574

Maitland, R. (2013), 'Backstage behaviour in the global city: tourists and the search for the "real London"', *Procedia – Social and Behavioral Sciences*, **105**, 12–19. doi:10.1016/j.sbspro.2013.11.002

Markusen, A. (2006), 'Urban development and the politics of a creative class: evidence from a study of artists', *Environment and Planning A*, **38** (10), 1921–40. doi:10.1068/a38179

Musikyan, S. (2016), 'The influence of creative tourism on sustainable development of tourism and reduction of seasonality – case study of Óbidos', Master's thesis, School of Tourism and Maritime Technology, Polytechnic Institute of Leiria, Portugal, accessed 9 October 2018 at http://www.iconli ne.ipleiria.pt/bitstream/10400.8/2147/1/Final_thesis-Srbuhi updated.pdf.

Richards, G. (2014), 'Creativity and tourism in the city', *Current Issues in Tourism*, **17** (2), 119–44. doi:1 0.1080/13683500.2013.783794

Richards, G. and L. Marques (2012), 'Exploring creative tourism: editors introduction', *Journal of Tourism Consumption and Practice*, **4** (2), 1–11, accessed 9 October 2018 at http:// www.mendeley.com/research/exploring-creative-tourism-editors-introduction/?utm_ source=desktop&utm_medium=1.16.3&utm_campaign=open_catalog&userDocumentId=%7B67 77c647-bb2a-4af2-ae36-e52db551fc4e%7D.

Richards, G. and C. Raymond (2000), 'Creative tourism', *Atlas News* no. 23, 16–20, accessed 10 October 2018 at https://www.academia.edu/1785786/Creative_Tourism_-_Richards_and_Raymond_2000.

Richards, G. and J. Wilson (2006), 'Developing creativity in tourist experiences: a solution to the serial reproduction of culture?', *Tourism Management*, **27** (6), 1209–23. doi: 10.1016/j.tourman.2005.06.002

Russo, A.P. and G. Richards (2016), *Reinventing the Local in Tourism: Producing, Consuming and Negotiating Place*, Bristol: Channel View Publications.

Tan, S.-K., D.-B. Luh and S.-F. Kung (2014), 'A taxonomy of creative tourists in creative tourism', *Tourism Management*, **42**, 248–59. doi:10.1016/j.tourman.2013.11.008

Ville de Montréal (n.d.), *La médiation culturelle – Montréal. Ville de Montréal*, accessed 9 October 2018 at http://montreal.mediationculturelle.org/.

Ville de Montréal – Service de la Culture (2015), *Nouvelles tendances en pratique artistique ama-teur*, Montréal, accessed 9 October 2018 at http://loisirculturel.ca/wp-content/uploads/2015/12/ NouvTendancesPratiqueArtAmateur_Automne2015.pdf.

Vivant, E. and D.-G. Tremblay (2010), 'L'économie créative', *Revue des travaux francophones – Note de recherche de la Chaire de recherche du Canada sur les enjeux socio-organisationnels de l'économie du savoir*, **10** (2), 71. Accessed 9 October 2018 at http://www.teluq.ca/chaireecosavoir/pdf/NRC10-02.pdf.

Websites

Art Hives: http://arthives.org/blog/ruches-dart-de-montr%C3%A9al-montreal-art-hives-0

Ateliers Créatifs: http://ateliers.creatifs.org (in French only)

Ateliers et Saveurs: http://www.atelierssaveurs.com

Attractive Japan: https://attractive-j.com/engtop/

AURA Notre-Dame Basilica Illumination: http://www.aurabasiliquemontreal.com/en/

C-2 Montréal: http://www.c2montreal.com

Chats de ruelles: http://tohu.ca/fr/m/programmation/detail/2016-2017/chats-de-ruelles/ (in French only)

Creative France: http://www.creativefrance.fr/

Culture Montréal: https://culturemontreal.ca/ (in French only)

Food trucks/Street cuisine: http://cuisinederue.org/

Griffintown Art School: http://griffintownartschool.ca/

Je fais Montréal: https://fairemtl.ca/en/je-fais-montreal

La Chasse-Balcon: http://www.lachassebalcon.com/a-propos

La Fabrique Culturelle: http://www.lafabriqueculturelle.tv/

La Grande Tournée: http://www.375mtl.com/en/decouvrez-la-grande-tournee/?gclid=EAIaIQobChMI h7qP88ax1gIVSJ7ACh1pRQsBEAAYASAAEgJoG_D_BwE

Les Ateliers C: http://les-ateliers-c.com/ (in French only

Les Fenêtres qui parlent: http://www.fqpmontreal.ca/a-propos/?lang=en

Magneto Balado: http://www.magnetobalado.com

Maisons de la culture: http://ville.montreal.qc.ca/culture/lieu-culturel

Mange ta rue: http://www.375mtl.com/en/programming/mange-ta-rue-690/

Marché des Possibles: https://popmontreal.com/en/section/marche-des-possibles/

MAtv: http://en.matv.ca/montreal

Moment Factory's Illumination of Jacques-Cartier Bridge: https://momentfactory.com/work/all/all/jacques-cartier-bridge-illumination

Montréal en histoire/Cité mémoire: http://www.montrealenhistoires.com/en/cite-memoire/

Montréal en histoire/Cité mémoire: https://fairemtl.ca/fr/montreal-histoires (in French only)

Montréal's 375th anniversary: http://www.375mtl.com/anniversary/celebrations

MT Lab: https://mtlab.ca/en/about

Mural Festival: http://2017.muralfestival.com/en/about/

Mutek International Festival: http://www.mutek.org/en/about

Osez la plume: http://www.osezlaplume.com (in French only)

Sonder – Local Living.Hotel Service: http://www.sonder.com

Tourisme Montréal: http://www.mtl.org/en

Regroupement arts et culture Rosemont-Petite-Patrie: http://www.racrpp.org/a-propos/ (in French only)

Urban Sketchers: https://urbansketchersmontreal.wordpress.com/

Village Au Pied-du-Courant: http://www.aupiedducourant.ca/english/

PART III

Creative tourism in local development

9 Creative tourism in Santa Fe, New Mexico

Brent Hanifl[1]

Creative tourism in Santa Fe, New Mexico, was started by the drive and passion of Councillor Rebecca Wurzburger who, at the time of the Santa Fe International Conference on Creative Tourism in 2008, was Mayor Pro Tem of Santa Fe. Councillor Wurzburger fully realized the impetus of the conference when a dignitary from Spain was invited to Santa Fe. During this time, Ms Wurzburger spent a lot of time with the dignitary, showing her one of the 'richest cultural environments' in the United States. Towards the end of the trip, she spoke about her last few days in Santa Fe as an enlightening and beautiful experience. However, Wurzburger was floored because the dignitary had not previously known that Santa Fe existed – this interaction became a catalyst for Wurzburger to try and put Santa Fe on the global map. In this chapter I describe how creative tourism was used to raise the profile of Santa Fe and to support artists keen to link with visitors. I discuss the chronology of events that occurred in the city's embrace of creative tourism, and present the results of an economic impact study of creative tourism in Santa Fe. On the basis of these experiences, I suggest future research directions on the links between creative tourism and local creative enterprises.

Santa Fe as an ideal location for creative tourism

Debra Garcia y Griego, current Executive Director for the City of Santa Fe Arts Commission, sees the traditional arts and crafts as providing important creative inspiration for the city. The creative heritage of Santa Fe includes Hispanic and Native American cultures, as well as the early twentieth-century arrivals from the east. The notion of the 'tri-cultural influence' is based on 400 years of interaction between these different cultures in the region. The contemporary art scene is also integral to creative tourism, including different types of performance and art experiences, 'so you get a good diversity of range of offerings in what is a very small area' (Garcia y Griego, personal communication, 12 November 2012). Another reason for the city's artistic strength is the 'geographic density' of Santa Fe, New Mexico. This town of 80,000 is a powerhouse in the art scene and, in terms of art sales, is consistently ranked 'up there with New York, San Francisco, Chicago, L.A.' (Garcia y Griego, quoted in Hanifl, 2015b, p. 59). Santa Fe boasts more artists per capita than any other American city and prizes the 'density' of its arts and cultural offerings.

The cultural and creative riches of Santa Fe also attract many visitors, which allows local artists to see 'an entirely different way of approaching their business' (Garcia y Griego), and provides them the opportunity to create a new revenue stream for themselves – creative tourism can be a stimulus for artists to rethink the business they are in. When Garcia y Griego asked a family friend and well-known artist how he spends his day, he responded: 'I'm always doing something because it's a business . . . just like you wake up every day and go to work, I wake up every day and go to work.' He went on: 'And I may not be painting every day, some days I'm cleaning the studio, some days I'm sketching, some days I come into the gallery and meet with people, but I'm always doing something.' Garcia y Griego notes that 'creative tourism has been a really good way to introduce some artists to the concept of arts as a business'.

Creative tourism is also about participation:

> People who are attracted to becoming artists, love to share and they love to learn, and they love to interact. That's a vital part of the creative process. Socializing is part of the creative process. And strong faith communities have strong social networks. So you give that sort of, given that social nature of art, the opportunity to interact with people, to teach your form, to learn from their mistakes, to learn from what you're teaching them, I think is a whole other aspect of creative tourism that's incredibly important for artists to participate. (Garcia y Griego, quoted in Hanifl, 2015b, p. 60)

There is little doubt that the artistic community in Santa Fe has a lot of potential for developing creative tourism. The big challenge for the city has been to link artists with visitors to develop engaging creative tourism experiences. In particular, the city was interested in making links not just with visitors from the rest of the United States, but also internationally.

Santa Fe International Conference on Creative Tourism

Around the same time that Santa Fe began seeking international contacts, the United Nations Educational, Scientific and Cultural Organization (UNESCO) was launching its Creative Cities Network. Santa Fe became the first US city to be designated a member of the network, becoming a Creative City of Folk Art and Design in 2005. As a direct result of contacts made by Santa Fe through the Creative Cities Network, the first International Conference on Creative Tourism was hosted in Santa Fe in 2008.[2]

Out of the initial planning for this conference, a definition of creative tourism was articulated: 'Creative Tourism is tourism directed toward an engaged and authentic experience, with participative learning in the arts, heritage or special character of a place' (Wurzburger et al., 2009, p. 17). Ingrained in this definition is the inclusion of a hands-on experience that immerses a visitor in a culturally authentic activity.

The conference sought to address the questions: What is creative tourism? Why should creative cities worldwide, and specifically those in the UNESCO Creative Cities Network, collaborate in creative tourism? How can creative tourism be best organized to enhance economic benefits to cities and provinces and countries globally (Wurzburger et al., 2009)? The conference was organized through a collaboration between the City of Santa Fe and other members of UNESCO's Creative Cities Network, which at that time included Aswan, Egypt; Bologna, Italy; Berlin, Germany; Buenos Aires, Argentina; Montréal, Canada; Popayan, Colombia; and Seville, Spain.

Delegates from 18 countries gathered to discuss 'emerging ideas and best practices in the development of creative tourism as a powerful economic development tool for cities, provinces, states and countries' (Wurzburger et al., 2009, p. 15). Thought leaders in creativity, tourism, and entrepreneurship led panels and discussions with participants from the United States and international delegates from Canada, Nigeria, China, Japan, Australia, Pakistan, the Bahamas, and various European countries. During the conference, attendees also participated in over 40 creative tourism experiences, including workshops and classes on pottery, puppet making, cooking, tinsmithing, physical theatre and musical activities, fibre arts, and painting.

A particularly interesting aspect of the conference was that locally born and raised Santa Feans were experiencing something they grew up with in a new way. Debra Garcia y Griego, current Executive Director of the City of Santa Fe Arts Commission and participant at the 2008 conference, described her experiences with different workshops:

> Those traditions have just always been part of my working reality. But the experience of going through actual workshops with artists made me understand them and experience them in a way that I never have before. And gave me an appreciation of my own culture that I've grown up in. And so to me the potential impact for a visitor, you know, you come here, you see the tin workshop, you see the micaceous clay, you eat the food, that's all well and good. But when you have that one-on-one experience with somebody who sits there and sort of holds your hand and makes a really deep personal connection, you suddenly understand that in a way that you never appreciated before. (Debra Garcia y Griego, personal communication, 6 November 2012)

Developing creative tourism in Santa Fe

The Santa Fe Creative Tourism Initiative emerged out of the 2008 conference. The Creative Tourism Initiative worked with artists and arts businesses to develop and promote workshops that allow visitors to experience Santa Fe's unique culture in a hands-on fashion. After the conference, the conference website was repurposed into an artist's business workshop directory of over 235 year-round arts-related workshops. These workshops were grouped under numerous categories, including: agritourism, assemblage and collage, mixed media and book arts, culinary arts, glass and jewellery, painting, sculpture, photography, pottery, science, theatre, dance and music, spiritual classes, and the more traditional artwork of New Mexico (fibre arts, tinsmithing, and woodworking). Beginning 2010 until 2015, the website generated over US$297,000 in reported income for artists providing workshops to visitors. From 2009 to July 2015, over 500 artists and business owners received consultations and instructive classes on developing creative tourism workshops and experiences. The website's offer of creative workshops rose from 40 to 222 workshops, with a high of 235 ongoing workshops in 2015. Artists listed on the Santa Fe Creative Tourism website reported increases in workshop bookings from their association with the Santa Fe Creative Tourism Initiative. The avenue of promotion for the Santa Fe Creative Tourism website was largely web-based marketing using content creation and social media. Artists were encouraged to supply the initiative with content for posts and interviews.

Over 80,000 words were written on workshop-related activities geared towards Santa Fe artists and businesses to entice visitors into participation. This content included how-to's, featured artist interviews, testimonials, tips and techniques, and a mix of artist-submitted content from personal storytelling to professional tips. The content was a vehicle to introduce potential clients to the community of artist workshops in Santa Fe.

The Santa Fe Creative Tourism Initiative also took an active role in training new artist workshop providers, taking place in both fall and spring of the year. The programme planned a ten-week business series class for artists interested in developing creative tourism programming with opportunities for one-on-one consultations with tourism, social media, and marketing professionals. According to the *Creative Tourism Report* for 2012/2013 (Hanifl, 2013), workshops presented by the initiative included: how to create and distributing press releases, how to create basic websites using blogs, how to harness social media, email marketing, and promoting artist work using digital video. Along with these classes came support from the community offering various trainings on professional web design, business tips, professional photo instruction, pricing artwork, and business marketing, among other topics. Organizations that presented included Santa Fe Web Design, WESST Business Incubator, City of Santa Fe Arts Commission, City of Santa Fe Community Gallery, representatives from the Santa Fe International Folk Art Market, City of Santa Fe Convention and Visitors Bureau, and various local curators, tourism professionals, and community members (Hanifl, 2013, p. 6). The artist-entrepreneurs who took advantage of these opportunities saw heightened promotion and profile for their business. For example, Elizabeth Mesh, owner of New Mexico Artist for Hire, remarked:

> Santa Fe Creative Tourism has helped to get the word out about my business in so many ways. They do this with innovative marketing, upkeep on the website, and continual promotional help in the form of published interviews, and marketing lectures. Best of all, I

see that, in general, they are passionate about supporting the work of artists in words and deeds. Santa Fe is a better town for having this kind of collaboration between artists and the city. (cited in Hanifl, 2015b, p. 66)

Another component of the Santa Fe Creative Tourism Initiative was the creation of DIY Santa Fe, which was a month-long festival of arts-related workshops throughout the month of March. In collaboration with multiple Santa Fe hotels, visitors had the chance to take packaged workshops from the many and varied artists in Santa Fe. Featured workshops included native tinsmith Sharon Candelario teaching traditional tin work in the village of Chimayo (located just outside of Santa Fe), Capoeira Regional Classes for Adults, Photo Collage and Mixed Media Workshop with Gail Buono, Photo Encaustic Demonstrations with Angel Wynn, and All Levels Trapeze Class at Wise Fools Studio. According to the *Creative Tourism Report* for 2014/2015,

> Participating artists offer workshops and classes at their homes or studios, throughout March. March visitors enjoyed special rates on accommodation at select locations, including: The Lodge at Santa Fe, Hotel St. Francis, Hotel Chimayo, Casa Cuma Bed and Breakfast, Two Casitas Vacation Rentals, The Inn and Spa at Loretto, Bishops Lodge; and various guesthouse rentals. Special social media-driven contests, sweepstakes, and giveaways help to promote DIY events, with participating artists and Heritage Hotels providing free workshops and lodging for winning entries. Entries came in from all over the country, with winners coming from Texas, Kentucky, and Minnesota. Since its inception, the March event has contributed a total of $69,314 in earned revenue for artists and participating accommodations ($20,763 in 2012; $20,099 in 2013, $14,067 in 2014, $14,385 in 2015). (Hanifl, 2015a, p. 11)

Julie Claire, an artist and creativity coach, reflected on her participation:

> I have been growing my intuitive painting and creativity coaching business in Santa Fe for over four years; and in the last year and a half that I have been part of Santa Fe Creative Tourism my business has finally become financially sustainable and successful. My painting workshops are often half full of people who have discovered me via the SF Creative Tourism website. Some of these participants make it a point to work with me seasonally and repeatedly, having found what they were looking for in Santa Fe as a creative experience. I regularly bring in more than $500/month and at times over $1000 in a month due to SF Creative Tourism. (Cited in Hanifl, 2015b, p. 68)

Surveying creative tourism artists

Anecdotal evidence from artists like Julie Claire indicated that Santa Fe Creative Tourism was creating economic benefits for artists. But there was a political and administrative need to develop quantitative measures of the economic impact as well.

Table 9.1   Reported earned revenue from Santa Fe Creative Tourism artists, 2010–11 to 2014–15

Year	Reported income (US$)	Per cent reporting (%)
2010–11	30 594	Information not available
2011–12	40 790	17
2012–13	62 782	21.5
2013–14	83 772	23.2
2014–15	79 528	23.3

Santa Fe Creative Tourism's standard reporting efforts were limited to economic benefits that can be traced directly to the programme's website, and while the information gathered provides a useful glimpse into the programme's effectiveness, it cannot capture the complete picture. Since the programme's inception, artist reporting has averaged at around 20 per cent, meaning a great deal of data goes uncollected. Furthermore, many reporting artists and organizations failed to gather accurate marketing data, such as where their students come from, how they find their workshops, and so forth. Thus, the continued efforts of the City of Santa Fe Arts Commission and Santa Fe Creative Tourism to reach and educate more local artists through the professional training series remain essential for a clearer understanding of the full impact that Santa Fe Creative Tourism, artists, and art education have on the local economy. Table 9.1 presents the reported income from creative tourism workshops for participating artists.

Table 9.1 shows that between 2010–11 and 2014–15, artists reported US$297,466 in revenue attributed to their participation in Santa Fe Creative Tourism. But with only 23 per cent of artists reporting, this probably represents a small proportion of total revenues. While Santa Fe Creative Tourism took steps to improve the integrity and efficiency of these reporting efforts, other research and data collection activities have helped to supplement unreported economic impact.

For example, in March 2014, I conducted a research project in fulfilment of requirements for a Master of Science in Arts Management at the University of Oregon's Arts and Administration Program. The project, entitled 'What is the Economic Value of Creative Tourism in Santa Fe, New Mexico?', set out to assess the scope, nature, and extent of creative tourism activities in Santa Fe; to evaluate the characteristics of a thriving arts and culture sector to support creative tourism activities; and to identify and assess the economic value of creative tourism activities in Santa Fe.

A critical portion of this project consisted of a survey of 100 artists and organizations providing arts workshops in Santa Fe County. For the purposes of this survey, students coming from outside of Santa Fe County were considered 'tourists'. The 35 survey respondents, all active participants in the Santa Fe Creative Tourism programme, reported over US$560,000 in workshop sales to tourists between January and December 2013, in addition to over US$485,000 in workshop sales to Santa Fe County residents, for a total of over US$1 million in workshop sales alone. Furthermore, these numbers do not factor in some of the Santa Fe arts community's largest and best-established members, including world-renowned organizations such as the Santa Fe Photographic Workshops, the Santa Fe School of Cooking, and the Ghost Ranch Education and Retreat Center. Even with these limitations, the survey indicated that Santa Fe Creative Tourism was an active player in a multi-million-dollar creative tourism industry.

Directions for future research

The experience of the Santa Fe Creative Tourism programme shows that creative tourism can generate significant economic benefits as well as other, less tangible benefits for artists and the local community. But the gaps in the empirical data generated by the programme also indicate that there are a lot of potential research areas that still need to be addressed.

While it was often suggested that creative tourism was the next big trend in experiential travel, a significant gap existed in New Mexico in examining the processes through which 'creative tourism' activities are contributing financially to the creative economy. Even though Santa Fe Creative Tourism has managed to generate information on the economic impact of activities booked via their website, the research conducted by Hanifl (2015b) indicated many other areas of impact that were not being measured (for example, workshops booked directly with other suppliers, as well as non-economic types of impacts). This situation is not unique to Santa Fe, but is found in many destinations developing creative tourism.

There is therefore considerable potential in developing value chain analyses of creative tourism destinations to provide a better understanding of the flow of resources between tourists, creative enterprises, tourism organizations, and the public sector. For Santa Fe, it appears that the development of a creative tourism programme by the public sector helped to create a flow of income to local artists. However, it is less clear what types of artists benefit most, or the extent to which the artists also need to engage in marketing activities in order to maximize their economic benefits. It would also be interesting to look at the development of revenues over time, and to consider the extent to which a creative tourism programme can increase revenues relative to other tourism marketing or development options. The cultural sector often complains that the development of cultural tourism, which depends on the attractiveness of culture, usually generates much more income for tourism enterprises than for cultural organizations. It would be interesting to see if the same problem occurs with creative tourism development, or if the closer personal contact between artists and tourists ensures that a greater proportion of total revenues accrue to cultural and creative organizations.

The Santa Fe Creative Tourism programme was also designed to reinforce the identity of the city as a creative place. But little research has been conducted on how creative tourism contributes to identity formation. Theoretically, creative tourism should help to develop place identity by supporting artists and particular art forms that are connected with the destination. These help to develop the look and feel of the place as well as provide an attraction for potential visitors. It might be interesting to investigate the relationship between well-known regions and associated art forms (for example, Pacific Northwest and glass, New Mexico and fibre arts, Italy and cooking) and how creative activities support the arts identity in that location.

There is also a lot of research that could be done in terms of branding and marketing creative tourism. As creative tourism is being adopted in various countries, and considering the unique cultural identity of each location, the shape of creative tourism has taken many different forms with active participation as its focal point. Many countries, cities, and regions around the world have developed creative tourism, and each defines creative tourism in their own way. Future research could usefully examine how different creative tourism communities brand themselves, for example, in terms of creative tourism as a 'thing to do' or activity versus trying to brand the destination specifically as a creative tourism destination. Some destinations show the visitors what they can do, so people are interested in the activity first, then the location. From a cursory review of many of these initiatives, it appears that many of these cities, online portals, and initiatives may have spent too much money and time trying to brand themselves as a creative tourism destination instead of developing activities that visitors are interested in.

Conclusions

Santa Fe Creative Tourism was just one example of the varied creative tourism marketing efforts happening internationally and nationally. Every initiative is different depending on the location, history, culture, and artists in the community. While creative tourism plays an important part in the overall tourism industry, further research is needed to establish if it is an economic engine for a given community. Creative tourism combined with other creative endeavours (for example, festivals, performances, exhibits, and so on) is only one component of the tourism industry as a whole. Creative tourism will continue to grow and establish itself as long as tourists seek new niche activities and experiences. Creative tourism is thriving and vital in Santa Fe because it creates value for artists to become, and continue to be, entrepreneurs, therefore diversifying income sources for artists. Creative tourism also provides a resource for tourism and cultural entities to collaborate to build a unique destination. Currently, cities and regions around the world continue to establish and identify new ways to compete for limited traveller dollars. New creative tourism initiatives will be established and it is important for communities and thought leaders to take note of the strengths and challenges of their programme and to understand the ways in which creative tourism can create value. This requires structured research efforts to establish the value of creative tourism.

Future research may inform and set the groundwork for successful creative tourism initiatives around the world.

NOTES

1 As a contractor for the City of Santa Fe Arts Commission (2009 to July 2015), I was active in connecting rural artists and businesses with tourists through the development of the Santa Fe Creative Tourism Initiative. I collected and analyzed the information as an employed Creative Tourism Consultant for the City of Santa Fe Arts Commission, using the lens of my own experiences and knowledge.

2 Membership in the UNESCO Creative Cities Network also created opportunities for Santa Fe to participate in professional development exchanges that benefit the local economy. Elected officials, civil servants, curators, and artists have travelled to other cities to take part in conferences and festivals, including Arts Commissioner Michael Namingha representing the city at a design symposium in Kobe, Japan, new media presentation at the Seoul, Korea, Creative Cities Network conference, and artist exchanges with Icheon, Korea. Joint economic development opportunities for Santa Fe and Icheon, Korea, have included Icheon master artist Mr Han Sug Bong participating in the Santa Fe International Folk Art Market and at the Gebert Contemporary Gallery in Santa Fe, as well as Santa Fe artists Rose Simpson, Heidi Loewen, and Todd Lovato participating in exchanges to Korea. Exchange visits with Korea, China, and Japan have also been organized.

References

Hanifl, B. (2013), *Santa Fe Creative Tourism 2012/2013 Report*, Santa Fe: City of Santa Fe Arts Commission, accessed 9 April 2018 at https://es.scribd.com/document/163257470/Santa-Fe-Creative-Tourism-2012-2013-Report.

Hanifl, B. (2015a), *Santa Fe Creative Tourism 2014/2015 Report*, Santa Fe: City of Santa Fe Arts Commission, accessed 9 April 2018 at https://es.scribd.com/document/280650991/City-of-Santa-Fe-Creative-Tourism-2014-2015-Report.

Hanifl, B. (2015b), 'What is the economic value of creative tourism in Santa Fe, New Mexico?', Master's thesis, University of Oregon, accessed 9 April 2018 at https://scholarsbank.uoregon.edu/xmlui/handle/1794/19478.

Wurzburger, R., T. Aageson, A. Pattakos and S. Pratt (2009), *Creative Tourism, a Global Conversation: How to Provide Unique Creative Experiences for Travelers Worldwide*, Santa Fe: Sunstone Press.

10 Local impacts of creative tourism initiatives

Jutamas (Jan) Wisansing and Thanakarn (Bella) Vongvisitsin

Introduction

In Thailand, creative tourism has been envisioned as part of community-based tourism, which is perceived to be one of the effective mechanisms to achieve better quality of life and well-being of local communities. The shared core element of both creative tourism and community-based tourism is to have multiple stakeholders actively engaged in all steps of creation and development, from conception to implementation, to equitably sharing in the benefits. Once an effective innovative and managerial system is put in place, the progress of the effort needs to be monitored. An essential prerequisite for a creative tourism project is to ensure that the planning process addresses issues such as: (1) what is the local heritage and how do local people want these resources to be innovated or preserved? (2) what does genuine progress look like? and (3) how can creative tourism be managed and marketed to make local people's lives better? Although there is extensive information on impact evaluations and indicators that can be used to measure various aspects of social, economic, and environmental sustainability and well-being, the idea of *a locally owned and led measuring process/tool* is relatively new.

The goal of the study presented in this chapter is to develop more micro-approaches that can gather information to inform local decision-making and policymaking. The idea of community-owned indicators of benefits gained from a Community Benefitting through Creative Tourism (CBCT) approach reflects a change in focus, from a macro and top-down imposition of what well-being, sustainability, and quality of life should look like for communities, to a bottom-up approach that emphasizes democratic participation and empowerment in the development of locally significant understandings of the community's own well-being and its measurement. Indicators and tools developed in this manner provide vast opportunities to encourage dialogue and democratic participation in envisioning a community's goals, to measure progress towards achievement of those goals, to raise awareness and focus attention on community priorities, to provide a feedback and accountability mechanism for decision-makers, and to actively choose future desired outcomes to suit each community's contexts and local situations (Page and Connell, 2006).

This chapter offers an integrated monitoring approach at a micro level, drawing lessons from a pilot project led by the Designated Areas for Sustainable Tourism Administration (DASTA), Thailand. The CBCT model has been designed and tested as a simple 'by locals for locals' monitoring tool to understand the impacts of creative tourism. The CBCT approach was designed to monitor impacts sustainably from *end to end*, across the entire tourism value chain. This integrated impact/benefit assessment provides a set of simple and comprehensive indicators for community leaders and members to fine-tune creative tourism activities, foster community development and empowerment, and tighten social capital (social networks and trust).

DASTA is a rare example of a public-sector tourism organization established solely to achieve a community-based approach towards sustainable tourism development in Thailand. While many tourism organizations have sustainability components in their mission, their roles vary. DASTA is committed to institutionalizing this mission by allocating resources and responsibilities to ensure that 'tourism is managed by communities for communities' (http://www.dasta.or.th). Responsible for six designated areas for sustainable tourism development in Thailand, all the initiatives (i.e., low carbon destination management, creative tourism, and other forms of tourism) are designed to be learning cases; thus, best practices and toolkits reflected from the execution are systematically formulated from experiential and experimental assignments. Such cases could be replicated and adapted to other contexts.

The 13 small communities used as a pilot case example for this chapter have engaged in a multi-staged approach to community-based tourism since 2007. The project has employed an Appreciative Inquiry technique, investing in accelerating top-performing teamwork, which guided the communities through self-determined changes. Positive dialogue among diverse multi-stakeholders enabled the community issues to be identified by local people and to put their solutions into action. The aims and objectives of the project were to: (1) engage communities in co-creating creative tourism best practices; (2) build community capability and capacity to maximize benefits from tourism; (3) create local pride and self-sufficiency, minimizing the degree of dependency on outsiders; (4) provide a learning platform for the nation to understand tourism as a tool for community development; (5) offer a development framework/model for change agencies to engage communities in community-based tourism and creative tourism; (6) create new ways to work across the tourism value chain; and (7) empower leaders who can share the community-based tourism approach. This chapter offers case examples and lessons learned from the field, providing insights based on the practicalities of community-based tourism and CBCT monitoring components and processes.

Literature review

Sustainability and creative tourism: a community-based approach

Sustainable development is increasingly accepted as a fundamental objective and guideline for public policymaking and tourism initiatives (Goodwin and Santilli, 2009). It encompasses balanced integration of the economic, environmental, and socio-cultural dimensions into the development processes. Researchers in the field have made it clear that a 'better' sustainable tourism planning approach should constitute benefits for all aspects of community livelihoods, including sociological (e.g., promotion of community stability, family solidarity, and cultural identity), economic (e.g., employment, income), and environmental (e.g., conservation/preservation). It is argued that the community will benefit more from tourism development if the community members participate genuinely in making decisions that affect their welfare and in implementing the desired actions/solutions. Therefore, community-based tourism is considered to be a better form of planning process because of its participatory orientation. The main principle of the community-based tourism approach is a quest for community inputs through their active participation in tourism development processes. This manifests a significant shift in tourism planning from being a centralized, top-down approach to being a decentralized, bottom-up approach (Huras, 2015). Such an integrative and inclusive approach to planning puts an emphasis upon an understanding of the whole tourism system based on rigorous evaluative research through extensive dialogues among all stakeholders involved. The goals for tourism development should therefore be derived from, and integrated into, the overall shared community visions and aspirations.

To date, achieving such an ambitious goal has been a challenging task, particularly at a local level in developing countries. Thailand has put in place an integrated and inclusive community-based tourism planning approach, which constitutes four key elements:

1. *Goal oriented*, with a clear recognition of the role to be played by local communities that tourism could be used as a mechanism in achieving broad community and societal goals.
2. *Systematic*, drawing on experiential research to provide conceptual and predictive support for planners, and drawing on the evaluation of action-oriented planning efforts to develop best practices and theory.
3. *Democratic*, with full and meaningful citizen input from the community level up.
4. *Integrative*, placing tourism planning issues into the mainstream of planning for local enterprises, education and heritage, conservation, land use, and social justices.

All forms of tourism can provide immense opportunities for local economic development, particularly in developing countries. Tourism can generate significant income and employment; if managed properly, local natural and cultural resources could turn into valuable tourism assets. It also provides local communities with the opportunity to express pride in their own culture, thus giving the impetus to revive threatened traditions and cultural practices (Prabhakaran et al., 2014). Tourism enables interaction among diverse groups of community members within a development area. Bringing local culture and pride to the forefront also creates a networking platform for individuals of different nationalities and backgrounds, thus fostering dialogue among cultures and encouraging cultural diversity and creativity. However, if not managed properly, creative tourism can also cause irreversible damage to and changes in culture and the environment (Richards, 2014). In the rush to develop tourism industries, locals could lose control to outsiders. Investors and governments, particularly in developing countries, have often focused the bulk of their investment on promoting the sites, while overlooking the need to make adequate preparations for local communities to take control of the management process to prevent the deterioration of their cultural, natural, and social assets brought about by uncontrolled tourism (Fletcher and Archer, 1991). It is therefore vital for local communities to manage their own future. Local governments, the tourism industry, developers, and members of the community should play a supporting role in formulating policies to mitigate the negative impacts of tourism on local culture and the environment. This can only be possible if all stakeholders have a clear understanding of the interaction between tourism, development, and heritage resources.

Once a local community decides to get involved in tourism development, they must also be able to map out the potential impacts and benefits from end to end, across the entire community-based tourism value chain (Wall and Mathieson, 2006). A comprehensive and local friendly tool remains elusive. Extensive information on indicators that can be applicable to measure various aspects of social, economic, and environmental sustainability at a community level are limited. In the following subsections, the relevant research literatures are summarized as a basis for the current research.

Social Impact Assessment

Social Impact Assessment involves the processes of analyzing, monitoring, and managing the intended and unintended social consequences, both positive and negative, of planned interventions (policies, programmes, plans, and projects) and any social change processes invoked by those interventions. These assessments can enable the authorities implementing a project to not only identify social and environmental impacts, but also to put in place suitable institutional, organizational, and project-specific mechanisms to mitigate adverse effects (Gollub et al., 2003). They can also aid in bringing about greater social inclusion and participation in the design and implementation stages of the project.

Community well-being

Impacts can also be monitored and evaluated based on the level of community well-being. The Institute of Wellbeing describes well-being this way:

The presence of the highest possible quality of life in its full breadth of expression focused on but necessarily exclusive to: good living standards, robust health, a sustainable environment, vital communities, an educated populace, balanced time use, high levels of civic participation, and access to and participation in dynamic arts, culture and recreation. (The Institute of Wellbeing, cited in Murphy, 2010, p. 4)

The connection between sustainable development and well-being is worth emphasizing. As the Organisation for Economic Co-operation and Development (OECD) states, sustainable development means increasing well-being over a very long time. For communities, sustainability hinges on resilient ability, meaning they could deal with changes, reconfigure available resources in a timely manner, and recombine financial capital, local skills, and natural resources in ways that create sustainable livelihoods. Communities seeking to monitor their cultural and creative tourism progress will typically need to understand the theory of change. The starting point of any change is to take stock of the currently available economic, environmental, and social resources; together develop a shared vision regarding the use of these resources; and develop a means to evaluate progress towards identified goals. However, this systematic thinking and planning for change is not put in place in most cases.

It has been suggested that measuring cultural and creative tourism progress should focus on developing a better local economy, rather than a bigger one. It also should focus on capitalizing on existing community social capital and strengths, including business clusters and networks, rather than relying solely on external support (Weaver and Lawton, 2002). The community should work to understand what kind of economic activity and ways of life it currently has and to envision what a sustainable livelihood in the future for their locality would look like. Assessment of the existing socio-cultural, economic sectors, and environmental resources is an integral part of this exercise.

One way to evaluate cultural and creative tourism performance is through a triple bottom line audit. This is an approach based on economic dimension insights that also incorporates the socio-cultural and environmental dimensions. It is an auditing and reporting framework for measuring economic, environmental, and socio-cultural performance. An audit is a process that assesses performance through changes over time. Improvement or progress could be monitored against a set of established baseline indicators from the starting point. Economic-oriented approaches often use money as the unit of measurement. This is useful because it allows for a more straightforward comparison across all tourism activities and tourism incomes generated from related goods and services. However, there are also limitations of this approach. The use of money or tourism revenue as a common measurement unit is problematic because the relationship between well-being and money is not always clear and some of the contributions made by money to well-being are hard to identify (Untong et al., 2006). For instance, studies have shown that even very poor people may feel happy and have positive well-being, and, conversely, that after a certain level, income no longer contributes significantly to increasing well-being.

Social capitals

Increasingly, many communities and researchers maintain that there are benefits of undertaking cultural and creative tourism with a participatory planning process; this is said to be independent of the outcomes. The participatory nature of community-based tourism helps strengthen the norms and networks that enable people to act collectively (Woolcock and Narayan, 2000, p. 226). Social capital is increasingly regarded as a source of human welfare, complementing conventional asset categories such as natural, physical, and human capital (Grootaert, 1998, p. 1). Undeniably, tourism has an influence on social structures in rural societies: with new sources of income, some groups have gained in status and others have lost ground. Tourism could also promote the formation of new institutions. It has also offered opportunities to develop and expand hierarchical, extra-community networks (Woolcock and Narayan, 2000).

Research literatures indicate that the monitoring system could be made up of a set of different indicators. It could be drawn up in a variety of ways into an instrument that any community at any scale of destination can pick up and implement as their own monitoring toolkit (Lacher and Nepal, 2010). It can be a useful way to track cultural and creative tourism performance and make better management decisions, as well as to influence policymakers in a more systemic manner for any required changes in policies and execution plans. The basic principle of the CBCT indicator system is that destination responsibility, ownership, and decision-making are shared. Engaging a group to come together and work together to collect and report information is a powerful way to undertake an effective monitoring system. Changes could be observed through the indicators listed in Table 10.1, which provides a set of CBCT indicators that have been generated by communities for communities from the pilot project.

Research methodology

An action research approach was used to capture the process and evidence-based cases. The aim was to build a theoretical foundation and a practical yet simple tool which can be used by community leaders and members. The researchers have been participating in the initiatives for the past five years, since their conception. Having realized the background of the pilot projects in detail, brainstorming techniques and focus group facilitation were employed with 110 key informants from the 13 communities to deepen understanding on how creative tourism was started and how the process has benefitted the community. The assessments were also informed by field visits to all communities and other local-level stakeholders to learn about their perspectives and priorities. The consultations made use of participatory assessment methodologies such as participatory rural appraisal (PRA). These methodologies provide tools for collaborating with local people in analysis and planning, and they can contribute to the scrutiny of the data collected, which can lead to development of action plans and participation strategies. Key elements

Table 10.1 Summary of Community Benefitting through Creative Tourism (CBCT) indicators

Economic quality indicators
1. Increase in local employment
2. Agricultural products are increasingly used in tourism sectors
3. Annual income increased
4. Younger generation returns home with job opportunities
5. New product development by local people
6. Local wisdom is valued and added to new product
7. New business development by locals
8. Market opportunities for handicraft and local artisans
9. Local sourcing and nearby communities benefit from tourism
10. Household debt decreasing

Socio-cultural indicators
1. Create jobs for women
2. Heritage preservation by younger generation
3. Family bonding
4. Health and wellness
5. Understanding cultural diversities
6. Revive cultures and traditions
7. Equality in participation of all ages and genders
8. Promotion of local senses of place and local history
9. Older generation is happy
10. Local pride

Environmental quality indicators
1. Waste decreased
2. Effective use of water
3. Lessen plastic uses
4. Increase in the use of natural materials
5. Energy consumption is managed effectively
6. Increase green spaces and areas
7. Increase environmental awareness
8. Young people are aware of climate changes
9. Increase in understanding about sustainable development
10. Waste management improved

Leadership indicators
1. Listen deeply and find agreed and shared solutions
2. Be more visionary in the future of communities
3. Build teamwork
4. Communication skills improved
5. Can see situations more systematically
6. Have courage to change
7. Ability to persuade others
8. Improve coordination skills

of all related tourism activities were mapped and visualized for each of the 13 communities studied. Community leaders and diverse stakeholders were invited to help elicit the structure of their creative tourism system and to depict creative tourism activities, the value chain, and the structure and system of existing income distributions. Tourist expenditures data were collected. A brainstorming technique was then used to co-analyse the data with multiple stakeholders. This was to identify a complete impact assessment, encompassing socio-cultural, economic, and environmental dimensions.

Developing the CBCT monitoring tool

The development of the locally owned monitoring tool employed DASTA's multi-stakeholders approach. An important step was to create a comprehensive definition of 'community'. A total of 140 full-time DASTA staff engages with complete tourism communities, from high-level policymakers, politicians, and business owners to young children and elderly residents in a small village. Staff travel throughout the year to help communities visualize sustainable tourism goals and align these with community priorities. This entails co-creating CBCT approaches by: redefining creative tourism expectations; specifying accountability, monitoring results, and rewarding progress; capacity building; and designing equitable dissemination of benefits.

To emphasize that tourism is not developed solely for the sake of tourism, a multi-stakeholder map was created. This identified the landscape of involved actors across the totality of what comprised the communities' well-being. Based on Global Sustainable Tourism Criteria, community-based tourism criteria were developed and executed with the following partners, representing a diverse range of sectors:

- Community members/leaders: 13 community tourism clubs and networks and expanded to 53 communities/clubs.
- Academic institutions: National Institute of Development Administration (NIDA), Thailand Research Fund, and Community-Based Tourism Institute (CBT-i).
- Development organizations: Tourism Department, Ministry of Tourism and Sports, Community Development Department, and Agricultural Department.
- Representatives of local administration: Thai Sub-district Administration Association and the National Municipal League of Thailand.
- Marketing bodies: Tourism Authority of Thailand, Tourism Council of Thailand (77 tourism-related businesses), Thai Ecotourism and Adventure Travel Association, and community-based tourism specialized travel consultants and agencies.
- Community representatives (role models): from Bangnamphueng Sub-district administration, community-based tourism of Baan Prasat, and ecotourism community of Baan Maekampong.
- Working collaboratively with the Global Sustainable Tourism Council

(GSTC), Asian Ecotourism Network (AEN), and Earthcheck to leverage additional positive opportunities.

The initial scale of the project involved a grassroots team of 495 individuals from 13 communities in six designated areas. These leading individuals created the CBCT shared goals, engaged their family members and sub-communities, and, in a later stage, were able to engage with larger groups in the communities (which have a total population of 68,069). The engagement of these larger groups created a ripple effect for positive changes in their districts and provinces, eventually gaining recognition in the region.

In the development of the CBCT monitoring tool, it was found that it is important to facilitate dialogue by addressing five issues respectively: (1) creative tourist activities; (2) tourist spending; (3) creative tourism income; (4) income distribution; and (5) community fund. Tourism economics jargon was avoided to ease the discussion. In a step-by-step process, economic benefits gained from creative tourism operations were highlighted. The framework aimed to capture how each community is benefitting through creative tourism (CBCT).

Conceptualizing leakages and linkages of their creative tourism operations through the tool permitted a critical and complete 'triple bottom line' evaluation of the creative tourism initiatives. Although the criteria used focused on income distribution, social impact assessment and environmental issues were also examined. Strategies to develop linkages were derived as a result of this close examination. Figure 10.1 presents the framework developed through in-depth discussions with all 13 pilot communities. The framework was used as a thinking tool to explain the monitoring system and then data were collected on a monthly basis.

Monitoring results and impacts

The CBCT – Linkages and Leakages economic monitoring showed an overall leakage rate (for all 13 pilot communities) to be between 18 and 43 per cent prior to implementation of the projects. Each community collected monthly data as shown in Figure 10.2, which has been developed and is used as a simple Excel file. An aggregated total of about 3 million baht (US$85,000) is earned each month from tourism for 13 communities. The tool stimulates communities to open up a dialogue on how they could do better to retain benefits within their area and also to distribute income more efficiently. These data could also help indicate sources of energy consumption and wastes.

The communities carefully monitored the management of procurements of food ingredients and the food production process because it was found that a high percentage of economic leakages fall into the cost of procurement of ingredients and raw materials (predominantly food and beverage and souvenir production). Agricultural-based assets and locally grown produce have since been nurtured and

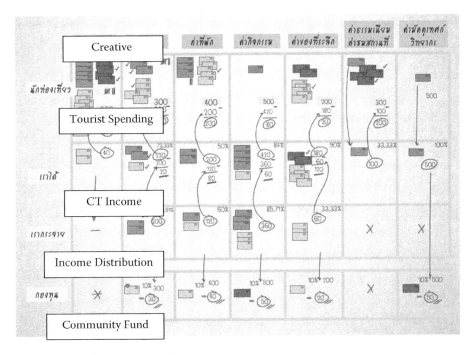

Source: Created by Jutamas Wisansing.

Figure 10.1   Community Benefitting through Creative Tourism – Linkages and Leakages monitoring tool

Linkages and Leakages

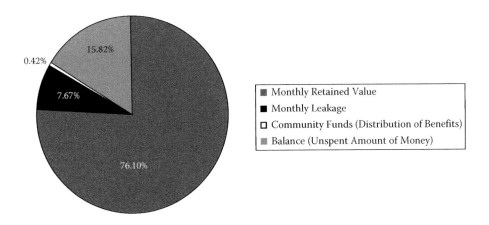

Figure 10.2   Tourist expenditures and data collection (monitoring system): an example

Table 10.2   Community Benefitting through Creative Tourism – Linkages and Leakages monitoring result

January				
Monthly Tourist Expenditure				Total
Number of tourists		288		
Expenditures per person		498.26		143 500
Revenue		Total	%	Notes
	Transportation	99 000	69	
	Food and beverage	20 000	14	
	Accommodation	–	0	
	Activities	–	0	
	Souvenirs	–	0	
	Attraction fees	–	0	
	Guides/interpretation	–	0	
	Others	–	0	
	Community fund contribution	24 500	17	
Total revenue		143 500	100	
Expenses		Retained Value	Leakage	Total
Transportation	Transportation	89 200	9800	99 000
F&B	Cook and housekeeping	20 000	–	20 000
	Ingredients	–	–	–
Accommodation	Accommodation	–	–	–
	Utilities	–	1200	1200
	Laundry	–	–	–
Activities	Manpower	–	–	–
	Materials	–	–	–
Souvenirs	Cost of procurement	–	–	–
	Production	–	–	–
Attractions	Entrance fees		–	–
Guides	Guides/interpretation fees	–	–	–
Other expenses	Others	–	–	–
Total expenses (for outside tourism club)		109 200	11 000	120 200
Expenses (paid to tourism club)				–
Profits	Administration fees (management team)	–	–	–
	Utilities	–	–	–
	Income tax	–	–	–
	Contribution to community fund	–	–	–
	Marketing and PR	–	–	–
	Others	–	–	–

Table 10.2   (continued)

January			
Expenses	Retained Value	Leakage	Total
Total expenses (paid to tourism club)	–	–	–
Retained value/leakage	109 200	11 000	120 200

Community Funds (Distribution of benefits)		
Community funds (distribution of benefits)		23 300
Fund	Welfare tourism club members	–
	Infrastructure	–
	Environmental quality	–
	Heritage	–
	Local enterprises	–
	Others	600
	Distribution of benefits (community funds)	600
	Remaining	22 700

Linkages and Leakages		Total	%
	Monthly tourist expenditure	143 500	100.00
	Monthly retained value	109 200	76.10
	Monthly leakage	11 000	7.67
	Community funds (distribution of benefits)	600	0.42
	Balance (Unspent amount of money)	22 700	15.82

turned to use in creative foodie tourism activities, enabling leakages to be reduced to an average of 10 per cent and stimulating local employment in the agricultural sector. Gastronomic trails were designed for better value chain management. Souvenirs were developed from local stories and local materials – these created a 10 per cent increase in jobs for retired women and opportunities for local young designers. Furthermore, communities actively promote local seasonality for tourists, with local bio-diversities becoming more appreciated.

As the vision was implemented and expanded, communities with CBCT projects developed an evidence base of improvement in six key community issues: (1) health and wellness; (2) economics (job creation and income distribution); (3) family relations and happiness; (4) leadership and management skills; (5) environmental issues; and (6) transparency and democracy. Engaged communities apply CBCT leakages and linkages across the value chain to monitor the social, economic, and environmental consequences of their activities. Each community has, in effect, created an inventory of opportunities that can be further investigated, prioritized, and addressed. Rethinking their tourism activities and impacts through the CBCT model becomes routine. An array of positive impacts is evident, for example:

- An increase in diversity, with 50 per cent of the total team leaders being women.
- Five to 10 per cent of the young generation is returning home, attracted by new business opportunities.
- All the communities' sourcing emphasizes purchases from local producers, creating backward economic linkages and stimulating agriculture and local food production.
- Gastronomic trails are designed to tell rich stories about local heritage, strengthening local identities and sense of community. For example, the Takientia community now offers coconut trails. This creative programme includes local food foraging, cooking classes, and ancillary services, thus reducing economic leakages.

Discussion

Since the implementation of the CBCT project in 2007, each participating community has elevated their leadership in CBCT management and partnered their sustainability strategy with tourism industry actors; for example, the campaign 'village to the world' was launched with travel agencies, suppliers, and airlines. A creative incentive trip for corporations was also initiated for the MICE market (Meetings, Incentives, Conventions, and Exhibitions tourism segment) under the theme 'meet in the village'. DASTA invests in community empowerment and engagement by providing seed funds of US$1 million annually. The grassroots stakeholders now are institutionalized as a Tourism Club, and public and private partners have developed genuine business partnerships with these communities in the form of social enterprises. This CBCT model redefines the old form of charity-oriented partnership as a healthy co-created responsible value chain business model. DASTA is now acting as a facilitator to leverage continuous positive dialogue among multi-stakeholders and to sustain the longevity and approach of the CBCT throughout the country.

Directions for future research

This research has outlined a set of indicators that has been generated from specific cases and contexts. In particular, it has highlighted the benefits of locally led creative tourism in generating a range of quality of life benefits for local communities. The indicators used in the current study could be developed and applied in a range of different settings to analyze the costs and benefits of creative tourism development and to compare the effects of different creative development strategies. As well as addressing basic questions such as whether the benefits of creative tourism outweigh the costs, a broader quality of life approach to monitoring and evaluation could help to identify the specific ways in which creative tourism could help local communities. For example, can the development of creative activities help to increase feelings of local pride and/or stimulate more young people to remain in rural communities?

Such analyses might also help to identify how creative processes can help local communities to innovate and provide future development potential. Studies of communities in Thailand underline the potential for developing creative skills that can enhance the income-generation potential of local people, such as valorizing gastronomic skills and knowledge. It is also important to understand how such skills can be passed between generations and between different communities in order to develop sustainability and ensure the spread of benefits from creative tourism. Understanding the functioning of such creative processes can also help to guide the development of effective management systems in local communities.

References

Fletcher, J.E. and B.H. Archer (1991), 'The development and application of multiplier analysis', in E. Cooper (ed.), *Progress in Tourism, Recreation and Hospitality Management*, Vol. 3, London: Belhaven Press, pp. 28–47.

Gollub, J., A. Hosier and G. Woo (2003), *Using Cluster-based Economic Strategy to Minimize Tourism Leakages*, UNWTO, accessed 25 June 2017 at https://pdfs.semanticscholar.org/8167/f77ba6099b340c529da5a2beec07b734a578.pdf.

Goodwin, H. and R. Santilli (2009), 'Community-based tourism: a success?', ICRT Occasional Paper no. 11, German Development Agency (GTZ), accessed 6 May 2018 at http://www.haroldgoodwin.info/uploads/CBTaSuccessPubpdf.pdf.

Grootaert, C. (1998), 'Social capital: the missing link?', World Bank, accessed 25 June 2017 at http://siteresources.worldbank.org/INTSOCIALCAPITAL/Resources/Social-Capital-Initiative-Working-Paper-Series/SCI-WPS-03.pdf.

Huras, C. (2015), '"Community-based creative tourism" as a strategy for poverty reduction', Thesis, Taipei National University of the Arts.

Lacher, R.G. and S.K. Nepal (2010), 'From leakages to linkages: local-level strategies for capturing tourism revenue in northern Thailand', *Tourism Geographies*, **12** (1), 77–99.

Murphy, B. (2010), 'Community well-being: an overview of the concept', Nuclear Waste Management Organization, accessed 27 June 2017 at http://datacat.cbrdi.ca/sites/default/files/attachments/Best-Practices-in-Community-Well-Being-Monitoring%5B1%5D.pdf.

Page, S. and J. Connell (2006), *Tourism: A Modern Synthesis*, London: Thompson Learning.

Prabhakaran, S., V. Nair and S. Ramachandran (2014), 'Community participation in rural tourism: towards a conceptual framework', *Procedia Social and Behavioural Sciences*, **144**, 290–5.

Richards, G. (2014), *Tourism and the Creative Economy*, Paris: OECD Studies on Tourism.

Untong, A., S. Phuangsaichai, N. Taweelertkunthon and J. Tejawaree (2006), 'Income distribution and community-based tourism: three case studies in Thailand', *Journal of GMS Development Studies*, **3**, 69–81.

Wall, G. and A. Mathieson (2006), *Tourism: Change, Impacts and Opportunities*, Harlow, UK: Pearson Education.

Weaver, D. and L. Lawton (2002), *Tourism Management*, 2nd edn, Milton: John Wiley and Sons Australia.

Woolcock, M. and D. Narayan (2000), 'Social capital: implications for development theory, research, and policy', *The World Bank Research Observer*, **15** (2), 225–49.

11 The development of creative tourism in rural areas of Russia: issues of entrepreneurial ability, cooperation, and social inclusion

Marina Matetskaya, Alexandra Svyatunenko, and Olga Gracheva

Sustainable development in rural areas is one of the Russian government's current policy priorities (see Ministry of Agriculture of the Russian Federation, 2017; Ministry of Economic Development of the Russian Federation, 2017; Russia Tourism, 2017a). These areas are usually characterized by demographic decline, low quality of life, low income, and unemployment. Internal migration from rural areas to cities is growing because residents want to achieve better economic, social, environmental, and public health outcomes. The support of non-agricultural activities in these areas, particularly rural tourism, generates infrastructure and jobs for residents, primarily in the service sector.

In recent years, the commitment of stakeholders to rural tourism has been growing in the Russian regions. Entrepreneurs are becoming the creators of new tourist products through their interaction with local residents, businesses, and government authorities. But even with Russia's tremendous diversity, its natural and cultural monuments, and its historical and new crafts, the tourism industry continues to use only a small fraction of its rich potential. In order to develop an authentic touristic product for rural regions in Russia, it is important to create tourism-related programmes using a wide range of tools to successfully implement them in rural areas. However, the particular features of these areas, such as poor transport and underdeveloped hospitality infrastructure, mean that rural tourism initiatives differ from those of city tourism.

This chapter examines the experience of several projects initiated by the non-governmental organization (NGO) 'Kaykino Creative Projects' in the rural region of Leningrad, which aim to support the initiatives of local residents in the field of rural creative tourism (Kaykino Creative Projects, 2017). Along with other governmental support measures and private investments, we believe that these projects have a number of advantages in terms of collaborating with local communities, including craftspeople (artisans), who represent a specific type of business. These cases are contextualized through an academic literature review conducted as part of the case study research, which discusses issues such as management tools employed by tourism projects in rural areas, the approaches of community engagement in tourism-related projects, and creative tourism models in rural areas. The chapter

137

explores the issues of how to lead territorial development projects, techniques that could be used to integrate rural communities (including authorities, entrepreneurs, and farmers) in creative tourism and related decision-making, and the participation of craftspeople and artisans in the production of creative tourism products and services.

Developing rural areas through tourism

As a factor in the development of rural areas, tourism is a central research topic. Common issues include the role of local authorities and community engagement, opportunities and risks for small business, special governmental support in the form of loans and rural tourism initiative programmes (accommodation, handicrafts, social services, and so on), and the more general economic and social effects of tourism practices (e.g., infrastructure growth and social well-being). At the same time, a range of specific tools and algorithms to manage tourism initiatives in rural areas are in great demand. Methods of communication and interaction with local residents, entrepreneurs, and other actors are just beginning to be analyzed and discussed in research and practice (Richards and Hall, 2000; Moscardo, 2014; Kangas, 2017).

Today, there is no generally accepted definition of rural tourism because it is characterized by diversity in all its aspects, from types of accommodation to various options for hanging out in the countryside (Lane, 1994). In the research presented in this chapter, we follow the definition offered by Woods and McDonagh (2011), who described rural tourists as people whose activities focus on the consumption of rural experiences, cultures, landscapes, and artefacts that occur on farms or in rural communities. This definition is wider than that of agritourism, which normally implicates holidays on farms or those initiatives closely related to farm owners and farm activities (Arroyo et al., 2013).

Rural tourism became a regeneration mechanism as it began to attract new, often skilled, and well-resourced migrants from cities to the countryside – also known as lifestyle entrepreneurs (Ateljevic and Doorne, 2000) – who help to open up rural societies (Persson et al., 1997). Consequently, tourism activities have become more complex due to the manifold businesses now involved in providing them (Clemenson and Lane, 1997).

Tourism has proven to be efficient in the economic and social reconstruction of rural areas as well as in preserving existing lifestyles (Salehi and Nadi, 2014). Rural tourism brings in around 15 to 30 per cent of the total income of the European tourist industry (European Commission – Agriculture and Rural Development, 2013, pp. 256–7). However, according to the estimates of the Federal Agency for Tourism, the share of rural tourism in the Russian tourism market was no higher than 2 per cent in 2015 (The Russian Government, 2016).

There are some obvious leaders among the Russian regions: the Republic of Karelia; the Vladimir Region; the Altai Territory; the Leningrad, Pskov, Vologda, Yaroslavl, Kaluga, and Astrakhan Regions; and the Chuvash Republic. Comparatively new rural tourism destinations are the Krasnodar Territory, the Stavropol Territory, and the Republic of North Ossetia-Alania. The most popular tourism products are ethnic parks based on cultural traditions and experiences (e.g., 'Ethnomir' (http://ethnomir.ru/) and 'Mandrogi' (http://en.mandrogi.ru/); thematic tours (e.g., cruises in the Baikal, tours of Buddhist temples or tours of the Tea Route); rural events tourism (e.g., 'Goose Fights' and the 'Cucumber Festival'); and ecological, hunting, fishing, and jeep tours (The National Calendar of Events, 2017).

The huge scale and diversity of the Russian regions entails high transportation and other related costs as well as a variety of impressions and experiences. Russian national culture is unified, but each rural area has its own unique history, traditions, heritage, and people, which form the particular basis of each specific tourism product. In the following section, we outline some general principles and elements that facilitate the development of tourism in rural areas.

The evolution patterns of rural areas

A literature review shows that tourism-related projects and initiatives mainly depend on the active participation of the local population (McGehee and Andereck, 2004; Látková and Vogt, 2012) as well as their collaboration in networks. The management of these networks relies on models of more or less participative governance and guidance by more or less charismatic leaders. Local communities (especially those with small and medium-sized businesses, NGOs, and tourist information centres) stand out as central stakeholders in determining and shaping the development of territories (Dana et al., 2014).

Many Russian residents have suburban houses and plots, the scale, quality, and location of which depend on income level. Therefore, agritourism has not become a mass leisure activity for Russians themselves, even those living in the cities. However, new forms of leisure activities related not only to agriculture, sports activities, and natural resources, but also to cognitive activities such as learning and training, obtaining new experience or knowledge, and individual skill development and communication are in great demand. New forms of agritourism that include elements of recreation and entertainment could potentially become an attractive niche for entrepreneurs (Lane and Kastenholz, 2015). Thus, tourism in rural areas is not only limited to the travel services offered such as accommodation, luxury services, and visiting attractions but can be open to broad opportunities for designing creative tourism products and experiences based on learning, tasting, seeing, doing, cooperation, and involvement (Richards, 2011, pp. 1238–40).

Entrepreneurs must cooperate to provide a full package of offerings for tourists, as tourists expect high-quality services and extraordinary impressions: 'they want to buy feelings and not products' (Trauer, 2006, p. 183). Experiences are considered to be the new focus of the product in the tourist industry (Pine and Gilmore, 1999). For example, winemaking could be the primary reason for visiting the countryside but additional cultural, entertainment, and gastronomy services and participatory activities could broaden the experience and the horizons of tourists as well as increase the overall economic benefits gained from their visit (Smith et al., 2010). However, for many years, Russian rural fairs and festivals have remained on a low, 'consumer-style' level.

Researchers have emphasized that local food is an important part of the tourist experience in rural areas. High-quality cuisine and gastronomy based on organic products and unique recipes transforms culinary heritage into a popular tourism product (Renko et al., 2010; Sánchez-Cañizares and López-Guzmán, 2012; Folorunso Adeyinka-Ojo and Khoo-Lattimore, 2013). Moreover, the process of directly participating in cooking the dishes can be an engaging activity for tourists. To create a competitive tourism product, 'The Gastronomic Map of Russia' was implemented in 2016 with the support of the Federal Agency for Tourism (Foodika, 2017; Readymag, 2017; Russia Tourism, 2017b). The engagement of stakeholders in the development of this map aimed to generate new forms of tourism products, including the cooking and serving of food. Both gastronomy and traditional crafts can open a window into the historical past of the countryside and enable visitors to engage directly with 'the past' in the present, serving as important 'touchstones' towards the development of creative tourism in rural areas.

Another example of a successful project of creative tourism in rural areas around Russia is Altourism (http://www.altourism.ru/travel-to-russian-villages). Each Altourism programme suggests tourist immersions into the local life and context, not only through gastronomic or craft activities, but also using everyday activities such as weaving, building, restoration, gardening, and so on.

Prospects for creative tourism

Creative tourism satisfies the need for an interactive experience that promotes personal development and an understanding of the uniqueness of the destination (Richards and Raymond, 2000). It directly depends on tourists' active participation in the co-production of valuable products and services (Richards and Wilson, 2006). To some extent, creative tourism can be seen as an innovative approach to place and tourism development. Interaction between tourists and local residents can be a tool for increasing the competitiveness of destinations, especially if they have no prominent heritage in terms of cultural and historical sites (Kiralova and Malachovsky, 2015).

This potential is accompanied by challenges related to product development and opportunity exploitation (Alsos et al., 2014). While activating the 'artisan–tourist' communication channel can contribute to a better lifestyle for the local population

(Zeppenfeld, 2017) and cooperation between craft centres and tourism organizations can promote the development of tourism and the construction of a local brand (Kiralova and Malachovsky, 2015; Sasu and Epuran, 2016), the co-creation of craft souvenirs is faced with issues such as a limited assortment of ideas, mixed styles, or unsatisfactory marketing strategies (Tan et al., 2013).

The development of rural tourism requires creative effort on the part of entrepreneurs to sustainably carry on agricultural and gastronomic businesses as well as the production of handmade arts and crafts (Solvoll et al., 2015). It remains crucial to initiate bottom-up, creative, and cultural industry-led cooperation with the ability to cope with the decentralized, multi-stakeholder nature of the rural tourism business. There is also a need to embrace the complexities and skill requirements of both new marketing media and experiential marketing (McGehee and Kim, 2004).

Creative tourism initiatives by the NGO Kaykino Creative Projects

In recent years, the activities of local resource centres run by NGOs are becoming broader than just interaction with local entrepreneurs. They try to assess the territory's tourism potential by showing inhabitants new opportunities for self-fulfilment and employment through providing information and countering the fear of starting a business. The NGO Kaykino Creative Projects is one of the main non-governmental centres in the Leningrad Region, which takes on all kinds of this type of work with the local community. Since 2012, Kaykino Creative Projects has been managing projects to develop territories and to support 'top-down' initiatives as well as to provide original solutions for the implementation of governmental programmes and the formation of communication channels between various stakeholder groups.

The activities of the NGO Kaykino Creative Projects are aimed at the development of an economically depressed zone, the Volosovo district of the Leningrad Region. This region includes one municipal village and 14 rural villages and has a total population of 51,923 people. It is situated 100 kilometres from St. Petersburg, on the Narva Highway, which runs up to the border with Estonia by the Narva River. It is the eastern-most stretch of European route E20, and carries significant traffic between Estonia and Russia. Its rich historical and cultural heritage remains unknown not only outside of, but also within, the region; therefore, the NGO promotes the Volosovo district as an entertaining and mysterious place of pilgrimage for enthusiastic tourists.

The case of the 'Kaykino, 10' projects in the Leningrad Region of the Russian Federation allows us to draw attention to the development of creative tourism on a micro scale. In this chapter, the experiences of four projects implemented in the Volosovo district and coordinated by the NGO Kaykino Creative Projects are analyzed: 'Volosovo Widers' (2015), 'Village Vacation' (2015–16), 'Pantry of Creativity' (2016), and 'Place Depends on People' (2017–18).

In 2015–16, the NGO implemented its first tourism-oriented projects in coop-eration with a team of students from the Higher School of Economics: 'Volosovo Widers' and 'Village Vacation'. The main aim of these projects was to establish com-munications between the various stakeholder groups, to identify active residents, and to come up with original prospective ideas for the development of tourism in the villages. As a professional centre for project management, communication, and coordination, the NGO has become an indispensable platform for creating teams, discussing ideas, and developing the skills of local residents.

As part of the 'Volosovo Widers' project, participants designed the first tourist map of the district and created a website on tourism (Migratory Birds, 2017) as part of the Tourism Development Centre, which was also formed within the NGO. During the 'Village Vacation' project, participants gained new socio-cultural experience by communicating with local entrepreneurs, government administrations, and exter-nal experts. They developed three project areas, the names of which became the distinctive brands of three villages:

- 'EcoSabsk' in the village of Sabsk, holding ecological events in one of the most picturesque locations in the Volosovo district.
- 'The bread place' in the village of Begunitsy, designing the image of a hospi-table, business-like location with a bread-making tradition based on strong enterprises such as the bakery 'Bread-house'.
- 'Learning is not dull! Available agronomy' in the village of Beseda, creating edu-cational workshops for new farmers and programmes for children and tourists, where they can be a young biologist, veterinarian, fisherman, or forester.

Significantly, the university students and consultants encouraged residents to come up with ideas from a new perspective, bringing with them a more business-oriented approach through researching the target audiences, determining the unique sell-ing point of each village, and developing its marketing strategy. Each stage of the 'Village Vacation' project was recorded and analyzed. It became an action research project as well, simultaneously conducting a study of the participants' interests, reflecting upon and discussing results, and developing new tools to achieve the project's objectives. All the projects applied project management principles and constantly adjusted to the needs and resources of the territories.

The 'Village Vacation' project began a new stage with the addition of the project 'Place Depends on People', which encourages and supports the residents themselves to focus on creating initiatives. Informed by the results of the previous projects, it became essential to rely on sustainable entrepreneurs and active residents in each territory.

Participatory inclusion of local residents

To encourage the continual development of creative tourism initiatives by rural residents, which techniques could be used to integrate rural communities (including authorities, entrepreneurs, and farmers) in creative tourism and its related decision-making?

At present, there is particular interest in using social inclusion technologies in the process of local place and tourism development (Richards and Hall, 2000). These tools can be adapted to suit a number of conditions: the features of each area, the characteristics of local communities (e.g., roles, tasks, motivation, and types of rewards and benefits), the accessibility of transport, economic welfare, and much more (Cornwall, 2008). To ensure the full and qualitative development of the territory, these tools and processes must take into account both residents and non-residents of a certain territory, as well as the presence of various community interests (Glazychev, 1984). With this in mind, the NGO Kaykino Creative Projects used three social inclusion technologies: (1) cultural events and business meetings; (2) interactive games with questionnaires; and (3) local newspapers, media, and social networks.

Seminars and distance work

As the Volosovo district is located 100 kilometres away from St. Petersburg, one- or two-day trips were organized so that the students and experts could obtain primary information about the area (e.g., its history, residents, and main resources). On-site seminars enabled and established communication and clarified project objectives. The organizing team managed to combine physical and intellectual activities during visits to farms, enterprises, museums, and cultural centres. This approach maintained a balance between business communication and friendliness while gathering different opinions.

To monitor the implementation of tasks, the participants sent short messages on their current assignments. Then, written and audio recordings were placed in a shared folder and sent to a webpage where all the project materials were kept, including books, articles, and presentations.

The project 'Place Depends on People' required the creation of additional maps showing the locations of farms, large enterprises, and cultural organizations as well as the competencies of the residents (skills, craftsmanship, or services). Information such as this is extremely important for generating ideas and appraising the real conditions under which they would be implemented (actors, forms of cooperation, and levels of motivation). The mapping technique encouraged the participants to learn more about each other and created further reasons for interaction.

One of the on-site seminars was dedicated to compiling a competency map using inhabitants' responses to a questionnaire, which started with 'I can and want to do things for my village'. People were asked to affix cards with their answers and contact information on an illustrated map of Begunitsy village. As a result, 14 responses were collected from middle-aged people taking part in a local celebration. Young people refused to interact, as they negatively perceived the technique as being 'another questionnaire', which demonstrates a significant drawback of this technology.

Entrepreneurship Council

The purpose of the Entrepreneurship Council is to unite the efforts and capabilities of local entrepreneurs with the aim of developing Beseda village. The additional function of the Council is to enable entrepreneurs to obtain new sources of revenue through advertising, representation at events, and so on. The meetings are usually professionally moderated by the NGO Kaykino Creative Projects. This allows members to keep to the agenda, to develop tools for interaction, and to manage controversial issues. Such meetings keep entrepreneurs active and direct their resources towards solving socially significant issues. In addition, entrepreneurs become aware of their importance and responsibility in developing the territory.

'Tourist Bus' interactive game

Local events and festivals have become the basis of residents' involvement and the implementation of various parts of the projects discussed here. The resource centre looks to such events to find out the various expectations of residents regarding the development of tourism, without imposing 'top-down' decisions. In this context, the 'Tourist Bus' interactive game aimed to carry out three specific tasks: (1) to figure out residents' opinions of their target audience and tourists' motivation to visit the destination; (2) to define the products and services that could further the offer provided to tourists; and (3) to identify activities that may be attractive to both local residents and tourists.

About 200 people took part in the Maslenitsa holiday[1] in the village of Beseda. However, only six fully completed questionnaires were received; but on top of this, there were 11 more suggestions for products and service offers for tourists as well as 15 more suggested events. Past unsuccessful experiences were mentioned as a reason for refusing to participate in the game and complete the questionnaire. For example, some respondents noted that although they are asked about their needs every year, nothing had changed.

Thus, a number of challenging issues were identified regarding the experience of social inclusion, with possible solutions also proposed:

- Regarding the weak engagement of locals: to develop a public relations strategy using social networks and local media (newspapers, radio, and television).
- Regarding the absence of competency maps: to examine new techniques for finding leaders capable of developing new tourist orientation products and services.
- Regarding competing interests: to consider the relationships between residents before building project teams.

Participatory inclusion of local artisans

How could craftspeople (artisans) participate in the production of creative tourism products and services? As has already been noted, local entrepreneurs are key stakeholders in the initial stages of developing a tourist destination, and are motivated by opportunities of business promotion, increased sales, and new consumers. However, they often lack the experience and knowledge to produce competitive services and goods. In the Leningrad Region, the products of craftspeople and designers often remain in their homes without gaining access to any market.

In order to unite artists and artisans to solve this complex problem, the 'Pantry of Creativity' project was initiated in 2016. As most craftspeople of the Leningrad Region do not dare to organize their business or to be officially registered as individual entrepreneurs, the project aimed to provide information and enhance local knowledge regarding the possibilities of developing a creative workshop and choosing an entrepreneurial status, such as partnerships or NGOs. The project collected information on 174 craftspeople in the Leningrad Region, and published 1,800 copies of a product catalogue with the contacts of the master craftspeople. Two mobile product exhibitions were organized as a joint promotion method. In light of these results, the research gave a broad overview of creative activity in the region based on the handicrafts sector in the Leningrad Region and Russia, providing crafts producers with ideas and models for creative tourism development.

Based on an analysis of the 'Russia Travel' website (https://russia.travel/), we singled out 109 objects claiming to be from centres of creative tourism based on handicraft and artistic activities. Regarding the form of ownership, state and municipal institutions make up a large part of the sample at 70 per cent (77 institutions), while private institutions represent 30 per cent (32 business entities). In the context of creative tourism, state (municipal) institutions are expanding their portfolio with services for both residents and tourists, and such services could be connected with learning (courses, master classes), tasting (experiences, open ateliers), and other activities (Richards, 2011). This change in direction is being brought about by the orders of new founders and the structure of consumer demand.

The second model spreading around Russia is that of private enterprises engaged in craft activities. To determine the current situation and to identify the main objectives of craft entrepreneurs, a survey of 89 participants in the 'Pantry of Creativity' project was conducted. This survey revealed that only seven of the 89 respondents had official entrepreneur status, while 34 of the respondents out of the remaining 82 expressed their intentions to open their own businesses in the field of crafts. At the same time, about 40 participants in the project had experience of teaching children at schools and in studios. This advantage serves as an incentive to develop programmes to teach crafts to tourists in the form of master classes.

According to the academic literature, services can be divided into the categories of simple services (resulting from a uniform activity) and complex services (a body

Table 11.1   Creative and cultural services by organizational type

	State institution	Private institution
Simple service (creative)	24	7
Complex service level 1 (creative + cultural)	24	12
Complex service level 2 (creative + cultural + ethnographic + event + gastronomic)	29	13

of simple services) (Gordin and Suschinskaya, 2007). In the current study, simple services can be considered as the products of creative tourism resulting from the artist's technology and knowledge that they passed on to tourists during master classes. Complex services were divided into two levels. The first level included the products of cultural and creative tourism gained by tourists as they became acquainted with the artist's lifestyle when visiting museum exhibitions and creative workshops. The second level encompassed products of event, gastronomic, and ethnographic tourism in combination with creative tourism (e.g., folk festivals, accommodation in a themed village, national cuisine, and so on). Their task is to recreate an authentic atmosphere so that tourists can immerse themselves in a culture of domestic crafts. Of the sample of 109 institutions, simple services were provided by 28 per cent (31 institutions), complex services included in the first level were provided by 33 per cent (36 institutions), while complex services included in the second level were provided by 38 per cent (42 institutions). Table 11.1 presents a matrix reflecting the number of craft organizations included in this creative tourism scope, organized by the nature of the services provided and the type of organization offering them.

The institutions primarily oriented to tourism and the creation of complex, second-level services are becoming increasingly relevant. Some craft centres are included in popular tourist routes, such as 'The Golden Ring of Russia' and 'The Silver Necklace of Russia'. Both state and private institutions can become members. The purpose of such projects is to develop domestic and inbound tourism, increase tourist flow, and increase the length of tourist stays. As a consequence, other institutions have been modifying their own activity to attract tourists and enter the tourism market.

Craftspeople are the main economic entities in these organizations, so their involvement determines the format in which the activities are commodified. As an example of best practice, we would like to present the Design Selo studio, which carries out various interactive events with the potential to become part of a tourist offer. Over the past two years, it has attracted great interest for its master classes for groups of up to 15 people on, for example, 'Gingerbread Shapes', 'Live Watercolour', or 'Granite Mosaics', as well as tourist sessions for groups of visitors lasting between three and four hours, such as 'Day with a Sculptor' or 'Manor of the Master' (open-air art master classes held in the framework of the project).

In 2016, the Design Selo studio opened an art gallery to present exhibitions of contemporary painting, sculpture, and design. This gallery creates an unexpected contrast between the traditional rural environment and the modern, stylish presentation of the art projects. The opposition of native nature and modern art forms is attractive to visitors, and people of all ages have experienced true passion and inspiration from participating in the master classes.

Ultimately, the research also identified the main limitations of creating creative tourism projects in the Leningrad Region, and we believe that these assessments are also true of most Russian regions. They are:

- The unequal development of and support for tourist information centres.
- The basic business and marketing skills of craftspeople, who are only just starting to act as creative entrepreneurs.
- A lack of tourist infrastructure and comprehensive coordination.
- Poor promotion of small creative tourism attractions and a lack of segmentation, targeting, and positioning strategies to build up marketing relationships with tourists.

Concluding reflections

Place management and marketing strategies are starting to develop in rural areas of Russia. The key stakeholders in this process are entrepreneurs and active residents in local communities who want to create competitive products and services for tourists to promote the authenticity of the countryside. In this chapter, we have drawn attention to projects being carried out in the Volosovo district of the Leningrad Region, with the NGO Kaykino Creative Projects emerging as a driver for cooperation between local communities and other stakeholders. Many of its projects purposefully sought to achieve changes in place development and to maintain their practice in a sustainable manner in the region. An assessment of their experiences indicates that a series of seminars for entrepreneurs and activities such as business meetings, cultural events, and educational programmes are essential to bring people together, to inspire them, and to support them.

We have found that creative tourism products are becoming more complex in rural areas, including new activities and experiences that combine creative and craft work, art practices, agronomy (e.g., gathering medicinal plants, visiting farms, and so on), gastronomic events, and health and wellness procedures. In this context, we consider the role of artisan-entrepreneurs from a new light – that they are active participants in the creation of cultural and creative experiences for visitors.

Research gaps

From the literature review and our experience of participating in the rural tourism development projects described in this chapter, we would like to point out the following issues as research gaps that can be addressed in the future:

- Examining the relative effectiveness of 'top-down' models of projects coordinated by NGOs or destination marketing organizations (DMOs) and grassroots projects for local development based on public–private partnerships.
- The operational aspects of creative tourism programmes – for example, the adaptation of social inclusion technologies to suit particular locations and communities, including motivation and team-building activities for residents, the distribution of administrative costs, and the design of effective online and offline communications.
- Product development and business solutions for entrepreneurs of creative tourism – with the rise of competition, it is essential to know more about the demand and expectations of the target audiences of creative tourism in rural areas.

Acknowledgements

This chapter was prepared within the framework of the Academic Fund Programme at the National Research University Higher School of Economics in 2017 and supported within the framework of a subsidy granted to the Higher School of Economics by the Government of the Russian Federation for the implementation of the Global Competitiveness Programme, 'The role of the destination brand in increasing territories' attractiveness for tourists'.

NOTE

1 Maslenitsa is an Eastern Slavic religious and folk holiday, celebrated during the week preceding Great Lent, that is, the eighth week before the Eastern Orthodox Pascha (Easter).

References

Alsos, G.A., D. Eide and E.L. Madsen (2014), 'Introduction: innovation in tourism industries', in G.A. Alsos, D. Eide and E.L. Madsen (eds), *Handbook of Research on Innovation in Tourism Industries*, Cheltenham, UK and Northampton, MA, USA: Edward Elgar Publishing, pp. 1–26.

Arroyo, C.G., C. Barbieri and S.R. Rich (2013), 'Defining agritourism: a comparative study of stakeholders' perceptions in Missouri and North Carolina', *Tourism Management*, **37**, 39–47.

Ateljevic, I. and S. Doorne (2000), '"Staying within the fence": lifestyle entrepreneurship in tourism', *Journal of Sustainable Tourism*, **8** (5), 378–92.

Clemenson, H.A. and B. Lane (1997), 'Niche markets, niche marketing and rural employment', in R.D. Bollman and J.M. Bryden (eds), *Rural Employment: An International Perspective*, Wallingford: CAB International, pp. 410–26.

Cornwall, A. (2008), 'Unpacking "participation": models, meanings and practices', *Community Development Journal*, **43** (3), 269–83.

Dana, L.P., C. Gurau and F. Lasch (2014), 'Entrepreneurship, tourism and regional development: a tale of two villages', *Entrepreneurship and Regional Development*, **26** (3–4), 357–74.

European Commission – Agriculture and Rural Development (2013), *Rural Development in the EU: Statistical and Economic Information – Report 2013*, Brussels: European Commission.

Folorunso Adeyinka-Ojo, S. and C. Khoo-Lattimore (2013), 'Slow food events as a high yield strategy for rural tourism destinations: the case of Bario, Sarawak', *Worldwide Hospitality and Tourism Themes*, **5** (4), 353–64.

Foodika (2017), 'All-Russian project "The Gastronomic Map of Russia"', accessed 17 August 2017 at http://foodika.ru/vserossijskij-proekt-gastronomicheskaya-karta-rossii/.

Glazychev, V. (1984), *Socio-ecological Interpretation of the Urban Environment*, Moscow: Science (in Russian).

Gordin, V.E. and M.D. Suschinskaya (2007), *Service Management: A Textbook*, St. Petersburg: Business Press.

Kangas, A. (2017), *Removing Barriers: Participative and Collaborative Cultural Activities in KUULTO Action Research*, Helsinki: CUPORE.

Kaykino Creative Projects (2017), 'About the NGO', accessed 26 August 2017 at http://creaprok.com/en/.

Kiralova, A. and A. Malachovsky (2015), 'Innovating the Czech and Slovak tourism through creative tourism', *Skyline Business Journal*, **11** (1), 101–17.

Lane, B. (1994), 'What is rural tourism?', *Journal of Sustainable Tourism*, **2** (1–2), 7–21.

Lane, B. and E. Kastenholz (2015), 'Rural tourism: the evolution of practice and research approaches – towards a new generation concept?', *Journal of Sustainable Tourism*, **23** (8–9), 1133–56.

Látková, P. and C.A. Vogt (2012), 'Residents' attitudes toward existing and future tourism development in rural communities', *Journal of Travel Research*, **51** (1), 50–67.

McGehee, N.G. and K.L. Andereck (2004), 'Factors predicting rural residents' support of tourism', *Journal of Travel Research*, **43** (2), 131–40.

McGehee, N.G. and K. Kim (2004), 'Motivation for agri-tourism entrepreneurship', *Journal of Travel Research*, **43** (2), 161–70. doi:10.1177/0047287504268245

Migratory Birds (2017), 'The Volosovo district: tourism and rest', accessed 26 August 2017 at http://volosovotur.ru/.

Ministry of Agriculture of the Russian Federation (2017), *Federal Targeted Programme 'Sustainable Development of Rural Territories for 2014–2017 and for the Period until 2020'* (in Russian), accessed 17 August 2017 at http://mcx.ru/activity/state-support/programs/territory-development/.

Ministry of Economic Development of the Russian Federation (2017), *Support Programs for Small and Medium-sized Businesses* (in Russian), accessed 17 August 2017 at http://economy.gov.ru/minec/activity/sections/smallBusiness/.

Moscardo, G. (2014), 'Tourism and community leadership in rural regions: linking mobility, entrepreneurship, tourism development and community well-being', *Tourism Planning and Development*, **11** (3), 354–70.

Persson, L.O., E. Westholm and T. Fuller (1997), *Two Contexts, One Outcome: The Importance of Lifestyle Choice in Creating Rural Jobs in Canada and Sweden*, Stockholm: Royal Institute of Technology.

Pine, B.J. and J.H. Gilmore (1999), *The Experience Economy: Work is Theatre and Every Business a Stage*, Cambridge, MA: Harvard Business Press.

Readymag (2017), 'Project presentation "The Gastronomic Map of Russia"', accessed 26 August 2017 at https://readymag.com/u75747694/gastrokartapdf/.

Renko, S., N. Renko and T. Polonijo (2010), 'Understanding the role of food in rural tourism development in a recovering economy', *Journal of Food Products Marketing*, **16** (3), 309–24.

Richards, G. (2011), 'Creativity and tourism: the state of the art', *Annals of Tourism Research*, **38** (4), 1225–53.

Richards, G. and D. Hall (eds) (2000), *Tourism and Sustainable Community Development*, New York: Routledge.

Richards, G. and C. Raymond (2000), 'Creative tourism', *ATLAS News*, **23**, 16–20.

Richards, G. and J. Wilson (2006), 'Developing creativity in tourist experiences: a solution to the serial reproduction of culture?', *Tourism Management*, **27**, 1209–23.

Russia Tourism (2017a), Federal Targeted Programme 'Development of Internal and Entry Tourism in the Russian Federation (2011–2018)', accessed 17 August 2017 at http://www.russiatourism.ru/contents/deyatelnost/programmy-i-proekty/federalnaya-tselevaya-programma-razvitie-vnutrennego-i-vezdnogo-turizma-v-rossiyskoy-federatsii-2011-2018-gody-/.

Russia Tourism (2017b), '"The Gastronomic Map of Russia" collecting country's regions at the New Year table', accessed 17 August 2017 at http://www.russiatourism.ru/news/11857/.

Salehi, H. and M. Nadi (2014), 'The development strategies of rural tourism with the goal of sustainable development', *Advances in Environmental Biology*, **8** (6), 1518–25.

Sánchez-Cañizares, S.M. and T. López-Guzmán (2012), 'Gastronomy as a tourism resource: profile of the culinary tourist', *Current Issues in Tourism*, **15** (3), 229–45.

Sasu, K. and G. Epuran (2016), 'An overview of the new trends in rural tourism', *Bulletin of the Transilvania University of Braşov/Series V: Economic Sciences*, **9** (58, no. 2), 119–26.

Smith, S., N. Davis and J. Pike (2010), 'Rural tourism development: a case study of the Shawnee Hills wine trail in Southern Illinois', *Journal of Extension*, **48** (5), 1–11.

Solvoll, S., G.A. Alsos and O. Bulanova (2015), 'Tourism entrepreneurship: review and future directions', *Scandinavian Journal of Hospitality and Tourism*, **15** (suppl. 1), 120–37.

Tan, S., S. Kung and D. Luh (2013), 'A model of "creative experience" in creative tourism', *Annals of Tourism Research*, **41**, 153–74.

The National Calendar of Events (2017), 'Russian events list', accessed 26 August 2017 at http://eventsinrussia.com/en/event/10277.

The Russian Government (2016), 'The concept of rural tourism development in Russia until 2030', accessed 17 August 2017 at http://static.government.ru/media/files/Fw1kbNXVJxQ.pdf.

Trauer, B. (2006), 'Conceptualizing special interest tourism – frameworks for analysis', *Tourism Management*, **27** (2), 183–200.

Woods, M. and J. McDonagh (2011), 'Rural Europe and the world: globalization and rural development', *European Countryside*, **3** (3), 153–63.

Zeppenfeld, R. (2017), 'Rural culture and rural structure', in H. Ryan and A. Shuler (eds), *Tourism in Rural Areas* (under scientific editor H. Chudnovsky), Moscow: Knorus Media, pp. 82–102 (in Russian).

12 Creative tourist regions as a basis for public policy

Magnus Luiz Emmendoerfer

Creative tourism as an object of public policy

Creative tourism is a relatively new economic sector and field of theoretical-empirical knowledge (Richards and Raymond, 2000; Richards, 2011). Its association with public policies for the development of regions has been even more recent. Empirically, public (government and community) and private (market) interests at local and international levels have been creating and developing areas in cities through creative tourism as a form of territorial specialization and new business generation. The public management of different places worldwide has treated this territorial specialization as a form of creative tourism-induced development and has designated these places as 'Creative Friendly Destinations' for the purpose of promoting creative tourism (http://www.creativetourismnetwork.org). In these destinations, the relationship between creativity, culture, and sustainability is highlighted, and such developments are often linked to discussions about the emergence of the creative economy (Hartley, 2005). The creative economy and creative tourism have been fostered in international policy agendas such as those of the Organisation for Economic Co-operation and Development (OECD), the United Nations Conference on Trade and Development (UNCTAD), and the United Nations Educational, Scientific and Cultural Organization (UNESCO), and in the public policies and national development plans of several countries, emphasizing the articulation of culture and creativity as important resources for local and regional development (Madeira, 2014).

While there are several definitions of public policy, it is common for public policy to be seen as addressing a public problem (Salamon, 1981; Secchi, 2016). In this way, public policies can be understood as activities of governments and other agencies of the state to mobilize resources to solve social problems or to address principles or values considered important by different groups in the population. In this sense, creative tourism can be a policy-enabled tool for addressing problems at the municipal level, particularly through place specialization via creative practices, which makes it possible to, for example: requalify public and private spaces; preserve material and immaterial heritage; generate work and income through the provision of organized cultural goods and services related to the creative economy; value popular activities; boost the local economy through tourism experiences; promote social cohesion; and provide new learning opportunities through leisure activities for children, adolescents, families, and the elderly. Such developments can, in turn, reduce migratory movements and stimulate increased identity attachment and a feeling of belonging to the city.

Creative tourism concepts and public policy

The main characteristics associated with the concept of creative tourism are co-production of cultural goods and services and acquisition of significant experiences, which generate learning in authentic communities that hold differentiated knowledge, attracting the interest of tourists (Richards, 2011). On the one hand, creative tourism depends on the tourist as a creative co-producing subject and as a consumer of experiences and, on the other hand, on the creative skills of the creators of experiences (Richards and Wilson, 2006). As a result, the guiding principle of creative tourism can be interpreted as the tourists' active involvement in cultural and community experiences and activities provided. A place provides creative opportunities, and it is up to the agents involved to construct their experiences according to their own subjectivities. These 'open' characteristics of creative tourism can generate doubts and concerns among policymakers, which can lead to superficial approaches and policy failures. This situation appears to be occurring when creative tourism and community-based tourism are related in research (Emmendoerfer et al., 2016).

Community-based tourism relies on organizations that offer tourists activities that are known as 'sharing experiences' (Grimm and Sampaio, 2011), with guests and hosts sharing the same activity as active agents. Such experiences are more latent, especially in visits to conservation units when the intimacy of the hosts with nature is perceived in the lodgings and houses of families and where relations become closer, intimate, and authentic, as well as in active participation in popular festivals and the local folklore, where the local culture is directly experienced. In these contexts, the experiences stimulate knowledge acquisition through lived experience. In this form of community-based tourism, the experiences occur in an integrative, contributory, and participatory way and the benefits are distributed to all involved.

The characteristics of community-based tourism and creative tourism are compared in Table 12.1 (developed after Emmendoerfer et al., 2016), which indicates that both community-based tourism and creative tourism aim to provide their users with a culturally authentic experience and integrated experiences. Consequently, it is striking to point out that community-based tourism depends on the articulation of the social strata to tourism activity, whereas in creative tourism, if there is no participative management in the sector, it can become merely economic in nature (Emmendoerfer et al., 2016). The descriptions of community-based tourism and creative tourism practices indicate that the aspect of greatest congruence is the contact with socio-cultural aspects and the local population of the tourist destination. Therefore, even though tourism is intentionality different within each of these concepts, creative tourism can be both a form of tourism per se and a strategy of incremental development of forms of tourism already existing in several countries, such as community-based tourism.

Table 12.1   Comparison of characteristics between community-based tourism and creative tourism for defining public policies

Community-based tourism	Creative tourism
Preferably rural	Predominantly urban
Internal managers of the community in *sine qua non* condition	External and/or internal community managers
Resident social actors, decision-makers, and leaders are of the host community	Social actors not necessarily from the receiving community
Benefits distributed in the host community	Benefits can be shared externally and more narrowly and/or distributed in the host community
Activities lived necessarily within the community, especially in their homes	Experienced creative activities not necessarily internal to the community
External infrastructure of the community is not necessary in the experiences, but important to reinforce the lifestyle associated with the habitat of the receiving community	Infrastructure outside the community can contribute or not to the creative process when making tourism in the territory, but it is important to create a friendly environment for creativity
Internal infrastructure is valued in the experiences with the receiving community	Internal infrastructure is valued and it stimulates creative processes in the territory
Creativity is authenticity identified as the identity of the host community	Creativity can compromise the authenticity of the host community if it is not monitored by stakeholders
Products and services also consumed by the host community	Products and services aimed at the external public (tourist) consumer
Leisure also experienced by the host community	Leisure directed at the external (tourist) consumer
Financing in local infrastructure is strategic and public administration assistance provides basis for tourist reception and development of activities	Activities linked to the production of experiences can be financed according to the specificity of the place: the creative organization that receives tourists can be financed by capital, government entities, and/or third-party capital
The experience is integrated, prioritizing the translation of the way of life of the receiving community	The experience shares and integrates community knowledge through the joint construction of experiences with the tourist
Way of life of the population as the main tourist attraction	Resources and activities that stimulate the creativity of tourists as the main tourist attraction
Tourist as an apprentice of the local culture and consumer of experiences, not necessarily in co-production with the inhabitants of the community	Tourist necessarily as a consumer of experiences and as an apprentice through the co-production of goods or services with the native inhabitants or not of the receiving community
Seeks the development of the community in territories not necessarily stimulating creativity	Contributes to the development of creative territories
Development predominantly associated with sustainability and the empowerment of communities in certain territories (especially rural) of the city or an agglomeration of cities, such as forest conservation units	Development predominantly associated with creative places or cities, with a focus on the production of symbolic value for the tourist and opportunities for direct creative interaction and connection

Source: Adapted from Emmendoerfer et al. (2016, p. 9).

Integrated spatial approaches as an option in the development of creative tourism

Creative tourism can be a factor for development because tourists seek singular experiences through the consumption of products in their place of origin, generating a fertile environment for local and regional development (Florida, 2014). According to Richards and Wilson (2006), there are three specific types of contexts in cities that nurture the development of tourism with creativity: creative places, creative events, and creative tourism. Although the terms are different, there is a set of common elements, namely: (1) individuals – participatory and authentic experiences that enable visitors to develop their creative potential and skills through contact with local culture and community; and (2) territorial – creativity that provides activity, content, and atmosphere for the development of tourism in the destination, which in turn supports creative activities developed by the inhabitants of the destination.

For cities to have their image projected and identified as 'creative' in some economic-cultural sector, it is necessary that the agents interested in the creative economy understand the peculiarities of existing spaces within a city. These peculiarities can be materialized in the imaginations of the people in the different parts of a city, and linked to the activities and sectors of the creative economy. There can be several creative territories, interconnected or not, in a creative city. They can become more visible and articulated to tourism through local government activity.

The creative city is a dynamic, interconnected, tolerant, interactive, and attractive place that seeks to value creativity and innovation as a generator of economy and quality of life, and is based in the history and culture of the population (Landry and Bianchini, 1995). This concept provides an inspiration for public sector managers to rethink urban planning and the local development of their cities, nurturing both the creative environment(s) and the people and organizations working in the culture-based sectors (creative industries) that 'drive' the creative economy (Howkins, 2001).

In recent communications about the UNESCO Creative Cities Network (e.g., UNESCO, 2017a), while the notion of space is not explicitly addressed in discussion of creative cities, it is relevant to understand the process of designating, classifying, or institutionalizing a creative city. Thus, this chapter proposes the notion of Creative Tourism Regions (CTRs) as multi-scalar spaces, built from a formative process adopted by a group of people over a period of time, who seek to offer authentic and singular cultural products resulting from creative and dynamic actions that are attractive and valued mainly through the subjective interpretation of the meaning (co-)created/produced by the inhabitants and travellers who experience these products in these spaces.

It is observed that this notion corroborates with Landry and Bianchini (1995) and Florida (2014) in conceiving culture as a basis for generating benefits and social and economic impacts, with the potential to add value through the development of a more creative environment and clear and facilitative governance with a long-term strategy. Thus, culture is recognized as the main basis for the CTR, which requires the individuals and organizations interested in the generation and development of creative industries to develop: integrated local/regional development policies; integrated urban planning and management; functional urbanism and innovative architecture; horizontal connections; cultural policies and diversified supply of activities; cultural awareness economy; creative management of companies and organizations; cultural and creative tourism; territorial marketing and branding; technological innovation, artistic creativity, and good business management of cultural products; stimulation of creativity and its recognition; building governance through a shared vision (public, private, and civil society); and the presence of creative people.

Elements of CTR recognition as a basis for formulating and managing public policy

The first step in establishing a CTR is defining the geographic space for the intentional fostering and development of creative tourism. It is important for the local government and other stakeholders to diagnose the space chosen and to identify the resources needed for public policy formulation. According to Emmendoerfer and Ashton (2014), there are three levels of creative territories that involve different types of spaces: (1) micro level (street, avenue, neighbourhood, historic town, village); (2) meso level (set of neighbourhoods, zoning, district, city, and municipality); and (3) macro level (set of cities, municipalities, regions, provinces, federal units). In defining 'creative territories' for policy and development, such a range of scales should be considered to avoid a 'misalignment', such as aiming to develop a creative city or region from a too small geographical base. In the development of creative tourism, it would be more appropriate to address the different scales that exist in the spatial planning policy of each country or city, in order to respect the diversity of existing socio-cultural capital in these spaces (Emmendoerfer and Ashton, 2014).

By employing the notion of 'creative places' as a constituent element of creative cities, we can avoid a particular activity or creative sector blocking out the others, due to the high profile usually given to a single creative activity in order to differentiate the city as 'creative' for designation and promotional purposes. This can be intensified or harmonized through public policies and tourism planning and promotion. Thus, every city can be a creative place, but not all creative places are necessarily creative cities. Moreover, this helps to focus on the formulation and management of public policies to encourage and support creative tourism actions.

In order to illustrate the application of the CTR concept, as well as other elements relevant to the diagnosis of the municipality for the purposes of formulating and managing creative tourism public policies, it is useful to present the case of Ouro

Preto. The city of Ouro Preto is located in the central region of the federal state of Minas Gerais, Brazil. Ouro Preto is both the name of the municipal-region (macro-territorial level) and the capital city (meso-territorial level) of a region that comprises 13 districts in total. This study focuses on the historical centre of the district, the city of Ouro Preto (micro-territorial level).

As a first step, it is necessary to diagnose the main features of the region in which one intends to develop creative tourism, elements that can be organized into three dimensions: economic, cultural, and organizational (Tomazzoni, 2009). For Ouro Preto, these were identified by Soares (2012) and updated in the current study. As Table 12.2 illustrates, the historic city of Ouro Preto is a tourist destination that is designated as a tourist territory mainly because of its natural and cultural heritage, the influence and tradition of its Portuguese heritage from the time when Brazil was a colony of Portugal. The cultural heritage of Ouro Preto consists of material goods (churches, chapels, and museums) from the seventeenth to the twentieth centuries, located mainly in the historical centre of Ouro Preto. The city of Ouro Preto is famous for the material goods that constitute its colonial architecture, with Ouro Preto decreed a National Monument City in 1933. It was the first Brazilian city to have its historical centre declared as a World Heritage Site by UNESCO in 1980 (UNESCO, 2017b). The city forms part of the Gold Circuit established by the Association of Municipalities, which recounts the colonial history of Brazil and Portugal. Cultural tourism was developed in Ouro Preto from 1960, mainly based on the Baroque architecture of the historic city (UNESCO, 2017b). A cultural winter festival has been developed, which brings together various artistic, cultural, and creative activities in partnership with the State University of Ouro Preto (UFOP).

The main reasons that stimulate regional, national, and international tourists and travellers to visit Ouro Preto have been its cultural heritage, architecture, and cultural venues, and its handicrafts, arts, and cultural events. These drivers are present in the historical centre and are closely associated with the creative economy sectors delineated in the UNCTAD model (UNCTAD, 2017), which formed the basis for the 2011–14 Plan for the Secretariat of the Creative Economy (SEC) (Brasil, 2012). In this plan, the creative economy is composed of five fields: (1) heritage: material, immaterial, archives, and museums; (2) cultural expressions: handicrafts, popular, indigenous and Afro-Brazilian cultures, and visual and digital arts; (3) performing arts: dance, music, circus, and theatre; (4) audiovisual, books, reading, and literature: film and video, publications, and print media; and (5) cultural and functional creations: fashion, design, and architecture. Based on the model of the Brazilian SEC, the historical centre of Ouro Preto encompasses the fields of heritage (i.e., material, immaterial, archives, and museums), cultural expressions (i.e., handicrafts, popular, and Afro cultures), and performing arts (music and theatre).

In the period 2012 to 2016, there were collective efforts of an organizational nature to promote and raise local awareness of the creative economy in order to strengthen Ouro Preto as a creative location. Events promoted by the Ouro Preto Art Foundation

Table 12.2   Information on Ouro Preto, Brazil, as a touristic destination

Economic dimension	Population: 70,281 people, 87% urban, 13% rural
	Territorial extension: 1,245,864 square km or 481.03077965 square miles
	Prevailing economic activity: Mining and Services
	GDP per capita (2014): R$79,116.61 or US$24,723
	Vocation: Historical-cultural tourism
	Hosting: 147
	Food services: 88
	Paved access: Yes
	Airport in operation: Confins – MG is the closest airport (141 km from the city of Ouro Preto)
	Bus station: Yes
	Regionally induces tourism: Yes
	Partnerships in tourism projects with other cities/Participate in touristic circuit: Yes – Gold Tourist Circuit (http://www.circuitodoouro.tur.br, only in Portuguese)
	Community awareness actions: No
	Convention centres: Yes
	Natural attractions: 19
	Other observations: Ouro Preto received awards from the Ministry of Tourism as follows:
	• 2009 – Planning and Management of Regional Tourism Category – Gold Tourist Circuit Case. Proponent: State of Minas Gerais
	• 2010 – Social Sustainability in Municipalities Category – Ouro Preto Case: Citizen's Patrimony. Proponent: Municipality of Ouro Preto
Cultural dimension	The history of the city is a renowned tourist attraction: Yes
	Effectively local handicraft production: Yes
	Cultural attractions: 36
	World Heritage Listed City: Yes – by IPHAN since 1938; Ouro Preto has been a World Heritage Site (UNESCO) since 1980
	Permanent events: 6
	Other observations: Ouro Preto received the following award from the Ministry of Tourism:
	• 2011 – Cultural Sustainability in Municipalities Category – Case of Intangible Assets Management in Ouro Preto: registration and safeguard
Organizational dimension	Municipal Tourism Council (COMTUR) with periodic meetings: Yes
	COMTUR president: Private sector member
	Municipal Plan of Tourism: Yes
	Profile of the municipal public power: Municipal Secretariat of Tourism, Industry and Commerce
	Entrepreneurs' profiles: They believe that tourism will happen anyway and do not invest in qualification and manpower. In addition, they expect a lot from the city hall
	Community profile: Recognize the importance of tourism for local development
	Performance of local schools and universities: Schools – not identified. University has a seat at COMTUR and is responsible for the Tourist Assistance Center
	Convention Visitors Bureau: Yes (http://www.ouropreto.org.br/convention-visitors-bureau)
	Missions and study trips with local actors: Yes. Training through federal and municipal government programmes and local development agencies
	Other observations: In 2014, Ouro Preto was granted the Award of the Ministry of Tourism of Business Capacity for the good performance and greater evolution in the Competitiveness Index of the National Tourism

Source: Adapted and updated from Soares (2012).

at the UFOP Seminar on Cultural Heritage in 2012 highlighted the importance of the creative economy for the development of the tourism industry based on its historical and cultural heritage. Cultural and educational activities related to the creative economy were included in the Winter Festival, one of the city's main cultural events, in 2013. From 2013 onwards, the City Council of Ouro Preto presented projects linked to the creative economy to animate public spaces and to support material and immaterial heritage, popular culture, and artists in the cultural and creative sectors. These measures aimed to stimulate the city's creative economy and create new job and income opportunities from cultural goods and services to improve the quality and competitiveness of Ouro Preto as a potential 'Creative Friendly Destination'.

It is important to emphasize that a diagnosis of public policies helps to characterize the focus of governmental action, with or without the partnership of society, and also allows the detection of weaknesses in the tourist destination, which needs to be organized and re-organized so that local stakeholders interested in tourism can legitimize the city as a creative territory. Three elements – cultural vitality, innovativeness, and connectivity – call for targeted attention:

- *Cultural vitality*: the city needs better conservation of its heritage and its cultural equipment, and better organization of its service sector with the professionalization of those who present the culture and history of the city to visitors and to the residents themselves.
- *Innovativeness* (innovations): the need to create an innovation ecosystem from a municipal innovation system to attract investment and product development in one or more of the creative sectors, and to strengthen partnerships with universities and technological institutes to improve the city's quality of urban life through teaching, research, and extension activities.
- *Connectivity* (social capital and networks): the need to strengthen the organizations interested in the historical centre of the city and to create a governance structure for the region based on dialogic spaces with community and market participation. In addition, there is low interaction between artists and professionals from different creative sectors, which hampers a politicization and synergies in favour of a 'creative territory'. The connectivity problem for the development of the creative economy in the city is reinforced by the low and fragmented social capital and participation of the community and the market in the city's tourism development.

These elements can be observed in Table 12.2. Even though the city of Ouro Preto does not yet have the structural and social conditions to apply for a designation such as a UNESCO creative city title, it is possible to begin a process of cultural and creative development based on the notion of a CTR. The historical centre of Ouro Preto can become a CTR if, in addition to contemplating, improving, and maintaining the elements of tourist development outlined by Tomazzoni (2009), the individuals and organizations interested in cultural and creative tourism can organize and coordinate the following five actions, which are presented here as guides or parameters for designing public policies for the configuration of CTRs:

Table 12.3 Potential elements and indicators for development of creative tourism public policies

Elements	Indicators
Technology and innovation	Amount of intellectual property per capita
	Wide access, easy and fast Internet in public places
	Number of revitalized degraded areas
	Presence of creative clusters for its artistic and cultural production
	Existence of investment policies in technological innovation
Talent	Number of residents with degrees in higher education courses
	Number of immigrant and migrant residents
	Number of resident artists
	Existence of public policy for culture and leisure
Tolerance	Existence of policies fighting inequality and violence
	Respect for diversity and differences of people (ethnicity, race, gender, age, physical abilities, social class, and sexual orientation)
	Training activities for citizenship
	Meeting the UN Millennium Development Goals
Connections	Amount of local clusters
	Existence of active public council managers
	Acting agencies of local development
	Number of cultural and art organizations in the city

Source: Elaborated by the author from Ashton et al. (2014) and Florida (2014).

1. *Understand the notion of creative regions.* This involves awareness raising and training people about cultural management and the creative sectors, which are also related to the fields of science, technology, and innovation. It is possible that several creative regions exist in the meta-territory of a city, and thus a wide knowledge of the community, the market, and the state is important. Furthermore, creative regions, and the creative tourism within them, are only legitimized if activities include co-creation or co-production involving local artists with tourists/consumers, a lively cultural agenda, and public access.
2. *Provide an environment for the development of creativity.* A creative region's monitoring indicators need to be planned and controlled by the agents involved. In this sense, as a proposal, one can argue that a CTR equates to the space that includes the elements and indicators listed in Table 12.3 (from Ashton et al., 2014), which are important to consider when formulating and evaluating public policies related to recognizing a CTR and for developing creative tourism. In public policies, defining such indicators before implementing the planned actions is of great value when later evaluating results in relation to the policy goals.
3. *Create a CTR governance structure.* This is an effective way of bringing

together the stakeholders interested in regional development. This structure is important to create links between the organizations in different creative sectors in the city. In this sense, governance could be tripartite, with representatives of the state, community, and market. As Woolcock (1998) argues, this enables the establishment of social identity in a CTR by inhibiting opportunistic behaviour and the transgression of established social and sustainability norms. The governance structure should also define the spatial scale to be developed for creative tourism within the city.

4. *Sensitize the community, economic/market actors, and the state to sustainable territorial development.* Having a flow of tourists in the city is insufficient for sustainable tourism development. In this sense, it is necessary to act collectively in valuing tourism and culture and involve stakeholders in awareness campaigns and training programmes for citizenship, cultural and heritage management, tourism planning, creative economy, and sustainability. Such campaigns and educational programmes aim to minimize the problem of discontinuity in governmental plans and actions and address the dominance of *top-down* institutional innovations promoted by the state.

5. *Design and validate the visual identity created for the city and/or its territories.* One way to strengthen a territory is to create mechanisms that generate collective identity, such as through the creation of logos and slogans that refer to the essence of the existing public value. The visual arts and design industries can play important roles in this action. Ouro Preto has a visual identity with the slogan 'Where every day is historic' to promote the city. However, this visual identity must be supported by communication and public relation actions, including the incorporation of cultural assets and the creative sectors, in order to be validated and legitimized by the community, the market, and the public sector.

Complementary to these parameters for public policies, the development of creative tourism in a destination could be started and stimulated through creative events as a way of raising awareness and encouraging creative tourism investments that require adequate infrastructure to support creative activities (Richards and Wilson, 2006). It is worth mentioning that this planning must be accompanied by municipal legal frameworks to ensure the idealized tourism development plan is feasible and is based on the city's real resources. A legal framework could regulate the use of the public space with measures of preservation of heritage existing in the historical centre, linked to monitoring and control by stakeholders. This is important as a starting point for thinking about Creative Tourist Territories as a guideline for public policies in cities.

Final considerations

This study has sought to show that the public sector, through the municipal government, can act as a promoter and coordinator of projects and public policies of creative tourism in cities where this form of tourism has not yet emerged. To begin, understanding the differences between creative tourism and community-based tourism is an important step to avoid inappropriate appropriation and reproduction of concepts in public policies.

The analysis presented in this chapter can guide public policies in the recognition and development of a CTR, which can evolve in different spaces in a city, including the historic centre. These elements allow us to generate and observe different levels of creative life in the context of urban tourism and help link creative tourism with public policies. It should be emphasized that the proposal presented in this chapter is not a model, but a possible guide to making this link.

The case of Ouro Preto in Brazil shows that having a tradition of international tourist flows based on historical attractions and a distinction through a UNESCO World Heritage Site designation are not enough to elevate this city to the status of a creative city. Therefore, the notion of CTRs becomes a significant way of starting a collective project for this purpose, as well as a possible strategy in public policies for territorial specialization, regional economic differentiation, and the city's own marketing.

Future research directions

The notion of CTRs as a basis for public policy suggests several research opportunities. One area of research is to identity and define theoretical categories (creative places, creative events, or both; Richards and Wilson, 2006) and empirical categories (such as those indicated in the contents of public policies for the development of CTRs; Emmendoerfer et al., 2018) that can serve as starting points for the configuration of creative tourism projects.

A second research topic is to examine underlying issues in practice, that is, in policy design and implementation, which weaken or undermine efforts towards collaborative governance and collective actions. As discussed in this chapter, the links between tourism and creative economy activities are still weak in Brazil, and will likely continue to be so for some time to come. On the one hand, stakeholders appear to have limited knowledge about the characteristics, congruencies, and peculiarities of these activities for sustainable local development. Consequently, there is a need for awareness-raising actions as well as research on perceptions and knowledge of tourism and creativity/creative economy, and the interrelations among stakeholders in these two fields. Questions that may support future research in this area include: What conflicts exist in the relationship among creative tourism stakeholders? What elements favour the collective work of stakeholders in the development of creative tourism and/or CTRs? How are images, and possible brands, related to CTRs designed by stakeholders? What are the productive agents and activities that lead and sustain the creative tourism development process?

On the other hand, there appears to be an absence of integrated actions that can promote synergies and added value for both activities in order to constitute a CTR. To address this second issue, there is a need to identify and foster the skills required for taking integrated actions in regards to the generation, recognition, and development of CTRs among stakeholders working in public and private organizations. These skills are related to stakeholder governance for coordinating public policies and CTR projects, which suggests other important research questions: What types of governance arrangements are most likely to assist the creative tourism and/or CTR? What is the degree of stakeholder participation in the development of CTR policies and projects? What are the consequences of governance structures and processes in the development of creative tourism/CTRs? How do governance arrangements contribute to or accompany public creative tourism/CTR policies? How effective are programmes or public policies in this context compared to other (more traditional options)? To what extent do governments assess such programmes? How can comparative research of the results and effectiveness of these programmes (at different scales – local, regional, national, international) be conducted? Does the adoption of a creative tourism/CTR policy or programme have an effect on the way in which other policies are viewed or implemented? As these possibilities of orientation for future research on creative tourism and public policies suggest, there is still much to be investigated in both theoretical and empirical terms on this subject.

Acknowledgements

This research was funded by the National Council of Technological and Scientific Development (CNPq – Process 310574/2016-1) and the Coordination for the Improvement of Higher Education Personnel (CAPES), Ministry of Education, Brazil.

References

Ashton, M.S.G., E.L. Tomazzoni and M.L. Emmendoerfer (2014), 'Elementos para a validação de cidades criativas como destinos turísticos competitivos' (Elements for the validation of creative cities as competitive tourist destinations), *TURyDES*, 7 (17), 1–15.

Brasil (2012), *Plano da Secretaria da Economia Criativa: políticas, diretrizes e ações 2011–2014 (Plan of the Secretariat of the Creative Economy: Policies, Guidelines and Actions 2011-2014)*, Brasília: Ministério da Cultura.

Emmendoerfer, M.L. and M.S.G. Ashton (2014), 'Territórios criativos e suas relações com o turismo' (Creative territories and their relations with tourism), *Revista Turismo e Desenvolvimento*, 4 (21–2), 459–68.

Emmendoerfer, M.L., W.V. Moraes and B.O. Fraga (2016), 'Turismo criativo e turismo de base comunitária: congruências e peculiaridades' (Creative tourism and community-based tourism: congruences and peculiarities), *El Periplo Sustentable*, 31, 1–14.

Emmendoerfer, M.L., A.S.A. Fioravante and J.F.F.E. Araujo (2018), 'Federal government actions for the creative territories development in Brazilian context', *Revista Brasileira de Gestão e Desenvolvimento Regional*, 14 (1), 400–24.

Florida, R. (2014), *The Rise of the Creative Class – Revisited: Revised and Expanded*, New York: Basic Books.

Grimm, I.J. and C. Sampaio (2011), 'Turismo de base comunitária: convivencialidade e conservação ambiental' (Community-based tourism: environmental coexistence and conservation), *Revista Brasileira de Ciências Ambientais*, **19**, 57–68.

Hartley, J. (2005), *Creative Industries*, London: Blackwell.

Howkins, A. (2001), *The Creative Economy: How People Make Money from Ideas*, London: Allen Lane.

Landry, C. and F. Bianchini (1995), *The Creative City*, London: Demos.

Madeira, M.G. (2014), *Economia criativa: implicações e desafios para a política externa brasileira (Creative Economy: Implications and Challenges for Brazilian Foreign Policy)*, Brasília: FUNAG.

Richards, G. (2011), 'Creativity and tourism: the state of the art', *Annals of Tourism Research*, **38** (4), 1225–53.

Richards, G. and C. Raymond (2000), 'Creative tourism', *ATLAS News*, **23**, 16–20.

Richards, G. and J. Wilson (2006), 'Developing creativity in tourists' experiences: a solution to the serial reproduction of culture?', *Tourism Management*, **27** (6), 1209–23.

Salamon, L.M. (1981), 'Rethinking public management: third party government and the changing forms of government action', *Public Policy*, **29** (3), 255–75.

Secchi, L. (2016), *Análise de políticas públicas: diagnóstico de problemas, recomendação de soluções (Analysis of Public Policies: Diagnosis of Problems, Recommendation of Solutions)*, São Paulo: Cengage Learning.

Soares, E.B.S. (2012), 'Planejamento público estadual e desenvolvimento turístico de destinos indutores em Minas Gerais (2007–2010)' (State public planning and tourism development of inductive destinations in Minas Gerais [2007-2010]), MSc in Public Administration thesis, Universidade Federal de Viçosa.

Tomazzoni, E.L. (2009), *Turismo e desenvolvimento regional: dimensões, elementos e indicadores (Tourism and Regional Development: Dimensions, Elements and Indicators)*, Caxias do Sul: Educs.

UNCTAD (2017), *Creative Economy Programme*, accessed 31 October 2017 at http://www.unctad.org/en/Pages/DITC/CreativeEconomy/Creative-Economy-Programme.aspx.

UNESCO (2017a), *Creative Cities Network*, accessed 31 October 2017 at http://www.unesco.org/new/en/culture/themes/creativity/creative-cities-network/who-are-the-members.

UNESCO (2017b), *Historic Town of Ouro Preto*, accessed 31 October 2017 at http://www.whc.unesco.org/en/list/124.

Woolcock, M. (1998), 'Social capital and economic development: toward a theoretical synthesis and policy framework', *Theory and Society*, **27** (2), 151–208.

PART IV

Creative tourism networks and platforms

PART IV

13 Good and not-so-good practices in creative tourism networks and platforms: an international review

Paula Remoaldo, Olga Matos, Isabel Freitas, Hélder da Silva Lopes, Vítor Ribeiro, Ricardo Gôja, and Miguel Pereira

A consensus has not yet been reached worldwide regarding the concept of creative tourism. Since 2000, it has generally been considered as a kind of tourism that can offer tourists the opportunity to co-create and develop their creative potential. To identify and analyze the nature of existing creative tourism practices today, we carried out an investigation to examine creative tourism networks and platforms internationally – providing a snapshot of the creative tourism field in 2017. In this chapter, we outline the difficulties in defining creative tourism and discuss the development of creative tourism spaces on an international scale through the creation of networks and platforms. The chapter provides an overview of the research findings and comments on the patterns, issues, and trajectories we perceived. At the end of the chapter, we provide a summary of future research directions.

This research was conducted as part of the CREATOUR (Creative Tourism Destination Development in Small Cities and Rural Areas) project. CREATOUR is developing an integrated approach to creative tourism by combining interdisciplinary, methodological, technical, and theoretical approaches to link the tourism and cultural/creative sectors in non-metropolitan areas of mainland Portugal. The project aims to promote a more sustainable and holistic development of rural and small city/town destinations with a strong historical and cultural past through the active and creative involvement of visitors and residents with local habits, traditions, and customs. The initiatives that are integrated within this project link creative, culture-based activities with various aspects of the 'authentic heritage' of the varied landscapes of the country for the benefit of both local residents and participating visitors.

Advances in creative tourism and existing networks and platforms

The concept of creative tourism

Creative tourism has become a focus of attention (Richards, 2011) due to recent tourism trends linked to meaningful and authentic experiences (Gilbert, 1989;

167

Poon, 1989) and to active involvement with culture and contact with real people (Richards and Wilson, 2008). In spite of this, there is no generally accepted definition (Richards, 2011), nor is there one single model or perspective (Richards and Marques, 2012). It is quite open and flexible in its adaptation to local contexts. The encounter between the conceptualization and different meanings of creativity from person to person, societies, and cultures (Klausen, 2010) makes it difficult to conceptualize.

Creative tourism, understood as a potential form of tourism, was first referred to by Pearce and Butler (1993), but they did not suggest a definition at that time (Richards, 2011). The first definition of creative tourism emerged in 2000, and was seen as tourism that offers visitors the opportunity to develop their creative potential. This is possible if the tourist participates actively in experiences and learning, themes, and activities, and if the activities are presented in the destination that is visited (Richards and Raymond, 2000).

In 2004, the UNESCO Creative Cities Network (UCCN) was created to promote intercity cooperation and learning in the use of culture and creativity for the sustainable development of urban areas. At the 2006 UCCN meeting in Santa Fe, New Mexico, creative tourism was identified as a new generation of tourism because it 'involves more interaction, in which the visitor has an educational, emotional, social, and participative interaction with the place, its living culture, and the people who live there' (UNESCO, 2006b, p. 26).

In 2007, a new vision of creative tourism emerged from Raymond (2007) as a result of his experiences in New Zealand, arguing that it is a more sustainable form of tourism. By providing a sense of authenticity of the local culture enhanced by small-scale practical workshops and informal creative experiences, it enables tourists to explore their creativity. In short, this kind of tourism provides the opportunity for tourists to really feel part of the place (Landry, 2010).

Creative tourism combines many different concepts: creativity, capacity development (Richards and Raymond, 2000; Briggs, 2005; UNESCO, 2006a), involvement with local people (Richards and Wilson, 2006; UNESCO, 2006b; Richards, 2011), local culture, active participation (Richards and Raymond, 2000; UNESCO, 2006b; Binkhorst, 2007), and the authentic experience (UNESCO, 2006; Binkhorst, 2007; Creative Tourism New Zealand, 2007). Perfume manufacturing workshops in France and cooking traditional dishes in Catalonia are some eloquent examples of unique experiences that involve engagement and developing skills. This idea of engagement and developing skills is also based on the move from 'seeing' to 'being' (Richards and Wilson, 2007), which refers to the importance of using other senses besides sight, such as smell and taste.

The wide range of creative tourism experiences has motivated some authors (e.g., D'Auria, 2009; Jelinčić, 2009) to analyze the transformation of cultural tourism into creative tourism as an evolution of cultural tourism focused on more authenticity.

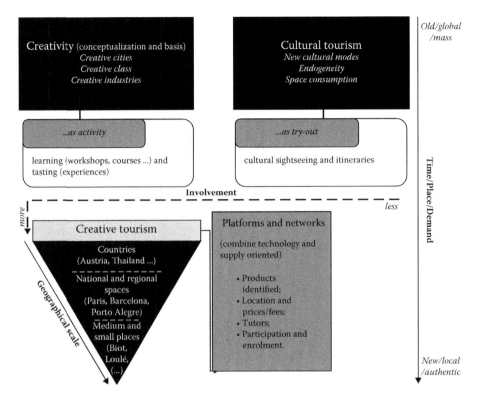

Source: Elaborated by authors.

Figure 13.1   From mass cultural tourism to creative tourism

In part, there is a greater fragmentation of cultural tourism because many creative activities are pursued by tourists who live postmodern lifestyles (Jelinčić, 2009). This fragmentation has also led to a variety of different views of creative tourism: as a form of cultural tourism (Richards, 2011) or niche tourism (Prentice, 2001; Richards and Wilson, 2006; Smith, 2006), or that creative tourism is the future of cultural tourism, which is already showing signs of saturation. A summary of our assessment of some of the main differences between cultural tourism and creative tourism is presented in Figure 13.1.

Many creative tourism networks have been developed, most notably the international Creative Tourism Network, which aims to promote destinations that have the potential to welcome visitors who are looking for new sensations and experiences both in the arts and participating with locals. This network includes national and regional capitals such as Paris, Barcelona, and Porto Alegre, Brazil, as well as small places such as the town of Biot in the south of France and the Tuscany region in Italy. There are also national networks in countries such as Austria, Guatemala, New Zealand, and Thailand, and more national and international seminars and conferences are being staged by these bodies (Richards, 2008, 2011).

We agree with Királová (2016) that creative tourism is fundamentally important in optimizing tangible and intangible heritage destinations and has a positive impact on safeguarding culture and the authenticity of places because of the value and interest shown by tourists in the practices and traditions of resident communities. It is a strong supporter of sustainability in tourism and can help combat seasonality. It also opens up the possibility of creating new destinations and new products based on a discovery of the real value of the culture(s) intrinsic to a landscape and a community.

According to Prentice and Andersen (2007), creative tourism is also more sustainable than cultural tourism based on consumption alone. It is not simply an activity to experience a ready-made product, but an opportunity to experience co-creation with other visitors, resident communities, and managers/promoters. In addition, creative tourists are interested in cultural diversity and can help to increase the cultural value of the destination and help local communities to appreciate the everyday aspects of their culture.

Richards (2014) expands on the idea of creativity in tourism within the framework of the aforementioned perspectives of product development and experiences, as well as noting its value in terms of cultural and creative valorization: revitalizing existing products, setting up spin-offs for creative development, and using creative technology – all placing value on culture-based and creative activity. There is no denying the individual value and the societal benefits of this co-creation through activities that generate great personal and emotional involvement.

Creative tourism can be an activity that can successfully develop in new spaces and, in particular, allow the development of less visited rural areas with fewer (traditional) tourist resources to become attractive to visitors. Creative spaces (creative cities and regions) can be developed that wish to opt for one of the avenues of creative tourism (Richards and Wilson, 2007).

Existing spaces, networks, and platforms in creative tourism

Gastronomy, painting, photography, crafts, music, dance, and wine tasting are experiences and activities found in many destinations where creative tourism is the main theme (Smith, 2009), and many networks and platforms have been established to develop and promote these kinds of experiences. These networks and platforms are the result of the conviction that creative tourism can involve cultural agents to take advantage of the potential of tourism to develop creative industries and activities.

The main objective of these networks is, therefore, to facilitate the development of cultural groups, exchanging knowledge, experiences, and best practices, while enhancing social development and promoting local economies (Itaú Cultural, 2012). As Scott (2005) has noted, 'By grouping together, companies will be able to save on their spatial interconnections, to obtain the multiple advantages of spatially concentrated labour markets, connect to the abundant flow of information and potential innovation that is present whenever many producers with different and complementary specialities come together' (cited by Itaú Cultural, 2012, p. 15).

The formation of a social network is typically associated with the need for a set of agents to receive some type of information or resource from others, thus creating an exchange through which investments and relationships will be determined by their levels of needs. In this network, the cultural agent is a node that represents an entity, either an individual or an organization (Uddin, 2017). Recent studies on tourism management have found that networking is a new and positive means of coordination, which is an important issue in this debate because there is a gap between the various stakeholders in tourism (Van der Zee and Vanneste, 2015). Networks support innovation and knowledge sharing, develop competitiveness and foster sustainability, and promote economic development for the stakeholders involved (Pavlovich, 2003; Novelli et al., 2006). Hall (2005) defines a network as 'an arrangement of interorganisation cooperation and collaboration' (p. 179).

Tourism networks have various positive factors. Networks function as systems that can organize and integrate tourism and destinations, improve the performance and quality of destinations, benefit tourism companies, and provide unique experiences to tourists (Zach and Racherla, 2011). Networks can bring together local people, contexts, and atmospheres to enable creative activities to develop in various locations (Richards, 2011). Learning traditional cuisine in Bangkok; making sculptures out of wood or bone based on tradition and local crafts in Portugal, Finland, Greece (Richards, 2005), and New Zealand (Raymond, 2007); dancing the Rumba in Barcelona or Sevillanas in Seville; blowing glass in Biot (French Riviera); producing chill-out music in Ibiza (Creative Tourism Network) – all these are unique and authentic experiences that take visitors to these destinations and definitely mark the experiences and memories of a place. Such diversified experiences, translated into networks and platforms, are recognized as ways to ensure the originality and authenticity of the offers, adapting them to the 'best practices of creative tourism' and promoting such locations as 'creative friendly'.

Research methodology

To chart the development of creative tourism worldwide, from March to August 2017 an Internet-based search was conducted using Google and the following keywords: 'creative tourism initiatives', 'creative cities', and 'best practices in creative tourism'. This research, which included Creative Tourism Network member institutions, helped us identify creative tourism initiatives being developed around the world. We found 24 institutions that are developing creative tourism initiatives and created a database of 20 topic items for each of them (e.g., institution responsible for implementing initiatives, year of implementation, website, types of activities developed, place of development, country, type of partners, and nature of local community involvement).

In September 2017, an in-depth analysis of each website was carried out to identify the activities undertaken by each institution. The analysis included topics such as: the typology of experiences promoted by the activities, the nature of visitor involvement, the typology of the offer, details about the animator and organizer of the creative activities, how long the activity takes, seasonality, prices, and the nature of the web-based information available for visitors. To analyze the type of creative activities offered, we used categories developed by ADDICT (Portuguese Agency for the Development of Creative Industries) and Augusto Mateus and Associados (2016) in terms of conception, creation, and product and process development. In addition, the creative tourism initiatives were categorized in terms of the creative sectors identified by the United Nations (Itaú Cultural, 2012), namely: crafts, audiovisual, design, media, performing arts, publishing, visual arts, and creative services including publicity, architecture, engineering, and other cultural services. A total of 160 creative tourism activities were categorized using the schemes proposed by ADDICT and the United Nations. A content analysis of the collected data and an evaluation of the offer of the institutions that said they practice creative tourism were carried out in order to diagnose the similarities and gaps in the offer.

In addition, representatives of each creative tourism institution were invited for an interview via Skype. The purpose of the interview was to complement the web-based information with insights on trends and issues from their perspectives and experiences. However, between July and November 2017, we received only seven positive answers from Europe and Brazil. This reflects the difficulty of reaching the institutions to obtain the information required.

Evaluation of good practices in creative tourism

The creative tourism initiatives and platforms we identified (Figure 13.2) show a strong concentration of projects in Europe. In total, our search found 24 sites with information for creative tourism: 1 network in Africa (Madagascar), 2 located in Asia (Thailand and Japan), 1 in South America (Brazil), 1 in Central America (Guatemala), 2 in Oceania (1 in New Zealand and 1 in Australia), and 17 in Europe (Spain, Portugal, France, Italy, Belgium, Austria, and England). Countries in southern Europe are more active in terms of developing creative tourism activities. One might ask: Is this because they have more saturated tourism markets and therefore need to develop new products and try to attract new audiences? Two of the platforms support general networks and receive and share information from other creative tourism organizations/institutions around the world. The most creative tourism platforms in Europe now hold a leading position in international creative tourism.

The platforms that were analyzed initiated their activities between 1988 and 2015, and most were created in the last few years. In spite of the current concentration

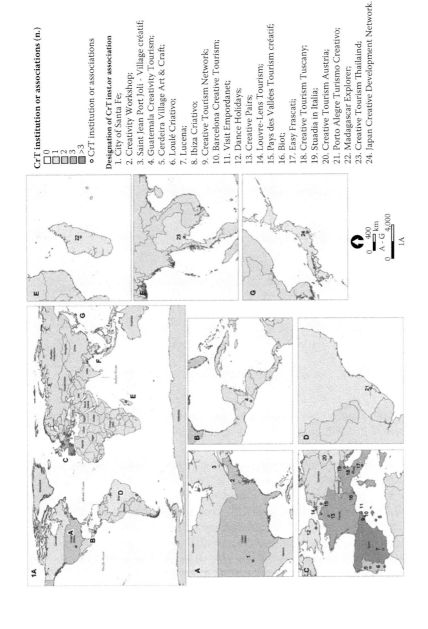

CrT institution or associations (n.)

0
1
2
3
>3

○ CrT institution or associations

Designation of CrT inst.or association
1. City of Santa Fe;
2. Creativity Workshop;
3. Saint Jean Port Joli - Village créatif;
4. Guatemala Creativity Tourism;
5. Cerdeira Village Art & Craft;
6. Loulé Criativo;
7. Lucena;
8. Ibiza Criativo;
9. Creative Tourism Network;
10. Barcelona Creative Tourism;
11. Visit Empordanet;
12. Dance Holidays;
13. Creative Pairs;
14. Louvre-Lens Tourism;
15. Pays des Vallées Tourism créatif;
16. Biot;
17. Easy Frascati;
18. Creative Tourism Tuscany;
19. Stuadia in Italia;
20. Creative Tourism Austria;
21. Porto Alegre Turismo Creativo;
22. Madagascar Explorer;
23. Creative Tourism Thailaind;
24. Japan Creative Development Network.

Source: Based on data from the Creative Tourism Network and maps from Google.

Figure 13.2 Number and location of places that organize creative initiatives, 2017

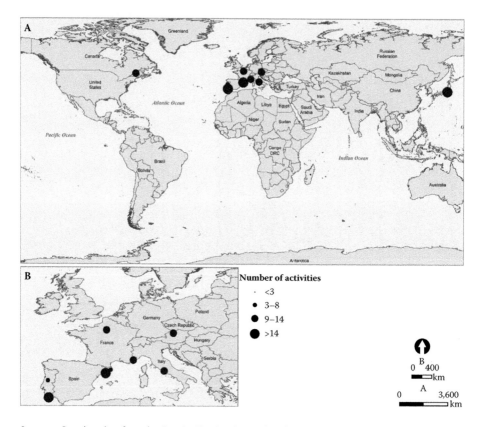

Source: Based on data from the Creative Tourism Network and maps from Google.

Figure 13.3   Number of creative initiatives identified in 2017

of creative tourism programmes in Europe, it seems that the first creative tourism networks appeared in Madagascar, the USA, and Japan (Figure 13.4).

In most (147) of the 160 activities listed on the creative platforms, tourists are invited to co-create. In 110 activities, the participants have the chance to take part and co-create with the maker/artist who organized the activity. From an analysis of 37 of these initiatives, it appears that the tourist can only be an observer of the activities, and the profile of these participants is not clear from the websites. In four activities, participants were involved in classes/training forums, thematic literary reflections, or wine tasting. In nine activities, it is difficult to define the type of experience given to the tourist because it is ambiguous or information is not given about the relationship between the tourist and the organizer. In only 98 out of 160 activities was it possible to understand the profile and only in 92 out of 160 activities was there information on periodicity. Moreover, only 83 out of 160 activities included the date the activity took place. This logistical information should be regarded as a weak point of creative tourism communication. The

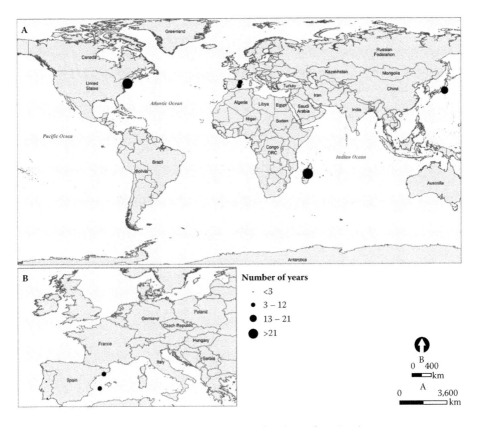

Source: Based on data from the Creative Tourism Network and maps from Google.

Figure 13.4   Number of years of creative initiatives identified in 2017

European countries previously mentioned (Spain, Portugal, France, Italy, Belgium, and England) also offer the most activities (Figure 13.3).

Creative tourism activities cover a wide range of creative sectors, including music and literature, film, design and media, gastronomy, folklore, and crafts. For example, in Thailand (Creative Tourism Thailand), experiences include massage, boxing, floral arts, gastronomy, fruit sculpture, traditional dances, singing, painting, pottery, and origami, while in Guatemala (Creative Tourism Guatemala), activities include exploring chocolate and coffee manufacturing workshops following the Mayan tradition. Barcelona Creative Tourism, one of the leaders in creative activities, runs workshops in Gaudi-style mosaics, Catalan rumba, and cuisine, and offers the chance to organize concerts in unique places. Experiences from Creative Tourism of Galicia (Spain) are linked to music and singing, where tourists can participate in local choirs, celebrations, and popular festivals. They can also make baskets, learn how to bake cookies, or even make cosmetic products. In Paris, the focus is naturally on the development of activities related to perfume, pastries (particularly croissants), and fashion in sewing workshops. Austria promotes creativity activities through traditional dances, handicrafts, and cuisine, while Creative Tourism Santa Fe (USA) offers opportunities to attend jewellery, painting, ceramics, photography, art, and cuisine workshops, as well as participate in visits to artist studios.

Creative tourism offers a wealth of experiences and activities in the most diverse fields of traditions and know-how, as well as intangibles and senses (smells, tastes, and sounds). In Portugal, Loulé Criativo (in the southern Algarve region) is notable in terms of its range of activities related to creating products from this area, for example, grapes in Quinta da Tôr, painting the legends of the Algarve, traditional Portuguese drums, and 'from the market to the kitchen' activities.

Table 13.1 shows the type of creative tourism activities being offered. The experiences are oriented mainly towards local products (93 activities) or towards products from other countries (45 activities). There are 20 activities related to creative work in visual arts, one to research, and one to contemporary society. Local products are preferred among the organization of creative tourism products, which provide a platform to transmit and share the local culture and local identity.

Four large investment areas in creative tourism can be found: visual arts (23 per cent), gastronomy and wines (21 per cent), handicrafts and traditional arts (18 per cent), and cultural tours or visits (13 per cent). Beyond these, we found a diversity

Table 13.1   Types of creative activities developed by institutions

	Per cent of activities (%)
Visual arts, including drawing and painting	23
Gastronomy and wines	21
Crafts and traditional arts	18
Tours and cultural visits	13
Performing arts	4
Historical recreation and heritage	4
Photography and video	3
Music	2
Creative writing and literature	2
Sports	2
Fashion design	2
Health domain (gymnastics, yoga, and Chinese therapy)	2
Furniture design	< 1
Cosmetics and beauty	< 1

Note: n = 160.

Source: Authors.

Table 13.2   Summary of the most relevant findings about the networks and platforms of activities in creative tourism

Characterization	Description
Areas of expansion of creative tourism	• Oceania, Africa, and America • Expansion to Europe • Mass and domain of Europe (appearance in Mediterranean Europe, with cases in Portugal, Spain or Italy)
Categorization of activities	• Significant proportion of activities related to arts (23%) and gastronomy and wines (21%)
Development stages	• *Phase 1* (activities oriented to cultural-creative tourism): before 2000 (Madagascar Explorer; Creativity Workshop; Creative Tourism New Zealand) • *Phase 2* (consolidation of concept of creative tourism and dissemination of Richards's theorization): 2000 to 2010 (Japan Creative Development Network; Barcelona Creativa) • *Phase 3* (maturity of concept and basis for increased value generation; reapplication in other areas and other products): post-2010 (Ibiza Creativa; Loulé Criativa; Cerdeira Village; Jean Port Créatif Joli; Creative Tourism Network)
Supply characteristics	• Short-term activities (usually less than 1 day) • Orientation to local products (in 54.7% of activities identified), especially in activities practised by European institutions • Majority are enrolled in co-creation (i.e., artistic moments; making local dishes) • Wide range of languages

Source: Authors.

of experiences not as widely adopted by creative tourism organizations, such as scenic arts, historical recreation, photography and video, creative literature, fashion and furniture design, and health and beauty (Table 13.1). This may reflect the preferences of visitors and/or creative organizations to invest in experiences that are tried and tested rather than new and innovative areas.

Some conclusions and future research directions

Opportunities arising from the connection between tourist activities and tourists in a co-creation relationship have spread from countries in Oceania, Africa, and the Americas, and finally to Europe. The Mediterranean countries have more recent projects, perhaps because tourist products are normally associated with 'sun and sea' tourism and they have felt a strong need to diversify their touristic offerings to maintain a competitive 'edge'. The evolution of creative tourism can be subdivided into three stages: (1) prior to 2000: implementing cultural tourism initiatives adopting a creative approach, although creativity was not the primary purpose; (2) 2000–10: with the theoretical contribution of Greg Richards and the implementation of initiatives in other countries and geographic areas, with expanded participation in activities by tourists; and (3) post-2010: generating revenues, involving new audiences, improving projects based on creative tourism, and including additional geographical areas (Table 13.2). Rural areas are part of this new attempt to develop creative activities, but it tends to be rare to include them in creative destinations. Rural areas are interested in introducing new domains of activity, but are mainly focused on culture and popular art, as well as (now popular) activities related to arts/festivals, gastronomy, and wine.

Concerning international practices in creative tourism networks and platforms, there will be a challenge in the coming years to develop a more complete offering of creative experiences. Our review indicates that there are a number of areas where there is potential to develop additional information or to provide new creative experiences through regional, national, or international platforms:

1. There is not always full information provided on the nature of the creative tourism activity.
2. The activities analyzed are mainly done in English, although some of them are taught in other languages.
3. In some places, there is no information about the activities developed on their websites, as in the cases of Creative Tourism Thailand, Creative Tourism Tuscany, Ibiza Creativa, Pays de Valées, and Studia in Italia; for cases where there is information on the websites, often the activity data shown is related to activities developed in other years and not current ones.
4. The prices of activities vary, offering variations, in most cases, proportional to the duration of the activity and the materials needed to carry it out; the average price of these activities is between €25 and €50.
5. The activities developed are mainly related to traditional arts, visual arts, gastronomy, and wines, although they are sometimes not concerned with actively engaging the tourist.
6. The institutions analyzed are concentrated in Europe, especially in southern Europe, in countries such as Spain, France, and Italy. In these countries, there seems to be a greater concern, through new types of activities, to attract audiences that can rejuvenate destinations. (Related to this, in the near future we intend to study how new activities can be implemented and how new audiences can be attracted. This information can be useful in re-targeting destinations.)
7. In the near-term future, existing creative tourism experiences can be diversified. As nowadays most people use computers and cell phones to write, calligraphy workshops will be most welcome. Book illustration, screen printing, risography, and binding are also alternatives to existing initiatives. And why not encourage the opportunity to be an actor for a day? This can be a memorable experience in some destinations.

In conclusion, creative tourism and its platforms have been developing more and more rapidly around the world and increasingly attracting a consistent number of participants. But research on the development, nature, and functioning of such networks and platforms remains sparse. We therefore suggest some fruitful avenues for future research.

Future research directions

One of the biggest gaps in our knowledge relates to the profile and motivations of the creative tourist. What types of people are attracted to creative tourism experiences, why do they participate, and what do they take away from the experience? Are they mainly domestic tourists, or are international travellers increasingly important? What kind of information sources do creative tourists use to find the experiences they participate in? The answers to these questions might also help us to understand the relationship between creative tourism and other forms of tourism. For example, given the concentration of creative tourism programmes in areas of Europe that already attract large numbers of tourists, to what extent are these experiences providing an alternative to the conventional tourism offer? What aspects of the experience help to differentiate them from other tourism products (for example, less participatory cultural tourism experiences) in the same region or destination?

Understanding the creative tourist and the relationship of creative tourism to cultural tourism can also provide important information relating to the ability of creative tourism to spread tourism to new areas. In the context of the CREATOUR project, for example, it is important to understand how creative tourism projects can help attract tourists to non-metropolitan and rural areas. It may also be interesting to investigate the extent to which creative tourism can help to combat seasonality in rural areas and also in traditional tourism destinations. This is important because a flow of creative tourists to areas with low population density can arguably help to support the creative life of small communities.

It is also important to understand the profile, activities, and skills of the providers of creative tourism experiences. What motivates people to develop creative tourism supply? Are new experiences developed to satisfy the creative drive of producers, or to tap into tourism as a new source of economic support? What do the producers learn from the tourists, and to what extent is active co-creation taking place? In the context of the CREATOUR project, it will be interesting to analyze the way in which producers in small communities manage to develop and sustain their initiatives. Does the peripheral location of many of these experiences make it difficult to ensure a flow of tourists, and therefore provide year-round, permanent access to experiences? To what extent does a flow of creative tourists help the producers to continue their creative activities?

Finally, in regard to the creative tourism networks and platforms, further research is needed on the best approaches to developing and managing these networks as both promotional hubs and capacity-building and knowledge-sharing entities. In addition, fruitful ways to distil and share the experience-based learning embodied within these organizations remains under-examined.

Acknowledgements

This research was conducted within the framework of the project 'CREATOUR: Creative Tourism Destination Development in Small Cities and Rural Areas' (no. POCI-0145-FEDER-016437), which is funded by the Portuguese Foundation for Science and Technology (FCT/MEC) through national funds and co-funded by FEDER through the Joint Activities Programme of COMPETE 2020 and the Regional Operational Programmes of Lisbon and Algarve.

References

Augusto Mateus and Associados (2016), *A economia criativa em Portugal. Relevância para a competitividade e Internacionalização da Economia Portuguesa*, Lisbon: ADDICT.

Binkhorst, E. (2007), 'Creativity in tourism experiences: the case of Sitges', in G. Richards and J. Wilson (eds), *Tourism, Creativity and Development*, London: Routledge, pp. 125–44.

Briggs, S. (2005), *Cultural Tourism: How You Can Benefit – A VisitBritain Advisory Guide*, ed. A. Bevan, London: VisitBritain, accessed 23 October 2018 at http://www.tourismknowhow.com/uploads/4/8/5/6/4856328/culturaltourism.pdf.

D'Auria, A. (2009), 'Urban cultural tourism: creative approaches for heritage-based sustainable development', *International Journal of Sustainable Development*, 12 (2/3/4), 275–89.

Gilbert, D. (1989), 'Rural tourism and marketing: synthesis and new ways of working', *Tourism Management*, 10 (1), 39–50.

Hall, C. (2005), *Tourism: Rethinking the Social Science of Mobility*, Harlow: Prentice-Hall.

Itaú Cultural (2012), *Relatório de Economia Criativa 2010: Economia criativa uma opção de desenvolvimento*, São Paulo: Secretaria da Economia Criativa, accessed 26 September 2017 at http://unctad.org/pt/docs/ditctab20103_pt.pdf.

Jelinčić, D. (2009), 'Splintering of tourism market: new appearing forms of cultural tourism as a consequence of changes in everyday lives', *Collegium Antropologicum*, 33 (1), 259–66.

Királová, A. (2016), 'Creativity as a tool of tourism development', in A. Királová (ed.), *Driving Tourism through Creative Destinations and Activities*, Hershey, PA: IGI-Global, pp. 67–93.

Klausen, S.H. (2010), 'The notion of creativity revisited: a philosophical perspective on creativity research', *Creativity Research Journal*, 22 (4), 347–60.

Landry, C. (2010), 'Experiencing imagination: travel as a creative trigger', in R. Wurzburger, T. Aageson, A. Pattakos and S. Pratt (eds), *Creative Tourism: A Global Conversation*, Santa Fe, NM: Sunstone Press, pp. 33–42.

Novelli, M., B. Schmitz and T. Spencer (2006), 'Networks, clusters and innovation in tourism: a UK experience', *Tourism Management*, 27 (6), 1141–52.

Pavlovich, K. (2003), 'The evolution and transformation of a tourism destination network: the Waitomo Caves, New Zealand', *Tourism Management*, 24 (2), 203–16.

Pearce, D. and R. Butler (eds) (1993), *Tourism Research: Critiques and Challenges*, London: Routledge.

Poon, A. (1989), 'Competitive strategies for a "new tourism"', *Progress in Tourism, Recreation and Hospitality Management*, 1, 91–102.

Prentice, R. (2001), 'Experiential cultural tourism: museums and the marketing of the new romanticism of evoked authenticity', *Museum Management and Curatorship*, **19** (1), 5–26.

Prentice, R. and V. Andersen (2007), 'Creative tourism supply: creating culturally empathetic destinations', in G. Richards and J. Wilson (eds), *Tourism, Creativity and Development*, London: Routledge, pp. 89–106.

Raymond, C. (2007), 'Creative tourism New Zealand: the practical challenges of developing creative tourism', in G. Richards and J. Wilson (eds), *Tourism, Creativity and Development*, London: Routledge, pp. 146–57.

Richards, G. (2005), 'Textile tourists in the European periphery: new markets for disadvantaged areas?', *Tourism Review International*, **8**, 323–38.

Richards, G. (2008), 'Cultural tourism: global and local perspectives', *Journal of Cultural Economics*, **32** (3), 231–6.

Richards, G. (2011), 'Creativity and tourism: the state of the art', *Annals of Tourism Research*, **38** (4), 1225–53.

Richards, G. (2014), 'Creativity and tourism in the city', *Current Issues in Tourism*, **17** (2), 119–44.

Richards, G. and L. Marques (2012), 'Exploring creative tourism: introduction', *Journal of Tourism Consumption and Practice*, **4** (2), 1–11.

Richards, G. and C. Raymond (2000), 'Creative tourism', *ATLAS News*, **23**, 16–20.

Richards, G. and J. Wilson (2006), 'Developing creativity in tourist experiences: a solution to the serial reproduction of culture?', *Tourism Management*, **27** (6), 1408–13.

Richards, G. and J. Wilson (2007), *Tourism, Creativity and Development*, London: Routledge.

Richards, G. and J. Wilson (2008), *From Cultural Tourism to Creative Tourism – Part 1: The Changing Context of Cultural Tourism*, Arnhem: ATLAS.

Scott, J. (2005), *On Hollywood*, Princeton, NJ: Princeton University Press.

Smith, M.K. (2009), *Issues in Cultural Tourism Studies*, London: Routledge.

Smith, W.L. (2006), 'Experiential tourism around the world and at home: definitions and standards', *International Journal of Services and Standards*, **2**, 1–14.

Uddin, S. (2017), 'Social network analysis in project management', *Journal of Modern Project Management*, May/August, 106–13.

UNESCO (2006a), *The Global Alliance for Cultural Diversity: Understanding Creative Industries*, Santa Fe, NM, accessed 26 September 2017 at http://www.ico-d.org/connect/features/post/229.php.

UNESCO (2006b), *Towards Sustainable Strategies for Creative Tourism*, Santa Fe, NM: UNESCO Creative Cities Network.

Van der Zee, E. and D. Vanneste (2015), 'Tourism networks unravelled: a review of the literature on networks in tourism management studies', *Tourism Management Perspectives*, **15**, 46–56.

Zach, F. and P. Racherla (2011), 'Assessing the value of collaborations in tourism networks: a case study of Elkhart County, Indiana', *Journal of Travel and Tourism Marketing*, **28** (1), 97–110.

Websites

Creative Paris: http://www.creativeparis.info/en/
Creative Tourism Austria: http://www.kreativreisen.at/en
Creative Tourism Network: http://www.creativetourismnetwork.org
Creative Tourism New Zealand: http://www.creativetourism.co.nz
UNESCO Creative Cities Network: http://en.unesco.org/creative-cities/home

14 Towards a research agenda in creative tourism: a synthesis of suggested future research trajectories

Nancy Duxbury and Greg Richards

As the chapters in this volume have demonstrated, creative tourism is a young and dynamic field that has already spawned a wide range of topics for investigation, theoretical reflections, methodological frameworks, and empirical approaches. In this closing chapter, we provide an overview of the main themes for future research that have been suggested in this volume and point out potentially fruitful future research avenues within the creative tourism field and related to it. In putting together this chapter, we chose to elaborate a breadth of research needs and trajectories in creative tourism research rather than narrowing to a 'top five priorities' list. In doing this, we feel we are reflecting the needs of a growing and diversifying area of activity and of the research that is accompanying this development. We also hope this provides a richer array of options for constructing individual research agendas in creative tourism. Accordingly, we have organized the chapter into nine thematic areas: the creative tourist, creative tourism experiences, creative supply, marketing creative tourism, the development of creative tourism experiences and destinations, assessing creative tourism development, the role of local communities in creative tourism, placemaking through creative tourism, and creative tourism networks and platforms.

The creative tourist

Who is the 'creative tourist'? Can we actually talk about one type of creative tourist, or are there many different types of tourists and creative experiences? Arguably, people – the creative tourists and their hosts – should be at the heart of the creative experience. But we still know relatively little about these people, or what motivates them to engage in (co-)creative experiences. As Remoaldo et al. suggest, there is still much research to be done on issues such as what types of people are attracted to creative tourism experiences, why they participate, and what they take away from the experience. Are they mainly domestic tourists, or are international travellers becoming increasingly important? What kind of information sources do creative tourists use to find the experiences they participate in? The work of Delisle also suggests other areas of investigation, such as the gender and age profiles of creative tourists, and the main origin areas from which they come.

Profiling the creative tourist can also help us understand the relative importance and role of creative tourists in the creative sphere as a whole. For example, is creative tourism driven by the growth of cultural tourism or, in other words, by a rejection of traditional 'mass cultural tourism'? Or is it driven by a growing interest in creativity per se in society? For example, the work of Angela McRobbie (2016) charts the rising popularity of various creative professions, which, in turn, might be expected to drive creative tourism demand as a means to learn new creative skills. Or it might be linked to the growth of the 'creative class', as suggested by Richard Florida. Some studies have already attempted to trace the link between the creative class and creative tourism (e.g., Gretzel and Jamal, 2009; Whiting and Hannam, 2014), but there is still much work left to do on the relationship between creative occupations, activities, and tourism.

Creative tourism experiences

Many of the contributions to this volume argue that creative tourists are attracted by the creative experiences that destinations have to offer. But what does the creative tourism experience actually consist of? Previous studies have underlined the complex nature of experiences, which arguably are holistic in nature and therefore very challenging to measure (De Geus et al., 2015). So the operationalization of the creative aspects of creative tourism experiences and the measurement of the experiences of different types of visitors in different contexts and locations becomes an important research issue. There is a lot of potential for developing scales to measure creative tourism experiences, and to understand the creative content of tourism experiences. Towards this end, Richards (2017) emphasizes the need to move away from prescriptive models towards more creative modes of creativity (Table 14.1).

One of the supposed effects of creative tourism is the ability to develop transformative experiences. As Tan and Tan point out, transformative learning can be used to nurture creative tourists, guide industry practitioners, and foster an affective sense of place towards heritage sites among local residents. Jelinčić and

Table 14.1 Comparison of 'creative model' and 'creative mode' approaches

	Creative Model	Creative Mode
Way of thinking	Prescriptive	Open
Way of being	Following	Leading
Way of moving	Fast	Slow
Way of relating	Top-down	Bottom-up
Way of inspiring	Gurus	Everyday creativity

Source: Richards (2017).

Senkić also argue that creative tourism can offer experiences that have the power to transform the visitor, thus leaving memorable traces. They also suggest that a transdisciplinary research approach grounded in culture, arts, and neuroscience can provide useful information on experience by focusing on the way in which different cultural/creative visual, aural, olfactory, gustative, and tactile stimuli can stir emotions. This is a direction also suggested by the work of Miettinen et al. in their use of creative tourism topography in Lapland. The development of new technologies can be very useful in tracking emotional responses to creative experiences.

There is also potential to explore the way in which different contexts help to trigger or support creative experiences. For example, Matetskaya et al. note the specific nature of rural areas in providing creative inspiration, and Brouder considers the context provided by peripheral locations. Many research questions could be related to the links between the experience context and other factors, such as personality or acquired skills, in contributing to the final visitor experience. Research along these lines is now emerging in the field of visitor studies (e.g., Falk, 2016).

At a fairly basic level, we also still need to understand what distinguishes creative tourism experiences from other forms of tourism. To what extent are these experiences providing an alternative to the conventional tourism offer? In the CREATOUR project in Portugal, to distinguish creative tourism activities from other experiential tourism activities, particular emphasis is placed on the creation process and the capacity for the visitor to engage in an activity with the potential for self-expression (Duxbury et al., 2019b). Further research is needed on what aspects of creative experiences differentiate them from other tourism products (for example, less participatory cultural tourism experiences) in the same region or destination. Do creative tourists actually do more 'creative' things than other tourists? Do they feel they are being more creative (and why)?

Creative supply

Although there is an emerging body of work on the supply of creative tourism offers (as Remoaldo et al. show), we still know relatively little about the profile, motivations, and experiences of those who provide or co-create the supply of creative experiences. What motivates people to become involved in creative tourism? Are new experiences developed to satisfy the creative drive of producers, or to tap into tourism as a new source of economic support? What do the producers learn from the tourists, and to what extent is active co-creation taking place?

Relatively little research has been done on the 'supply side' – the creative producers, such as artists, artisans, specialists, tutors, suppliers, service providers, and so forth (Delisle). It will be important to understand the pre-requisites for offering such activities, both in terms of the individual creative producers (micro-scale) and the umbrella organizations linking together and promoting such offers (meso-scale). Do creative tourism suppliers act out of economic motives (as Hanifl's research in Santa Fe might suggest), or are they more likely to be 'lifestyle entrepreneurs' who are more interested in supporting their own creative lifestyle than in making money?

Furthermore, as Matetskaya et al. indicate, we also know relatively little about the business models adopted by creative tourism entrepreneurs. Are creative tourism businesses truly innovative, new ideas, or do they act as an extension to existing tourism products? How are creative tourism activities contextualized and 'packaged' with other experiences to attract creative travellers, sometimes across significant distances to small towns and rural areas? How are synergies produced in these initiatives? How do various approaches resonate in different geographical and cultural contexts, and with different types of offers?

Differentiating creative tourism offers to explore more deeply the different types of creative tourism supplied, for example, by making a distinction between serious leisure and casual leisure, or the degree of active participation offered to tourists, or different art forms and aesthetic experiences, is also needed. What makes a 'successful' creative tourism offer? To what extent do tourists actually get involved in the co-creation of experiences? Seo suggests some interesting new perspectives emerging at the intersection of the attention economy and the experience economy, where creativity may need to be served up in ways that cater to reduced attention spans. As Delisle points out, research might also consider the input needed by the creative producer as a host compared to the one expected by the visitor.

The intermediation role of creative suppliers seems to be increasingly important, and Tan and Tan suggest that they can provide a bridge between cultural heritage and creativity in the context of tourism. Bakas et al. (2018) observe the emergence of artisan entrepreneur-mediators who connect artisans to creative tourism in small town and rural contexts in Portugal. These entrepreneur-mediators take on multiple roles as networking agents who design, organize, promote, and offer creative tourism experiences, providing the missing link between artisans and tourists. This requires a high level of skill from the intermediary, and a high degree of social embeddedness in the community in which they operate. Beyond organizational skills, these intermediaries also need to foster a deeper understanding of cultural heritage and its conservation within the wider community, with appropriate creative strategies to revitalize these resources for community benefit.

Marketing creative tourism

The branding and marketing of creative tourism is an area of research that has not received much attention to date. Hanifl addresses the need for marketing creative tourism experiences in order to increase the economic benefit of creative tourism to producers. Artists are not always keen to market their products, so this might present a challenge for some individual producers. Bringing creative experiences and producers together in networks might help to pool marketing expertise and resources to reduce this problem, but there has been little research to show whether networks are more effective than individual artists/artisans in marketing creative tourism. To what extent can a creative tourism programme increase revenues relative to other tourism marketing or development options?

Furthermore, the operational aspects of creative tourism programmes, for example, the adaptation of social inclusion technologies to suit particular locations and communities, including motivation and team-building activities for residents, the distribution of administrative costs, and designing effective online and offline communications are also in need of research attention to help ensure community benefits derive from a destination's creative tourism initiatives (Matetskaya et al.).

From a macro/destination perspective, how do different creative tourism communities brand themselves, for example, in terms of creative tourism as a 'thing to do' or activity versus trying to brand the destination specifically as a creative tourism destination (Hanifl)? What is the added value of a creative tourism brand compared to other brands? What is the recognition of creative tourism and individual creative tourism brands among producers and consumers? As creative tourism is often positioned as a means of creating relationships, how do these add to the quality of the experience, and do consumers see creative experiences as more 'authentic'?

How are images, and possible brands, strategically related to creative tourism destination regions (Emmendoerfer)? How can we measure the impact of media and celebrities on creative tourism promotion and marketing strategies? In the broader context of investigating how the creative industries, mass media, and social media contribute to form place identity, what is the relationship of celebrity and media with creative tourism (Seo)?

The development of creative tourism experiences and destinations

Creative tourism is relatively new, and one might expect the field to exhibit a high level of innovation. We still know relatively little about how creative tourism ideas emerge, or how they are transferred between different entrepreneurs or communities. In the context of Bali, Blapp and Mitas suggest that there is a high level of copying of concepts, leading to the 'serial reproduction' of creative tourism products. One of the issues to be examined in this context is the extent to which a certain critical mass of creative resources or knowledge might be needed to support real innovation in creative tourism experiences. Seo argues that there is room to examine the evolution of creative tourism in terms of product diversity, and whether there is diversification based on creative convergence or the hybridization of activities to create new items. Future research could also consider the balance between strategic and accidental creative tourism developments.

We still know little about how different cultures, generations, and stakeholders interact and inspire 'sparks' to inform innovation processes and strategies in creative tourism. As Tan and Tan argue, it is interesting to assess the 'strengths' of each stakeholder involved, and how their interactions may inspire innovation. Thinking of this innovation as a socially embedded process with potentially wider implications, how can creative tourism ideas and processes help local communities to innovate and provide future development potential? And how can skills be passed between generations and between different communities in order to nurture cultural sustainability and ensure the spread of benefits from creative tourism? Greater knowledge is needed about how such processes function to guide the development of effective management systems in local communities (Wisansing and Vongvisitsin). What elements favour the collective work of stakeholders in the development of creative tourism? What conflicts exist in the relationship among creative tourism stakeholders? What are the productive agents and activities that lead and sustain a creative tourism development process (Emmendoerfer)?

As creative tourism develops, new research opportunities will also emerge in tracing development trajectories. How do producers in small communities manage to develop and sustain their initiatives (Remoaldo et al.)? Does the peripheral location of many creative tourism experiences make it difficult to ensure a flow of tourists, and therefore provide year-round access to experiences? Studies of the early stages of creative tourism development may turn into long-term studies of the virtuous spiral of creative tourism evolution as the concentration of tourism supply in rural peripheral places is expected to consolidate further in future creative outposts (Brouder). To what extent does a flow of creative tourists help the producers to continue their creative activities? As Delisle suggests, there are few empirical data about successes and pitfalls of creative tourism, and the viability of such activities is seldom addressed.

Assessing creative tourism development

Studying such development processes makes it imperative to monitor and evaluate the outputs and impacts of creative tourism. As Brouder suggests, measurements need to be made over a long period of time because the less tangible benefits of creative tourism development may only become evident over a period of years. Any measures need to be refined enough to fully value the local gains made in creative and other processes over the longer term. The metrics used to measure immediate returns or 'innovation' may not capture all necessary dimensions, and a focus on community relationships and processes of interaction may expand this lens to incorporate wider and more dispersed community changes. Creative outposts – places where the isolation from the regional core is offset by strong *in situ* cooperation and interaction – provide valuable settings for this type of research.

The outputs of creative tourism also need to be assessed relative to the aims. In many cases this may be the generation of economic impacts of different types. What are the effects of personal contacts between producers and consumers, or the physical process of co-creation? Does the closer personal contact between artists and tourists ensure that a greater proportion of total revenues accrue to cultural and creative organizations (Hanifl)? In the assessment of economic impacts, many areas of value are not being measured (for example, workshops booked directly with other suppliers, as well as non-economic types of impacts). Developing network value analyses (Colombo and Richards, 2017) of creative tourism destinations could provide a better understanding of the flow of resources between tourists, creative enterprises, tourism organizations, and the public sector.

The objectives of creative tourism initiatives may also involve benefits such as spreading tourism in space and time. One of the questions addressed by the CREATOUR project in Portugal (http://www.creatour.pt), for example, is the extent to which creative tourism can help combat tourism seasonality in traditional tourism destinations, and spread the dispersion of tourists to 'new' visiting areas, such as smaller communities and rural areas. Going beyond a tourism focus, how can creative tourism development provide a stimulus for the revitalization, diversification, and sustainability of rural and remote communities, while retaining local control and direction?

Identifying the true value of creative tourism for communities also implies taking a broad quality of life approach to monitoring and evaluation to identify the specific ways in which creative tourism could help local communities. For example, can the development of creative activities help to increase feelings of local pride and/or stimulate more young people to remain in rural communities (Wisansing and Vongvisitsin)? Can creative tourism activities help develop and strengthen social bonds among different residents in a community, contributing to intergenerational exchange and cultural sustainability? Interlinked with these dynamics, through what means can the introduction of creative tourists in a locale contribute to inter-cultural exchange, knowledge sharing, and co-creation, enriching the lives of both local residents and visitors? Could creative tourism provide an attractive base to support and develop creative life and vitality in rural communities, and potentially distinguish some areas as attractive for an influx of new residents?

Assessing the effectiveness of policies directed at developing creative tourism is also important, as Emmendoerfer suggests. There is relatively little research on the design and implementation of creative tourism policies, or the extent to which these may incorporate efforts towards collaborative governance and collective actions. We need to evaluate the synergies and issues encountered in the inter-relations among stakeholders in the tourism and creative fields, and the effect of creative tourism development on community leaders and decision-makers' perceptions and knowledge of culture-based and creative development and the creative economy. Can creative tourism initiatives provide a platform for wider discussions regarding cultural and creative development in a locale?

By comparing creative tourism development strategies with other, more traditional options we can assess what new kinds of value these can create. Comparing programmes at different scales (local, regional, national, international) can also yield useful insights into the effects of creative tourism development in different contexts. In such research, it is important to assess what is actually accomplished in any given creative tourism development. As Brouder notes, creative developments are often idiosyncratic and place-dependent, and many nascent successes are undone over time. This means looking beyond product and/or project 'failures' to the learning and increased community cohesion which comes from the process of creative tourism development since the knowledge gained becomes a resource for future development regardless of the present outcomes. Further development and application of indicators in a range of different settings is needed to analyze the costs and benefits of creative tourism development and to compare the effects of different creative tourism development strategies (Wisansing and Vongvisitsin).

The role of local communities in creative tourism

Although local communities are often considered to be at the heart of creative tourism, relatively little research has been done on their involvement in creative tourism. Does creative tourism development support or hinder community participation in tourism? How can local communities participate in the co-design of tourism products to have greater influence on the way they are presented and visualized? How can we improve dialogue, communication, and collaboration between the tourism industry and local communities, especially in peripheral regions (Miettinen et al.)?

How can local residents be meaningfully engaged and their skills and knowledge mobilized in creative tourism? Through participative processes such as cultural mapping (Duxbury et al., 2015, 2019a), how can local cultural resources, narratives, and other distinctive assets and places be linked to creative tourism initiatives? And how can local community benefit be assured in the strategic actions and processes that result?

What types of governance arrangements are most likely to assist the involvement of local communities in creative tourism? What is the degree of stakeholder participation in the development of creative tourism policies and projects (Emmendoerfer)? It would also be interesting to reflect on the role of creativity as a desirable form of development for many administrations. In the same way that cultural tourism has often been seen as a 'good' form of tourism, the creative label has also apparently helped to convince many cities and regions to follow this development path. How much of this attractiveness is due to exogenous factors (such as the influence of creativity 'gurus' like Richard Florida and Charles Landry) and how much is embedded in the local desire for creative expression and endogenous development potential?

Placemaking through creative tourism

Relatively superficial place marketing or place branding initiatives are gradually being supplemented by more holistic placemaking approaches. Borrowing from Lefebvre (1974 [1991]), Richards (2017) argues that an effective placemaking process involves consideration of the resources, meanings, and creativity present in a specific place. Places are not simply constructed through the assemblage of physical materials, but also shaped through the meanings and creative use of physical and intangible resources. Many creative tourism initiatives, such as the Hieronymus Bosch programme in the Dutch city of 's-Hertogenbosch or the Barcelona Creative Tourism programme, owe their success to a skilful use of creative resources to develop engaging narratives about places and the people who inhabit them (Richards and Duif, 2018).

The essential links between place, community, and tangible and intangible resources are also traced in the work of Wisansing (2015) in Thailand. Linking these elements can increase the pride of the local community in the places they inhabit, which in turn can be bolstered by having people from elsewhere come and share in their creativity. However, we still know relatively little about the processes that underlie such developments. What aspects of the creativity of a place are most likely to appeal to the local community as development tools, and how do these map onto the creative demands of tourists? In what ways do creative activities help to define the identity of places? Given the strong links between art and place narratives and images, how do creative activities support the arts identity of particular art-locales (Hanifl)?

Creative tourism networks and platforms

The roles and functions of creative tourism networks and platforms have received very little research attention to date, yet collectively form a significant soft infrastructure for this tourism domain. How have they developed and how are they sustained? What are the best approaches to developing and managing these networks as both promotional hubs and capacity-building and knowledge-sharing entities? How can such organizations distil and share their experience with others (Remoaldo et al.)?

Related to this, there is also a need to identify and examine different organizational models of creative tourism and creative tourism governance. There is plenty of scope to examine the relative effectiveness of 'top-down' models of projects coordinated by non-governmental organizations (NGOs) or destination marketing organizations (DMOs) and grassroots projects for local development based on public–private partnerships (Matetskaya et al.). The categorization of different models might be approached in terms of the power relations inherent in the organization (top-down versus bottom-up) and the level of organization of the participants (individual versus collective initiatives) (Figure 14.1), and associated with the different types of environments in which these models are developed and implemented.

Level of organization

Type of organization	Individual	Collective
Top-down	Local producer networks	Destination networks/ Creative regions
Bottom-up	Artists' workshops	Local creative cultures

Source: G. Richards.

Figure 14.1   Framework for examining organizational models of creative tourism and creative tourism governance

In closing

Creative tourism is an evolving, dynamic field in which policymakers and researchers are struggling to comprehend its changing nature; the demand for creative tourism experiences; the most effective and innovative approaches to the design, marketing, and execution of offers; the roles and influences of new technologies; and the broader consequences of creative tourism strategies and programmes for the sustainable development of local communities. On the ground, practitioners designing and implementing creative tourism offers are also looking for informed guidance in these matters.

Creative tourism does not fit well within traditional tourism research paradigms because it is not a mass market with significant economic impacts in urban and traditional holiday locales. However, in more and more places (and particularly in peripheral, rural places), creative tourism is fostering significant 'soft' impacts, which are now beginning to be mapped through new research processes and approaches. We are observing a growing range of disciplinary and theoretical perspectives brought to creative tourism, including many researchers from outside the tourism field, producing an interdisciplinary nexus. This confluence of multidisciplinary perspectives and approaches provides a rich platform for interlinking conceptual frameworks and innovating research methodologies to critically examine creative tourism in its multiple wider contexts.

As a field informed both by academic research and the changing dynamics of practice, research in creative tourism can critique and inform development practices for the benefit of both local communities and travellers in many different international contexts. In the current context of 'overtourism' in traditionally visited places and the ever-growing desire among travellers for meaningful, creative, and bespoke travel experiences, creative tourism is (potentially) positioned as a leading niche area from which future tourism trajectories and trends can be detected. And it may even illuminate the importance of imagination, creative activities, and self-expression in creating a more humane, mobile, and connected world.

References

Bakas, F.E., N. Duxbury and T. Vinagre de Castro (2018), 'Creative tourism: catalysing artisan entrepreneur networks in rural Portugal', *International Journal of Entrepreneurial Behaviour and Research*, **24**. doi:10.1108/IJEBR-03-2018-0177

Colombo, A. and G. Richards (2017), 'Eventful cities as global innovation catalysts: the Sónar Festival network', *Event Management*, **21** (5), 621–34.

De Geus, S., G. Richards and V. Toepoel (2015), 'Conceptualisation and operationalisation of event and festival experiences: creation of an event experience scale', *Scandinavian Journal of Hospitality and Tourism*, **16** (3), 274–96.

Duxbury, N., W.F. Garrett-Petts and D. MacLennan (eds) (2015), *Cultural Mapping as Cultural Inquiry*, New York: Routledge.

Duxbury, N., W.F. Garrett-Petts and A. Longley (eds) (2019a), *Artistic Approaches to Cultural Mapping: Activating Imaginaries and Means of Knowing*, London: Routledge.

Duxbury, N., E. Kastenholz and C. Cunha (2019b), 'Co-producing cultural heritage experiences through creative tourism', in *Managing Cultural Heritage in Tourism*, textbook for Moodle online-course, 'Basics of cultural heritage management in tourism', linked to the European project E-CUL-TOURS.

Falk, J.H. (2016), *Identity and the Museum Visitor Experience*, London: Routledge.

Gretzel, U. and T. Jamal (2009), 'Conceptualizing the creative tourist class: technology, mobility, and tourism experiences', *Tourism Analysis*, **14** (4), 471–81.

Lefebvre, H. (1974), *The Production of Space*, reprinted in 1991, trans. D. Nicholson-Smith, Oxford: Basil Blackwell.

McRobbie, A. (2016), *Be Creative: Making a Living in the New Culture Industries*, London: Polity Press.

Richards, G. (2017), 'Creative tourism: opportunities for smaller places?', Paper presented at the CREATOUR international conference, 'The State of the Art in Creative Tourism: Leading Research/Advanced Practices/Future Trajectories', Cúria, Portugal, 1 June.

Richards, G. and L. Duif (2018), *Small Cities with Big Dreams: Creative Placemaking and Branding Strategies*, New York: Routledge.

Whiting, J. and K. Hannam (2014), 'Journeys of inspiration: working artists' reflections on tourism', *Annals of Tourism Research*, **49**, 65–75.

Wisansing, J. (2015), *Redesign Tourism*, Bangkok: DASTA.

Index